Critical Acclaim for *HELP! Paradox for Windows*

"A gold mine of information to the beginner and even a seasoned PW user will pick up valuable advice. They're the kind of tips that will let you operate at a level that would take many months to achieve using PW by yourself."

"An excellent comprehensive guide to interactive Paradox for Windows."

"Biow consistently delivers more than you might expect."

"To achieve this size, some books are stuffed with blank space, fancy emblems, and elaborate space-consuming titles and subtitles. HELP! is not one of them—it's a legitimately big book. Ms. Biow has done an outstanding job of filling each page with helpful and well-organized information. In fact, *HELP! Paradox for Windows* is the best of its kind to date."

—**Jerry Coffey,** *Paradox Informant*

Critical Acclaim for the first book in the How It Works Series

PC/Computing How Computers Work

"A 'real' book, and quite a handsome one…The artwork, by Mr. Timothy Edward Downs, is striking and informative, and the text by Mr. White, executive editor of [*PC/Computing*], is very lucid."

—**L.R. Shannon,** *New York Times*

"…a magnificently seamless integration of text and graphics that makes the complicated physics of the personal computer seem as obvious as gravity.

When a book really pleases you—and this one does—there's a tendency to gush, so let's put it this way: I haven't seen any better explanations written (including my own) of how a PC works and why."

—**Larry Blasko,** *The Associated Press*

"If you're curious but fear computerese might get in the way, this book's the answer…it's an accessible, informative introduction that spreads everything out for logical inspection. To make everything even clearer, White introduces the explanatory diagrams with a few concise, lucid paragraphs of text. Readers will come away knowing not only what everything looks like but also what it does."

—**Stephanie Zvirin,** *Booklist*

"Read *PC/Computing How Computers Work* to learn about the inner workings of the IBM and PC-compatible."

—Ronald Rosenberg, *Boston Globe*

"…the text in *How Computers Work* is remarkable free of jargon and distractions. Readers are left with a basic impression of how a particular component works; they're not overloaded with information they may never use or remember."

—Gordon McComb, *Copley News Service*

"For most PC users, the brief introduction of the subject of disk caching in *How Computers Work* is all they need to understand the basics behind the technology. This is a boon to readers who may have been totally stumped by a more technical description of the process, and who may have avoided the more in-depth article. Whether you're new to computers or want a refresher course in the latest technology, *How Computers Work* offers a solid and colorful introduction."

—Gordon McComb, *Copley News Service*

"Computer users at all levels will enjoy and profit from this book."

—Don Mills, *Computing Now!*

"From mouse to CD-ROM, the treatment manages to convey 'how it works' without being simplistic or overly complex. A very good overview for those curious about how computers make their magic."

—*Reference & Research Book News*

HOW TO

Use Your Computer

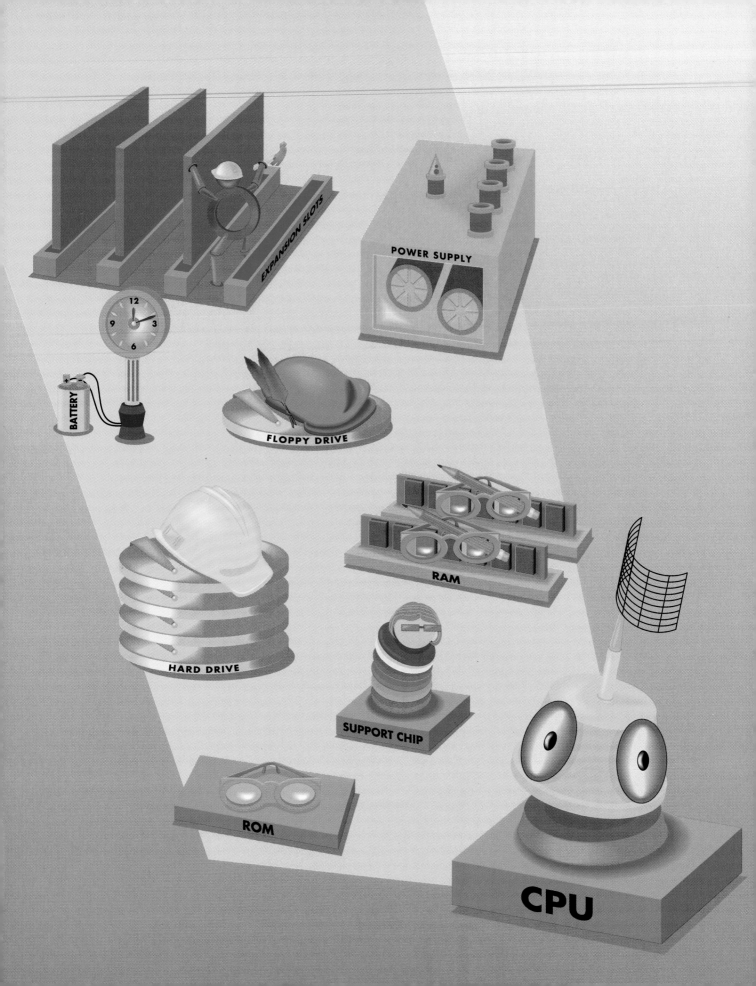

EXPANSION SLOTS

POWER SUPPLY

12
9   3
6

BATTERY

FLOPPY DRIVE

RAM

HARD DRIVE

SUPPORT CHIP

ROM

CPU

HOW TO

Use Your Computer

LISA BIOW

With illustrations by
PAMELA DRURY WATTENMAKER

ZIFF-DAVIS PRESS
EMERYVILLE, CALIFORNIA

Development Editor	Valerie Haynes Perry
Copy Editor	Deborah Craig
Technical Reviewer	Richard Ozer
Project Coordinator	A. Knox
Proofreaders	A. Knox and Cort Day
Cover Illustration	Pamela Drury Wattenmaker
Cover Design	Carrie English and Kenneth Roberts
Book Design	Dennis Gallagher/Visual Strategies, San Francisco
Technical Illustration	Pamela Drury Wattenmaker
Word Processing	Howard Blechman, Cat Haglund, and Allison Levin
Page Layout	M. D. Barrera
Indexer	Lisa Biow

Ziff-Davis Press books are produced on a Macintosh computer system with the following applications: FrameMaker®, Microsoft® Word, QuarkXPress®, Adobe Illustrator®, Adobe Photoshop®, Adobe Streamline™, MacLink® *Plus*, Aldus® FreeHand™, Collage Plus™.

Ziff-Davis Press
5903 Christie Avenue
Emeryville, CA 94608

How to Use Your Computer
FIRST IN A SERIES

ISBN 1-56276-155-2

Manufactured in the United States of America
10 9 8 7 6 5 4 3 2

To Deborah,
again

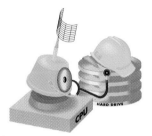

TABLE OF CONTENTS

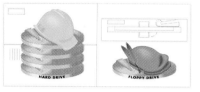

CHAPTER 6
USING WINDOWS

CHAPTER 7
THE MACINTOSH OPERATING SYSTEM

CHAPTER 8
APPLICATIONS SOFTWARE

CHAPTER 9
MORE ABOUT HARDWARE

CHAPTER 10
TELECOM- MUNICATIONS

ACKNOWLEDGMENTS

Literally dozens of people helped make this book happen. In particular:

Pamela Wattenmaker created the beautiful and sometimes zany artwork that adorns these pages. She consistently transformed my often vague ideas into clear and evocative images, and was a pleasure to work with as well.

My friends and collaborators Heidi Steele and Miriam Liskin read most of the chapters in the book, each providing her own unique and invaluable kind of criticism. The book is far better for all their efforts.

Sue Scope read the first two chapters and provided much-needed moral support.

Deborah Craig provided the perfect copy edit (thoughtful, intelligent, filled with funny Post-Its). She also contributed several of the best ideas for illustrations.

Richard Ozer, technical editor, knows as much or more about different types and facets of computers than anyone I can think of. He also burned the candle at all possible ends—juggling duties as programmer, consultant, and dad—to get all his astute comments in on time.

Gerry Kaplan spent many hours answering questions about video and printer drivers and teaching me everything there is to know about Macs.

Valerie Perry, development editor, is one of the most patient and gracious people I've ever worked with. She provided much needed encouragement throughout the book. She also contributed many important ideas to the structure of this book, which is the first in the series.

Dennis Gallagher is responsible for the beautiful book design. It inspired me in the beginning of the book when I saw the design boards and again at the end of the book when the first page proofs arrived.

Ami Knox, my all-time favorite project editor, did another exceptional job of keeping all the pieces together, managing (as always) to stay wry and unwrinkled under the tightest of deadlines.

Several terrific production people worked on the book. Elisabeth Beller, production manager, allowed an unreasonable (and much appreciated) number of modifications to the art. Charles Cowens, production services manager, worked out many of the details of the book design. M.D. Barrera, layout artist, spent hours arranging and rearranging pages and creating the wonderful chapter openers. Carrie English and Ken Roberts are responsible for the great cover design. Dan Brodnitz, systems manager, kept me amused on all my trips into ZD and kept files moving smoothly through the system.

Word processors Howard Blechman, Allison Levin, and Cat Haglund somehow managed to decipher my abominable handwriting and follow my convoluted instructions for cutting and pasting.

Richard Lesnick generously loaned me an extra computer and answered miscellaneous hardware questions.

Dennis Lindholm donated some of his original sheet music for one of the figures.

Last but not least, Cindy Hudson, publisher, threw me this pearl in the first place, figured out exactly what was missing in an early draft, and put up with at least one semi-hysterical phone call.

INTRODUCTION

Over the last ten years, personal computers have moved from the hobbyist's basement to most of the offices, storefronts, factories, banks, supermarkets, farms, and classrooms in the United States. They've found their way into almost a quarter of the homes as well. Given this, the question has become not whether you'll have to deal with computers, but whether you'll understand them when you do.

In most cases, the difference between someone who likes computers and someone who doesn't is a matter of knowledge. If you see the computer as a tool that can assist you in work or play, and that you can use for your own ends, then you'll probably like it. On the other hand, if you see the computer as a mysterious contraption that you have to tolerate and/or appease in order to keep your job, you may need some time to warm up to it. This book is aimed at helping you turn the computers in your life from metal sphinxes into willing helpmates.

I've written the book for four types of readers:

▶ *People who have recently been confronted with a computer, either at work or at home.*

▶ *People who don't have a computer, but are either thinking about getting one or simply wondering what the fuss is about.*

▶ *People who've been using a computer for a while (a week, a month, three years) without ever feeling comfortable with it.*

▶ *People who are fairly proficient with one particular program or one particular area of computer use, but who want to round out their knowledge.*

If you're totally new to computers, this book will tell you a little about everything you need to know. By the time you're through, you'll know what a computer is, what it's good for, and how it works in general terms. In short, you'll know the basic terms and concepts you'll need no matter how you plan to use your computer.

This book will also tell you enough about different ways of using computers to help you decide what areas you want to delve into further. When you're through, you may decide to learn all about spreadsheet programs so you can do your own financial projections. Or you may want to experiment with telecommunications so you can start working out of your home. In any case, you'll get enough of a background that you'll know where you want to head next. You'll also get the foundation you need to explore computers further on your own. One of the hardest aspects of learning about computers is that most computer books and classes—even ones allegedly designed for beginners—assume that you already know the fundamentals (as if people were born knowing the term "random access memory"). By starting from the very beginning, this book gives you the knowledge you need to use other resources such as books, classes, computer users' groups, and technical support staff. It will even enable you to converse with and understand computer salespeople and repair technicians.

If you're already using a computer, you can use this book to fill in the gaps in your knowledge. If you've spent years throwing around terms like memory, bits, and bytes without ever quite knowing what you're talking about, this is the book that will finally explain them to you. It will provide you with the concepts and skills you need to use your computer with more confidence, to move from knowing what keys to press to knowing what those key presses are doing (and what to do when they don't work).

HOW THIS BOOK WORKS

The heart of this book is pictures. Not just pictures of what a particular computer program or piece of equipment looks like, but pictures that illustrate concepts like how the parts of a computer interact, or how information is organized inside a computer, or what you can do with a particular type of program.

Many of the figures (and much of the text) draw analogies between computer components and things that are more familiar to you. You'll find parts of the computer compared to a set of mailboxes in a post office, for example, or to a sports stadium. You'll also find various computer components and programs personified in some of the pictures—not because I really believe there are little people in there, but because such images can help you visualize and remember the events taking place inside your computer.

This book covers the two major types of personal computers—PCs (meaning IBM computers and "compatibles") and Macintoshes. (You'll learn more about these two types in Chapter 1.) Information that applies to only one of those two types of computers is represented by the following symbols: **PC**   **MAC**

ABOUT THE SIDEBARS

Throughout this book, technical information is presented not for its own sake but so you can understand what's going on when you use a computer. The emphasis throughout stays squarely on the practical: details you need to use a computer effectively.

For those of you with a technical bent or a wealth of curiosity, there are also sidebars that look just like this one. These sidebars present additional technical information—extra details or related topics that will prove interesting to at least some of you but are not necessarily essential. Feel free to skim these or skip them altogether if you'd rather stick with the basics.

THE BASICS

1

Learning to use computers is like learning a new language.

Along with the new vocabulary and skills you will inevitably acquire some new ways of thinking about and interacting with the world. Even if all you learn to do is plug in the computer and compose letters, the computer may change the way you write, or at least change the process of writing, by making it so much easier to revise what you've written. Learning about computers will also give you access to new ways of obtaining and working with information. Once you know how to operate a computer, you can easily use it to chat with people across the country or the globe, about everything from the "new world order" to recipes for bouillabaisse to Chinese word processing programs. If you have an office job, computer literacy may even enable you to carry out some of your work from home—letting you communicate with the office computer using your own computer and a telephone. Finally, you may gain glimpses of what the future might be like, when computers are sure to be far more ubiquitous and capable than they are today.

In short, learning about computers will probably change your life, at least a little. Consider it an adventure.

COMPUTERS ARE NOT FRAGILE

Before you start using your computer, there is one critical thing you should know. Contrary to much popular opinion, computers are hard to break. There is no key or combination of keys that you can press that will damage the machine. Shy of dropping the computer on the ground or spilling soft drinks on it, there is little havoc you can wreak that is irreversible or even more than annoying. The one fragile part of the whole setup is your computer's disks, which do not take kindly to magnets, extreme

COMPUTERS ARE NOT FRAGILE

Contrary to much popular opinion, computers are hard to break.

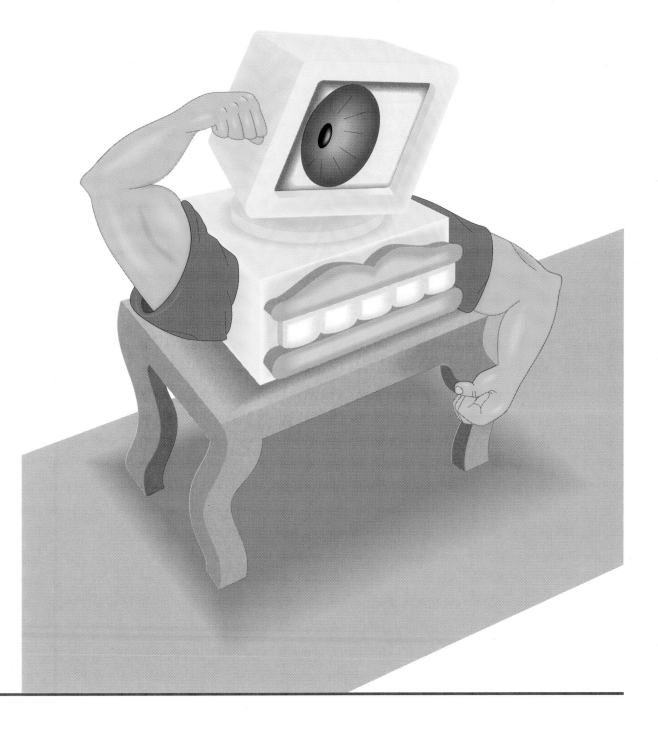

heat, or spilled coffee. But for the most part, your computer is a sturdy object, without any auto-destruct sequence or ejector seat.

Computers are also very forgiving. Even if you blindly press every key in sight, the worst possible result is that you will delete some of the information you just entered. (Even this will take a little doing and, if you notice the mistake immediately, can often be corrected with a single command.) If you issue an instruction that doesn't make sense, the computer will usually let you know by displaying a message on the screen. As soon as you acknowledge the message (often by pressing another key), it disappears and the computer discards all knowledge of the misdeed. Worse comes to worst, you will inadvertently tell the computer to do something other than what you intended. Once you notice the problem, you can almost always find a way to undo what you just did and then try again.

N O T E   *This is not to say that computers never break down. They do. But they break because of electronic or mechanical failure rather than because you pressed the wrong key at the wrong time.*

HOW TO LEARN ABOUT COMPUTERS

The prospect of learning about computers can be very intimidating for the following reasons:

▶ *People who already know about computers speak a dialect guaranteed to frighten off newcomers.*

▶ *It seems that everyone else, including all the five year olds on the block, already know how to use them.*

▶ *Maybe it's been a while since you've explored such thoroughly new terrain.*

For those of you who feel a little anxious or inadequate at the thought of "learning computers," here are some suggestions for approaching the learning process itself:

Tip 1: **ASSUME THAT YOU HAVE THE CAPACITY TO DO THIS.** Just about anyone can learn to use a computer. You don't need to be good at math. You don't need mechanical aptitude. And you don't need to be geared toward logical or linear thinking. You do, however, need some patience. And you need enough self-confidence and determination not to give up when something doesn't work the first (or even the second or third) time you try it.

Tip 2: **ACQUIRE NEW KNOWLEDGE IN BITE-SIZED PIECES.** Don't try to read about and absorb everything at once. Instead, learn only as much as you can comfortably assimilate in a single session, and then review and/or practice until you have mastered the material. Then go back and learn some more.

Tip 3: **MAKE IT CONCRETE.** Whenever possible, try to put at least some of the information or skills you acquire to immediate use: Your new knowledge is much more likely to "stick" if you find some way to put it to work. When you read about computer equipment, see if you can locate the various components in your own computer system. Try to figure out exactly what type of equipment you have. When you read about a particular type of computer program, try to imagine how you might use such a program (or whether you'd have no use for it at all). Or at least imagine how other people or businesses you know might use the program.

Tip 4: **CULTIVATE CURIOSITY.** The best way to get really good at computers is to experiment, to question, to wonder if you can do *x* or what would happen if you did *y*. Don't just passively accept what you read here or in computer manuals. Try to figure out at least some things on your own.

Tip 5: **DON'T TRY TO BE PRODUCTIVE IMMEDIATELY.** If at all possible, keep the learning process free of deadline pressure. (For example, don't decide to learn how to produce a newsletter the day before the newsletter needs to be finished.) Try to make learning about computers a task in itself rather than a means to an immediate end, scheduling plenty of time for the process and, if possible, working on something that interests or amuses you.

Tip 6: **WHEN IN DOUBT, DON'T PANIC.** Your aim, in learning about computers, should not be to avoid mistakes, but to discover what to do when they happen. I'll give you lots of hints for what to consider when the thing is not behaving itself, and suggestions about where to go for more help.

Tip 7: **AVOID BAD TEACHERS.** Thousands of people have learned to hate computers at the hands of well-meaning friends, spouses, and coworkers—someone who tries to tell them everything they need to know about computers in fifteen minutes, or who forgets that there was ever a time they didn't know what a CD-ROM drive is. If you feel stupid every time a certain someone tries to teach you about your computer, you can probably assume that the problem lies in the teaching, not in you or in the subject matter itself. Tell them gently but firmly to leave you alone.

If you want someone to hold your hand while you learn computers, make sure it's someone you're not afraid to ask "stupid questions," someone you don't need to impress. For most of us, this means avoiding a teacher who's either a boss or an employee, and quite possibly a spouse or child as well.

Tip 8: **REMEMBER: YOU DON'T NEED TO BE A COMPUTER EXPERT TO USE A COMPUTER.** The purpose of the computer is to help you do something. You shouldn't (and don't) need a Ph.D. in electrical engineering to get some work done. Although you can make a career or a permanent hobby out of learning about computers, it's fairly easy to do the easy things. If you just want to use your computer to compose and print simple letters, you can probably learn everything you need to know in an hour or two. If you want to learn to produce a professional-looking newsletter, expect to spend weeks. (If you want to learn to converse with computer salespeople, you may need months.) In any case, learning everything you want to know about computers may take a while, but you can fairly quickly learn enough to get some work done.

Tip 9: **HAVE FUN WHENEVER POSSIBLE!**

There's one last thing to know about computers before you start. As you may have already heard or experienced, computers are completely and often maddeningly literal. If you spell something wrong or accidentally press the wrong key, they don't even *try* to guess what you mean. There is, however, a positive side to this trait: Namely, when you do everything correctly, it works. In most cases, computers provide immediate and decisive feedback. When you press the right keys, you get the right results; when you don't, you don't. If you have a job (or a life) in which it's sometimes hard to tell how well you're doing, you may find such clarity refreshing.

WHAT IS A COMPUTER?

A computer is a general-purpose machine for storing and manipulating information. Beyond this, there are two very different schools of thought.

▶ *Computers are dumb but very fast machines; equivalent to extremely powerful calculators.*

▶ *Computers are thinking machines, capable of awe-inspiring, almost limitless feats of intelligence.*

Both of these things are true. In themselves, computers have a very limited set of skills. They can add numbers, compare numbers, and store numbers. This probably seems very strange. The computers we know or have heard about seem to do far more than this. They manipulate text, display graphic images, generate sounds, and do lots of other things that, to us, seem nonmathematical.

But internally, the computer handles all information as numbers, and everything it does involves storing and manipulating those numbers. In this sense, computers are like fancy adding machines. But assuming that you know how to "talk" to a computer in the language of numbers, as some programmers do, you can get it to do some amazing things. Any kind of information that can be represented numerically—and this includes everything from music to photographs to motion picture videos—can be manipulated via a computer, assuming someone knows how to provide the computer with the proper instructions.

This does not mean that you need to know how to learn to program computers (write your own instructions) in order to use them. Chances are you will simply buy and use programs that other people have created. Then you simply need to learn how to use those programs, a task that is far easier and less demanding than learning to write programs of your own.

PERSONAL COMPUTERS

Even if you have yet to encounter a computer at work or buy a computer for home, you probably deal with computers on a daily basis, whether you want to or not. Every time you use an automated teller machine, or watch the checker scan the bar code on your milk carton into an electronic cash register, or use a hand-held calculator, you are using a computer. Some of those computers—like the calculator, for example—are designed to do a very specific task, and the instructions for performing that task are built into the equipment itself. The type of computer you will probably be dealing with at your home or office is more general purpose. It can do just about anything provided it is given appropriate instructions.

Computers come in a multitude of shapes, sizes, and types, ranging from those that fit in the palm of your hand or hide in the corner of your microwave or VCR to those that occupy entire rooms, from ones that are generally used by one person at a time to those that are simultaneously used by dozens or even hundreds of people. This book is about *personal computers*— that is, computers primarily designed for use by one person at a time.

Personal computers are newcomers to the computer scene. Although the first computers were built in the 1940s, the first personal computers were only introduced in the 1970s and were primarily the province of hobbyists, almost like new-fangled ham radios. In 1975, Apple produced the first Apple computer, followed by the Apple II in 1978. By 1980, there were a number of microcomputers on the market that could practicably be used in small businesses, but they were used only by people and companies that were either particularly adventurous or especially in need of automation. Then in the fall of 1981, IBM introduced the original IBM PC, whose instant popularity astounded everyone, including IBM. The success of the IBM PC was due to a combination of

THE COMPUTERS IN YOUR LIFE

Even if you have yet to encounter a computer at work or buy a computer for home, you probably deal with computers on a daily basis.

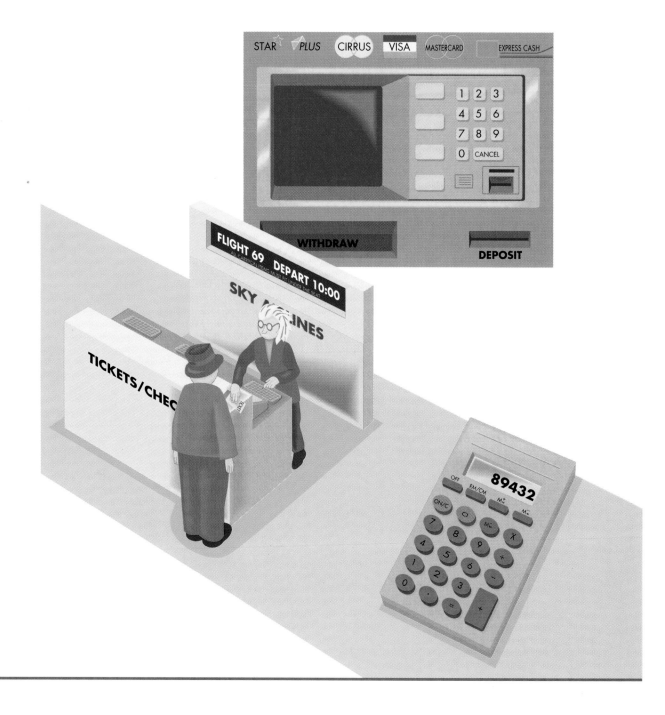

good timing (a lot of small to medium-sized businesses were itching for a financially feasible way to automate) and the IBM name, which lent new credibility to the whole notion of small desktop computing. The budding personal computer mania was further spurred by Apple's introduction, in 1984, of the original Macintosh computer: a type of computer specifically designed to be easy to learn, fun to use, and unintimidating for the nontechnical user. Meanwhile, the speed and capacity of the machines continued to increase almost as fast as their size and prices shrank, making them all the more practical and popular. (Today's personal computers are hundreds of times more powerful than those sold ten years ago, generally cost less, and can fit in packages the size of a notebook.) By the end of the decade, personal computers had gone from being the province of hobbyists and retired engineers, to being an almost ubiquitous fixture in the work world and a member (so to speak) of almost 20% of U.S. households.

N O T E *Just because personal computers are "personal" doesn't mean they can't talk to each other. Many businesses and other organizations have computer networks—groups of computers that are linked together so that they can share information, programs, and/or equipment such as printers. You'll learn more about networks in Chapter 9.*

THE TWO PERSONAL COMPUTER CAMPS

The majority of personal computers currently used in business fall into two camps:

▶ *IBM PCs and compatibles*

▶ *Apple Macintosh computers (often referred to simply as "Macs")*

THE MACINTOSH CAMP AND THE PC CAMP

The majority of personal computers currently used in business fall into two camps: the Macintosh camp and the PC camp

The terms *IBM clone* or *IBM compatible* mean a computer that uses similar components and a similar design to IBM-manufactured PCs, and therefore can use the same type of programs as IBM computers.

Macintosh clones are extremely rare, due to both certain technical complexities of the machine and Apple's very tightly held copyrights. In contrast, when it first created the PC, IBM decided to allow others to imitate its machines. The theory was that the more IBM imitations there were, the more likely it was the IBM would become the business standard. While this did probably enhance IBM's standing in the marketplace, it also spurred the development of literally thousands of brands of IBM "workalikes" (aka *clones*).

Several other types of personal computers are also widely used at home (Ataris and Commodores, for example), as school computers (Apple II's in particular), or in specific types of work (Amigas, for instance, are popular among musicians because they have built-in musical capabilities.) While some of these machines sell well in Europe, they are less widely used in the U.S., particularly within the business world. In offices, the standard is still IBM and clones, followed by Macs.

NOTE *Although the term PC was coined by IBM as the name for its first personal computer, its meaning has expanded over the years. Some people use PC as shorthand for any personal computer. Others, including myself, use it to mean IBM-type computers, including IBM compatibles. In this book, PC means any computer designed to work like IBM personal computers and capable of running programs designed for those computers.*

The main difference between PCs and Macs has to do with what is known as their *user interface*—that is, the way they present information on the screen and solicit and respond to your input. In general, Macs have a more playful, less intimidating interface, centered around pictures and *menus* (lists of options) on the screen. Originally, the PC interface tended to be a bit more stark and more text oriented, but this has begun to change within the last few years.

PROGRAMS: THE WIZARD BEHIND THE CURTAIN

People who are new to computers sometimes think that computers come ready and willing to do anything they want them to do, like electronic Wizards of Oz. Although computers can theoretically do just about anything, by themselves they do nothing at all. They are like player pianos without a roll of music, or VCR machines without tapes. What allows your computer to actually do something are programs: that is, sets of instructions that tell the computer what to do and how to do it. Programs are like the man behind the curtain, turning the knobs and pulling the levers, making your computer perform or seem to perform magic.

Let's take an example. If you want to use your computer to compose and print letters, you use a word processing program. (As I'll discuss shortly, word processing is essentially electronic typing.) The word processing program contains instructions that tell the computer what colors, characters, and/or images to display on your screen, and how to respond to your actions (such as pressing various keys). When you run this program, you get a kind of interactive word processing movie. Your screen appears largely blank, resembling the electronic equivalent of a blank sheet of typing paper. You may see a list of options at the top of the screen that allow you to perform word processing tasks, like setting margins or underlining or adding footnotes.

If you want to do something else with your computer—keep track of customers, for example, or play a game of solitaire—you need to find a program designed for that purpose. The computer is not "set up" to do that task, or any other task, on its own.

In a sense, you could say that the basic function of a personal computer is to "play" different programs—just as VCRs are designed to play VCR tapes. In both cases, the machinery is the same, but the resulting "movies" will be very different.

A single computer can and usually does hold several programs at once. When you buy a computer, it sometimes comes with one or more programs already *installed*—that is, already on your computer and set up to work with your equipment. You can install new programs whenever you like, and once they are installed, they remain stored inside the computer, ready for you to use. The number of programs that you can store in a single computer is limited only by the amount of disk space that you have. You will learn about disks and disk space in the next chapter.

WHAT YOU CAN DO WITH A COMPUTER

There are dozens of types of programs that you can run on a personal computer, from ones that teach typing to ones that prepare your tax returns. For now, we'll just outline some of the major categories:

▶ *Word processing programs let you use your computer to compose and print letters, papers, reports, and other types of documents. They offer much more extensive editing capabilities than typewriters—allowing you to insert new characters and delete existing ones, and to move blocks of text from one part of the document to another, all without retyping. Most also have features for handling page numbers and footnotes. They also generally include a feature, known as mail merge, that allows you to*

"PLAYING" A PROGRAM

The basic function of a personal computer is to "play" different programs—just as VCRs are designed to play VCR tapes.

generate personalized form letters by "merging" a letter with a set of names and addresses.

▶ *Desktop publishing (DTP) programs enable you to combine text, pictures, graphics, tables, lines, boxes, and other design elements in a single document. They let you perform the type of page layout operations required to produce documents such as newsletters, books, and flyers—the kind of operations otherwise performed in a typesetting shop.*

▶ *Spreadsheet programs are number crunchers. They let you perform almost any kind of mathematical calculations. Although they are most often used for financial calculations (budgeting, financial analysis, and forecasting), they can be used for scientific or engineering calculations as well. They also often have built-in graphics capabilities, permitting you to transform a set of numbers into a bar graph or pie chart, for example.*

▶ *Database management programs let you store, retrieve, and manipulate large collections of information, such as mailing lists, inventories, student rosters, or library card catalogs. They enable you to keep your data up-to-date, sort it, generate statistics, print reports, and produce mailing labels. Database programs also let you extract portions of your data based on some kind of selection criteria, listing all your customers in Oregon with a credit limit of over $100, for example, or all the inventory items of which there are less than three items in stock.*

▶ *Accounting programs help you manage your money. They let you track and categorize income and expenses, reconcile your bank statements, and produce standard financial reports such as income statements and balance sheets. At one end of the spectrum are simple personal money*

TYPES OF PROGRAMS

Word processing programs let you use your computer to compose and print letters, papers, reports, and other types of documents.

Desktop publishing (DTP) programs let you perform the type of page layout operations required to produce documents such as newsletters, books, and flyers.

Database management programs let you store, retrieve, and manipulate large collections of information, such as mailing lists, inventories, student rosters, or library card catalogs.

Spreadsheet programs are number crunchers. They let you perform almost any kind of mathematical calculation.

Note: Because spreadsheet programs are frequently used for financial calculations, many people have a hard time distinguishing them from accounting programs. Spreadsheets are completely open-ended: they can perform almost any calculation you can imagine, but only if you provide them with explicit instructions. Accounting programs, in contrast, already "know" how to handle accounting functions and generate standard accounting reports. All you need to do is type in your numbers.

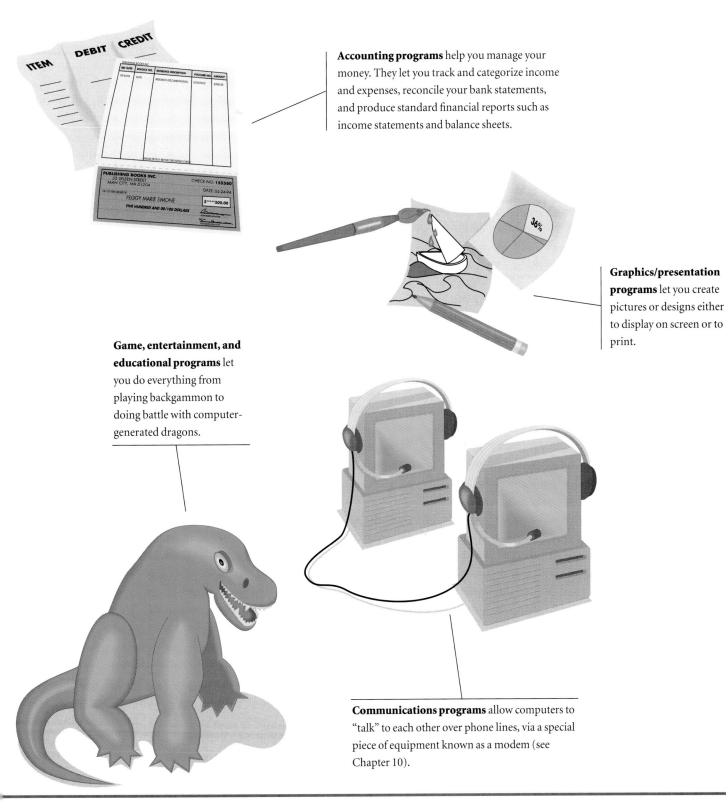

Accounting programs help you manage your money. They let you track and categorize income and expenses, reconcile your bank statements, and produce standard financial reports such as income statements and balance sheets.

Graphics/presentation programs let you create pictures or designs either to display on screen or to print.

Game, entertainment, and educational programs let you do everything from playing backgammon to doing battle with computer-generated dragons.

Communications programs allow computers to "talk" to each other over phone lines, via a special piece of equipment known as a modem (see Chapter 10).

management programs that let you balance your checkbook and track personal expenses. At the other end are sophisticated business accounting programs that generate extensive financial reports, produce invoices and statements to customers, handle accounts payable and receivable, print payroll checks and payroll reports, and track inventory.

▶ ***Graphics/presentation programs*** *let you create pictures or designs either to display on screen or to print. This category includes painting and drawing programs that let you either combine and modify existing pictures or construct your own. It also encompasses presentation graphics programs, which let you create line graphs, pie graphs, organizational charts and other types of diagrams and, in many cases, to combine these images into slide shows. (As mentioned, some presentation graphics capabilities are often built into spreadsheet programs as well.) This category also includes programs that let you edit or enhance photographic images.*

▶ ***Communications programs*** *allow computers to "talk" to each other over phone lines, via a special piece of equipment known as a modem (see Chapter 10). You can use this capability to access electronic bulletin boards and information services like CompuServe, Prodigy, Internet, and Lexus. These services let you do everything from sending messages to other people via "electronic mail," to conversing with others about topics ranging from global warming to vacation hot spots, to shopping in "electronic malls" (kind of like a computerized catalog and order-taking system), to discovering which airlines are flying to Albuquerque tomorrow morning or how your stocks are doing on Wall Street.*

▶ *Game, entertainment, and educational programs let you do everything from playing backgammon to doing battle with computer-generated dragons. There are programs that let you step inside detective and science fiction novels, work on your golf swing, and attempt to save the world from ecological disasters. There are also dozens of games for children, many of them educational in intent. There are programs that "read" children's stories, for example, highlighting each word on the screen while pronouncing it through the computer's speakers.*

In Chapter 8 you will learn more about the major types of programs, and how to select the right one for you.

HARDWARE VERSUS SOFTWARE

Now that you know what a program is (a set of instructions), you are ready for your first two pieces of computer jargon. In computer terminology, all computer equipment is referred to as *hardware* and all computer programs are known as *software*. These two terms emphasize the fact that the equipment and program are two essential parts of a working computer system. Hardware is the machinery and its physical accouterments, including the keyboard (the part that looks like a typewriter), the screen, and the printer. Software is the magic spell that brings the machinery to life.

Some people get a little confused about the difference between hardware and software. Part of this confusion has to do with the way software is packaged and sold. If you buy a new program, you get a box with one or more manuals explaining (hopefully) how the program works, plus one or more floppy disks on which the program is stored. When you get back to your home or office, you install the program by copying its instructions from the disks to your computer.

HARDWARE VERSUS SOFTWARE

Hardware is the machinery and its physical accoutrements. It includes all parts of the computer system that you can touch.

Software is more elusive. It is like the music recorded on a CD rather than the CD itself. You can't touch it, you can only see or hear its results.

As a result, many people think of disks as software. (If you've never encountered a *floppy disk,* they are round, flat wafers—kind of like small and flimsy records—that are encased in a square plastic wrappers. They are used to store both programs and data. You'll learn all about disks in Chapters 2 and 3.) In fact, they are hardware. The basic rule of thumb for determining if something is hardware or software is whether you can touch it: And since disks can be touched, they're in the hardware camp. Software, on the other hand, is much more elusive. You can't touch, see, or taste it; you can only witness its results.

When you buy a new program, then, the physical disks on which the program is stored are hardware. The program itself—the instructions stored on those disks—is software. The distinction here is a little subtle—like the distinction between the music and the records, magnetic tape, or compact disks on which that music is recorded. The music (which is analogous to software) is intangible; the part you can touch (the record, tape, or CD) is merely the medium on which the music is stored. Similarly, the disks you get when you buy a program are simply the medium on which the program is stored.

NOTE *From here on, I will be using the words program and software virtually interchangeably.*

THE TWO TYPES OF SOFTWARE

As mentioned, the native language of computers consists solely of numbers. Since very few of us are capable (or patient) enough to speak to a computer in this language, we almost never interact with the computer directly. We always "speak" to the computer through an intermediary, namely, a program whose function, among other things, is to translate our requests to the computer. And it is programs that enable the computer to "speak" back to us, by telling it how to displaying text or pictures on the screen, produce sounds, or printing characters on paper.

There are actually two different types of software: applications software and operating systems. *Applications software* is the software that you use to actually perform your work. This includes all the types of programs previously described under "What You Can Do with a Computer."

N O T E   *The term* applications *is often used in computer circles to mean "things that you do with your computer." So if someone asks you what types of applications you intend to run, they are really asking you what you plan to do with your computer—that is, what types of programs you plan to use.*

In contrast, *operating systems* are programs that act as the intermediary between you and the hardware and, to some extent, between the hardware and the applications software. As you will learn in Chapters 5 through 7, operating systems serve several different functions. For starters, the operating system controls various parts of the machine and allows them to talk to one another; in effect, it *operates* the hardware. The operating system also provides your basic working environment, the world you encounter when you first turn on the machine. Whether you see something like C:\> or a screen full of pictures when you power up your computer depends, in large part, on which operating system program you are using.

In addition, operating systems include various "housekeeping utilities" that allow you to find out what programs and data are stored on a disk, to copy programs and data to and from your computer, and to delete programs and data. And finally, it's the operating system that allows you to start up application programs. If you want to play chess on your computer, for example, you

THE THREE STANDARD OPERATING ENVIRONMENTS

THE MACINTOSH OPERATING SYSTEM

DOS

WINDOWS

issue a command that tells the operating system "Go find the chess program and fire it up."

Different operating systems are designed for different types of computers. If you are running a PC, you will probably use an operating system named DOS, possibly OS/2, or, more rarely, one called Xenix. If you are running a Macintosh, you will use the Macintosh operating system, which you may have heard called System 7 or the Finder.

For those of you who have heard of or seen the program Windows, you may be wondering where it fits into this division of labor between operating systems (programs that run your computer) and application programs (programs that let you "do something"). Windows is a special case: It is an operating system that cannot stand on its own. It must work hand-in-hand with either the DOS or, less frequently, the OS/2 operating system. (Future versions of Windows will probably work independently, rather than alongside another operating system.) Although Windows is built to run on PCs, it provides a more picture-oriented and, to some eyes, less intimidating environment than the DOS or OS/2 operating systems—in effect, making a PC look and function more like a Macintosh computer. You can learn all about Windows in Chapter 6.

THE TASK AHEAD

Now that you know about the difference between hardware and software, and between application programs and operating systems, you can understand a little more what's involved in learning about computers. In a nutshell, there are three topics you need to know about:

▶ *Your Hardware. The type of machinery and accessories you will be using and how they work*

▶ *Your Operating System. The essential program that makes your computer "go"*

▶ *Application Programs. The individual application programs that let you accomplish whatever you intend to do with your computer—be it typing letters, producing newsletters, handling mailing lists, preparing your tax return, or playing Dungeons and Dragons*

In terms of hardware, you need to learn at least a little bit about what the different components are and how they work. At a minimum, you need to know something about how data and programs are stored inside your computer (so that you understand what happens when you "save" data, for example, or when it's safe to turn off the computer). You should probably also know enough to buy new equipment as needed, which unfortunately involves mastering a daunting number of buzzwords.

Learning about hardware has another purpose: It makes you feel more in control of your machine. While some people have made jokes about the necessity of sacrificing lambs to their computer, there's little fun in feeling subjugated to a capricious deity. The more you know about your computer's innards the less likely you are to feel that there's an evil spirit in there, and the less fatalistic you're likely to be about hardware problems.

You also need to know some basics about the operating system that goes with your computer. At a minimum, you want to know how to use the operating system to start up various applications programs. You also want to know things like how to copy and erase programs and data.

Finally, you need to learn how to use particular application programs. If you want to use your computer to generate letters and other documents, for example, you need to pick out (if necessary) and then learn a particular word processing program. If you plan to crunch numbers, you'll need to find and master a spreadsheet program. Since there are literally thousands of application programs available, we can't explain how to use individual programs in this book. Instead, we'll discuss, in Chapter 8, how the major types of applications programs work, how to choose a program, and how to go about teaching yourself (including how to read computer manuals, locate good books, and obtain technical support).

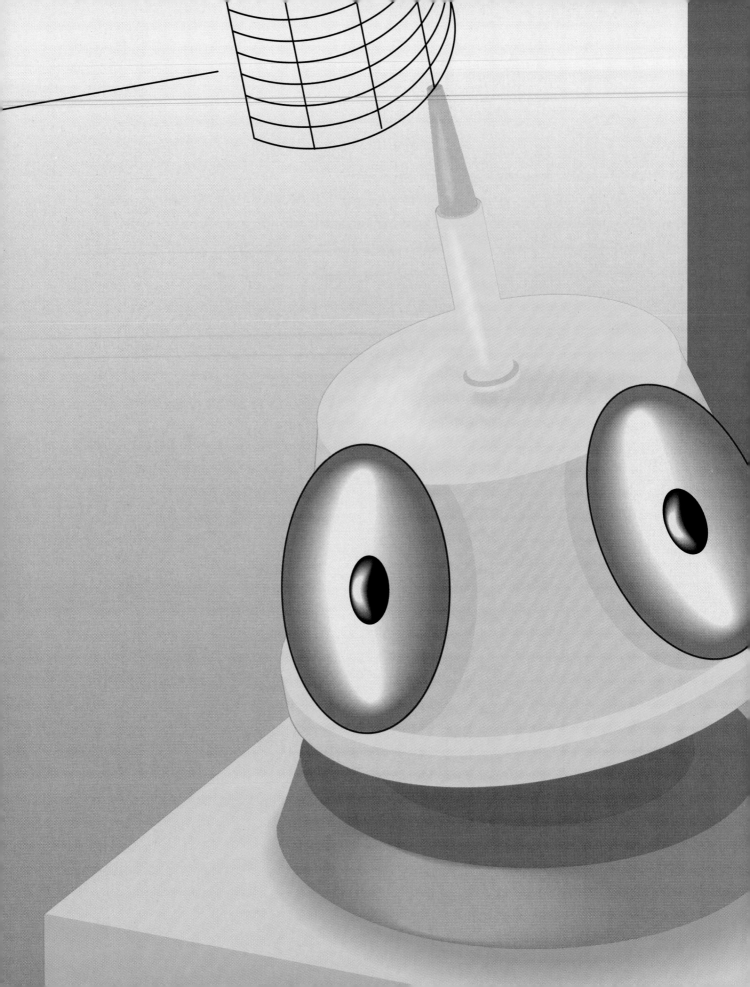

CHAPTER

2

ANATOMY OF A COMPUTER

2

In this chapter,
you will learn the fundamentals of computer hardware—what the essential parts are and how they interact with each other. I will start with the core elements of the computer—the parts that let you store and manipulate information, and allow you to communicate with your computer. Then at the end of the chapter I'll backtrack a bit and discuss the pieces that support and/or connect those core devices, turning the individual parts into a cohesive working system.

Probably the most important knowledge you will glean from this chapter relates to how your computer stores information. By the time you finish this chapter, you will know

▶ *What happens when you load a program*

▶ *Where the data you type into your computer goes*

▶ *What happens when you save data (where the computer puts it, and how you get it back again)*

Whenever possible, I'll use analogies to things you already know about and, for now, I'll give you just enough technical detail to get a feel for what's really going on inside your computer. You'll learn a bit more of the technical details in the next chapter and in Chapter 9.

THE BRAIN OF THE COMPUTER

At the core of every computer is a device roughly the size of a large postage stamp. This device, known as the *central processing unit*, or CPU for short, is the "brain" of the computer, the part that reads and executes program instructions, performs calculations, and makes decisions. The CPU is responsible for storing and retrieving information on disks and other storage media. It also handles moving information from one part of the computer to another. For this reason, some people compare it to a central switching station or control tower that directs the flow of traffic throughout the computer system.

In personal computers, the CPU (also known as the *microprocessor*) is comprised of a single integrated circuit. An *integrated circuit*, or IC, is a matrix of transistors and other electrical circuits embedded in a small slice of silicon. (*Transistors* are essentially microscopic electronic switches: tiny devices that can be turned on and off.) Like the dozens of other integrated circuits that inhabit your computer, from the outside, a CPU chip looks something like a square ceramic bug with little metal legs. These "legs" are designed to fasten the chip to a fiberglass circuit board which sits inside your computer, and to carry electrical impulses into and out of the chip. Inside the ceramic case is the chip itself, a slice of silicon about the size of a fingernail. At first glance, it's hard to imagine how this tiny device can run your entire computer. But under a microscope, the slice of silicon reveals an electronic maze so complex it resembles an aerial photograph of a city, complete with hundreds of intersecting streets and hundreds of thousands of minuscule houses. Most of the "houses" are transistors, and there are usually somewhere between one hundred thousand and three million of them on a single CPU chip.

The type of CPU that a computer contains determines its processing power—how fast it can execute various instructions. These days, most CPUs can execute on the order of millions of instructions per second. The type of CPU also determines the precise repertoire of instructions the computer understands and therefore which programs it can run.

THE SYSTEM UNIT

The CPU resides inside a box known as the system unit, along with various support devices and tools for storing information. (You will learn about

INSIDE THE CPU CHIP

When placed under a microscope, a CPU chip resembles an aerial photograph of a city.

these other residents of the system unit later in this chapter.) For now, just think of the system unit as a container for the CPU.

The system unit case—that is, the metal box itself—can either be wider than it is tall, in which case it usually sits on top of your desk, often underneath the screen, or it can be taller than it is wide, in which case it generally sits underneath your desk and is referred to as a *tower case*.

THE VARIOUS TYPES OF CPU CHIPS

In the PC world in particular, people often categorize computers by the model of CPU chip they contain, saying things like "I have a 386" or "My computer is a 486." The CPU chips currently used in PCs include the 8088 at the low end, 80286, 80386, 80486, and at the high end, the Pentium (the generation after the 486). People usually omit the first two digits when referring to 80286, 80386, and 80486 chips. So if someone tells you that they have a 386 computer, they mean an IBM-type computer with an 80386 chip. (You can tell it's an IBM computer or clone because they're the only computers that use 80386 chips.) The CPU chips used in Macintosh computers are, from slowest to fastest, the 68000, 68020, 68030, and 68040.

STANDARD COMPUTER SYSTEMS

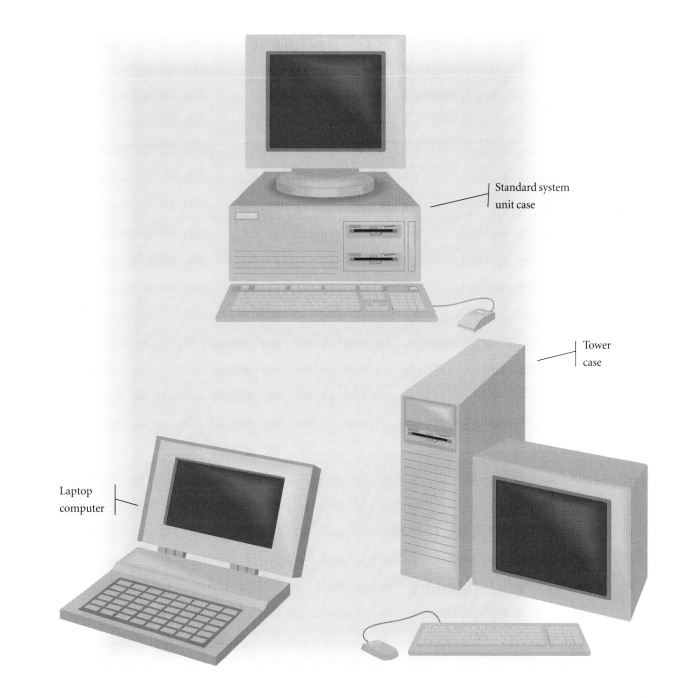

Standard system
unit case

Tower
case

Laptop
computer

Within each class of CPU, speed is measured in terms of the cycle time at which the computer was designed to operate. All computers have built-in clocks that help regulate the flow of information from one part of the computer to another, rather like a metronome. Each pulse of this clock is known as a cycle, and a CPU can perform, at maximum, one operation per cycle.

Every CPU is designed to work with a clock that "ticks" at a particular rate. A CPU may be designed to run at 16 megahertz (MHz) or 33 megahertz, for example, meaning 16 or 33 million cycles per second. Bear in mind, however, that this measurement is relative to the class of processor. In the PC world, a 25MHz 386 is faster than a 16MHz 386, for example, but a 25MHz 486 CPU runs much faster than a 25MHz 386 CPU.

The other parts of the computer system—that is, the parts outside the system unit—are primarily used as a means of communicating with the CPU—of sending in instructions and data and getting out information. Devices used to communicate with the CPU are known, collectively, as *input and output devices*, or simply *I/O devices*. Input devices are all those things that allow you to "talk" to your computer—to pose questions and issue commands. Output devices are what allows the computer to talk back, providing you with answers, asking you for additional information, or, at worst, informing you that it has no idea what you are talking about.

NOTE *You may also hear the term* peripherals *applied to I/O devices. Technically the term peripheral means everything outside the CPU (including I/O devices).*

In personal computers, the most common input device is the keyboard (the part that looks like a typewriter). The second most common input device is a mouse. The mouse is a handheld pointing device that allows you to point to words or objects on the computer screen. The mouse sits on your desktop or sometimes on a rubber pad, called a *mouse pad*, that allows it to move more easily than on the bare desktop. Moving the mouse forward and back, or left and right, causes an arrow on the screen (known as the *mouse pointer*) to move as well. And pressing the buttons on the mouse (called *pressing* or *clicking*, depending on how fast you do it) lets you make selections on your screen. You will learn more about using the mouse in Chapter 4. All Macintosh computer systems include a mouse, but the mouse is optional on PCs.

There are also lots of other input devices that you can use to communicate with your computers, including

▶ *A trackball, which is a pointing device that resembles a ball nestled in a square cradle, and serves as an alternative to a mouse.*

▶ *A scanner, which allows you to copy an image (such as a photograph, a drawing, or a page of text) into your computer, translating it into a form that the computer can store and manipulate.*

▶ *A joy stick, which lets you manipulate the various people, creatures, and machines that populate computer games.*

The most common output device is the display screen, which the computer uses to display instructions, ask questions, and present information. Computer screens go by many names, including monitor, VDT (video display terminal), and CRT (for cathode ray tube, the technology used in most desktop computer screens). (In laptop computers and their newer, smaller cousins the *notebooks*, both the screen and the keyboard are often built into the system unit itself.)

Almost all computer systems also include a printer for generating paper copies of your data. Like monitors, printers come in many shapes and sizes, and generate output ranging from the old grainy-looking computer printout to color printouts that rival the clarity of offset printing. (The main types of printers are discussed in Chapter 9.)

Finally, there is one type of device—called a modem—that serves as both input and output device. A *modem* is a gadget that allows computers to communicate with each other over phone lines. You can use modems both to send

INPUT AND OUTPUT DEVICES

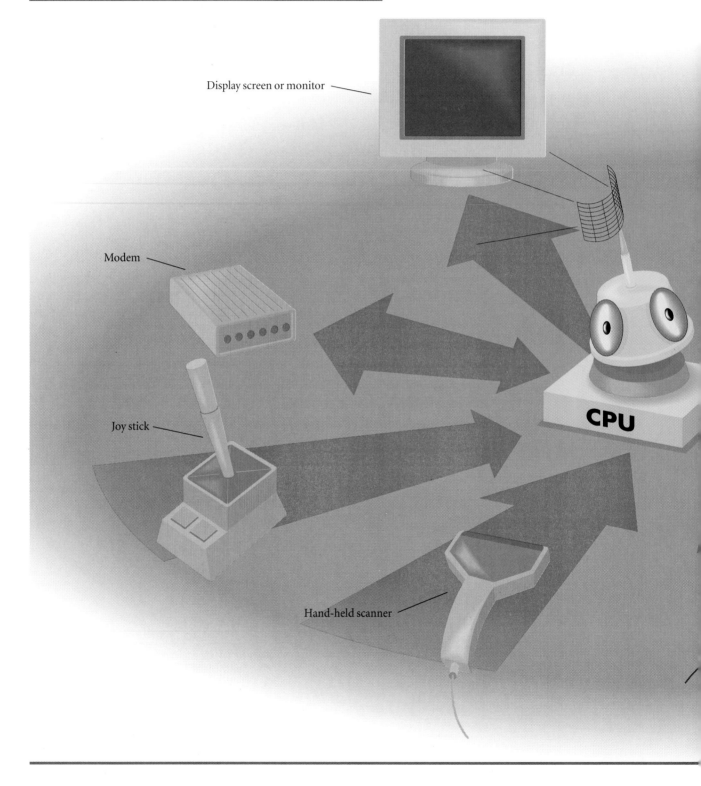

Display screen or monitor

Modem

Joy stick

Hand-held scanner

CPU

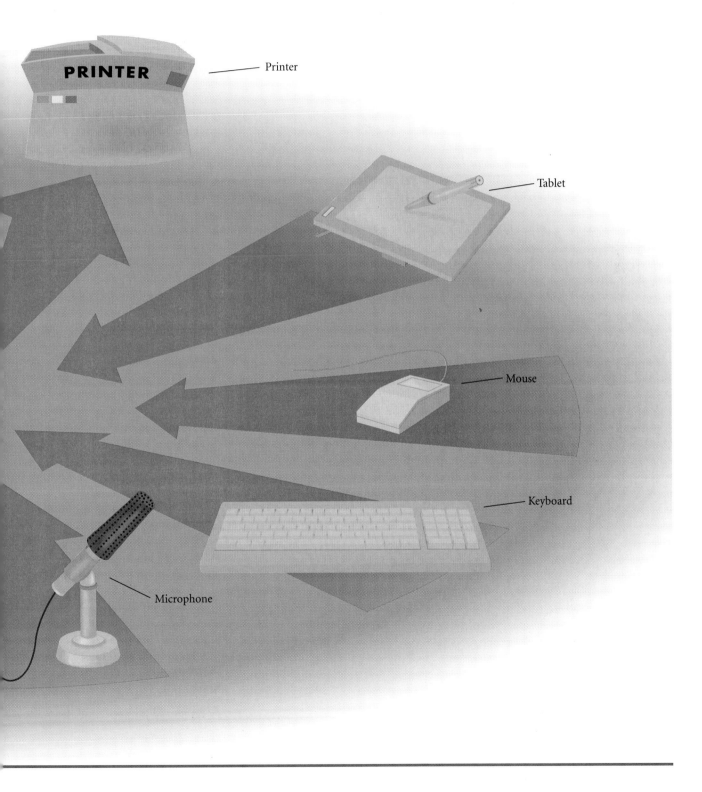

Printer

Tablet

Mouse

Keyboard

Microphone

COMPUTERS COMMUNICATING VIA MODEMS

Modems are devices that allow computers to communicate over phone lines.

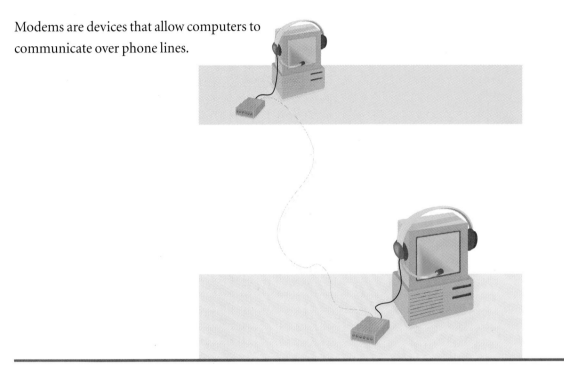

data and messages to your friends and coworkers who have computers, to tap into electronic information services such as Prodigy and CompuServe. Some modems even have fax capabilities built-in, allowing you to send and receive faxes via your computer.

NOTE *Some modems are separate devices that plug into the system unit. Others reside inside the system unit. You'll learn more about monitors, printers, and modems in Chapters 9 and 10.*

STORING INFORMATION

Now you know a little about the CPU of the computer and the devices that you use to communicate with that "brain." There is still one very large gap in our image of a computer system, however. There is no storage space.

Although the CPU is terrific at manipulating data and following instructions, it has almost no capacity for storing information. (Think of it as a brilliant but extremely absent-minded professor.) In order to function, your computer therefore needs a place to store both programs (the instructions that tell the CPU what to do) and data. You need, in other words, the electronic equivalent of a closet or filing cabinet.

NOTE *In computerese, the term* data *refers to whatever type of information you are trying to manipulate. Data therefore includes far more than numbers; it includes any information that you type or otherwise input into the computer. You can also think of data as the raw material that is processed or manipulated by application programs. If you are using a word processing program, data means the document (letter, memo, poem, novel, legal brief, whatever) you are typing and/or editing. If you are working with a database program, it may be a set of names and addresses you are adding to your company mailing list.*

In most computers, the primary storage places are disks—flat, circular wafers that resemble undersized phonograph records. (You may be used to thinking of disks as square because they are always housed inside square plastic jackets. But the disks themselves are round.)

Like phonograph records or compact disks, they store information that can be "played" by devices specifically designed for that purpose. The device that "plays" computer disks is known as a *disk drive*. It is in several respects the equivalent of a turntable or CD player. Like turntables or CD players, disk drives have components designed to access the information on a specific area of the disk. These parts are called *read/write heads* and are equivalent to the phonograph needle on a turntable or laser in a CD player. Like turntables, disk drives turn around, thereby spinning the disk so that different parts of the surface pass

TYPES OF DATA

The term data refers to whatever type of information you are trying to manipulate.

READ/WRITE HEAD

The read/write heads on a disk drive are like the phonograph needles on turntables or lasers in CD players, except that they can write (record) as well as read (play) information.

underneath the read/write heads (just as records spin underneath the needle). Most disk drives have at least two read/write heads—one for each side.

Unlike record players or CD players, however, disk drives can record new information on disks as well as play existing information. (In this sense, they're more like cassette tapes than records.) In computer terminology, the process of playing a disk is called *reading* and the process of recording onto a disk is called *writing*. (Hence the term read/write head.)

Computer disks come in two basic types: floppy and hard.

▶ *Floppy disks generally hold less information and are slower than hard disks. They can also be removed from their disk drives. In other words, you can "play" different floppy disks in the same drive by removing one and inserting another. The word floppy refers to the disk itself, which is a*

Computer disks and disk drives come in two basic types: floppy and hard.

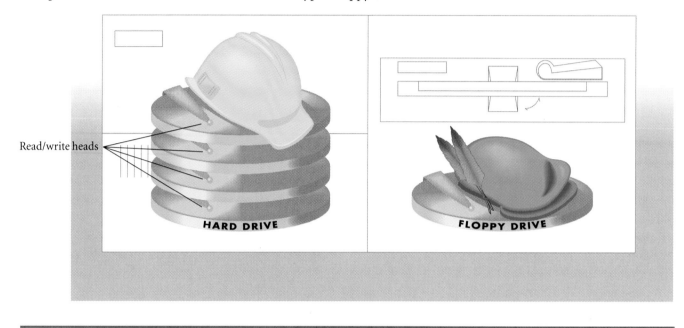

Read/write heads

HARD DRIVE   FLOPPY DRIVE

very thin, round piece of plastic on which information is magnetically recorded (much as music is recorded on the surface of plastic cassette tapes). This decidedly floppy disk is enclosed inside a sturdier, unfloppy plastic jacket to protect it from dust, scratches, liquid, and the oils on your fingers—all of which can erase or scramble the information recorded on the disk's surface. The disks used in personal computers are usually either 3½ or 5¼ inches in diameter.

▶ ***Hard disks*** *hold more information and spin faster than floppies (about twenty times faster). They are also permanently enclosed within their disk drives. You can think of hard disks as records that are encased inside their record players so that the record and the record player function as a single unit. Contrary to what you may think, hard disks are not always* *larger than floppies; they're simply capable of packing information more tightly, and therefore can store more data in the same amount of space. Most hard drives contain multiple disks, often called* platters, *which are stacked vertically inside the drive. Typically, each disk has its own pair of read/write heads. Since you never remove hard disks, hard-disk drives do not contain doors or slots, as do their floppy counterparts. This means that the drive itself is completely invisible (and sometimes hard to locate) from outside the system unit. In most cases, the hard drive is adjacent to the floppy drive.*

These days, most personal computers have one hard-disk drive and either one or two floppy-disk drives. In general, you'll use hard disks as the primary repository of data and programs—the place you store the information that you work with day to day. You'll use floppy drives mainly as a means of getting information into and out of your computer, by transferring information to and from floppy disks. Floppy drives are, in this sense, like doors to the outside world. In particular, you use floppy-disk drives to:

▶ *Install new programs, by copying them from floppy disks to your hard disk.*

▶ *Make extra copies of programs or data for safekeeping by copying from the hard disk to floppies. This is known as* making backups. *If you are working on the great American novel, for example, you will keep your main working copy on the hard disk but keep an extra copy on a floppy disk, in case there is a mechanical problem with the hard-disk drive or you accidentally erase the original. If you want to be completely safe, you might even keep this duplicate copy in a safe deposit box or a fireproof safe.*

▶ *Archive data that you don't use regularly (and therefore don't want taking up space on your hard disk) but that you don't want to discard altogether.*

▶ *Transfer data from one computer to another, by copying information from one computer's hard disk to a set of floppies, taking the floppies over to the other computer, and copying from those floppies onto the hard disk.*

There are several things that you need to know to work with floppy disks, including how to determine which type will work in your disk drive, how to prepare them for use, how to insert and remove them, and how to take care of them. (You'll learn to do all of these in the next chapter.)

Although disks and their disk drives are by far the most common means of storing data and programs, they are not the only ones. Other storage technologies currently in use include tape drives, CD-ROM drives, magneto-optical drives, and Bernoulli boxes. You will learn more about storage devices in Chapter 9.

MEMORY: THE ELECTRONIC DESKTOP

Given what you've learned so far, you might assume that when you run a program, the CPU fetches instructions from the disk one at a time and executes them, returning to the disk drive every time it finishes a single step. If this were actually the way computers worked, they would be so slow as to be unusable.

Left to their own devices, most personal computer CPUs are capable of executing between one million and one hundred million instructions per second. But because it is mechanical—that is, composed of moving parts—the disk drive cannot deliver program instructions anywhere near that fast. Reading an instruction from the disk involves both rotating the disk so that the proper section is below one of the read/write heads and then moving the head closer to or farther from the center of the disk until it is positioned

THE MANY ROLES OF A FLOPPY-DISK DRIVE

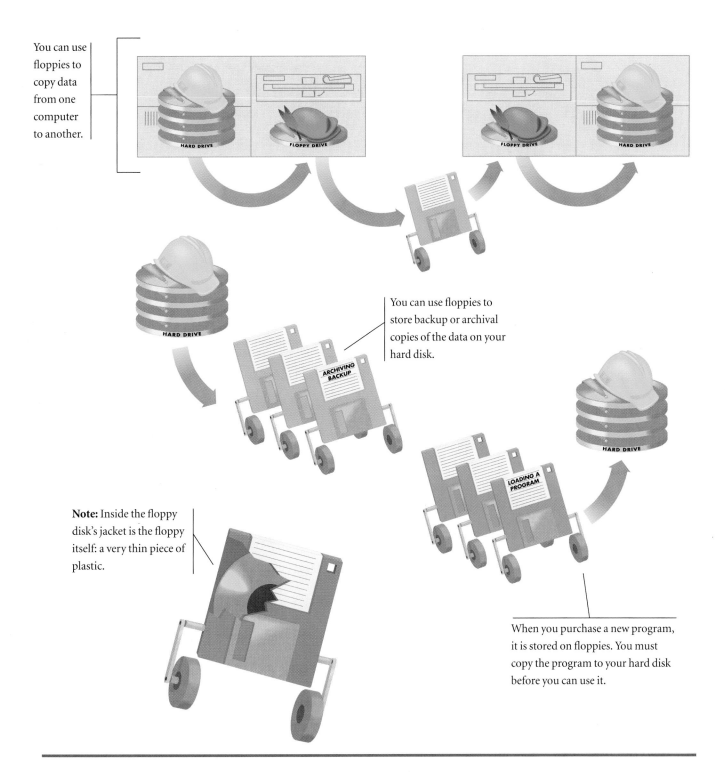

You can use floppies to copy data from one computer to another.

You can use floppies to store backup or archival copies of the data on your hard disk.

Note: Inside the floppy disk's jacket is the floppy itself: a very thin piece of plastic.

When you purchase a new program, it is stored on floppies. You must copy the program to your hard disk before you can use it.

directly above the spot where the instruction is recorded. Even on a hard-disk drive, this process generally takes between 9 and 25 milliseconds (millionths of a second).

Now if the CPU can execute millions of instructions per second and the disk drive can only deliver, say, one hundred thousand instructions per second, you have the equivalent of an assembly line in which one person on the line (the CPU) is moving somewhere between 10 and 100 times faster than the previous one (the disk drive). If this were really the way your computer worked, the speed of the CPU would be wasted while it waited for the disk drive to deliver the next instruction.

For the computer to function efficiently, it therefore needs some repository of information that is capable of keeping pace with the CPU. This extra piece is called *random access memory*, usually referred to as RAM or simply memory for short.

Physically, RAM consists of a set of separate integrated circuits (each of which looks something like a small CPU chip) which are often mounted on fiberglass boards; in practice, however, memory is treated as a single, contiguous set of storage bins. One useful way to envision memory is as a set of mailboxes, like those inside a post office. Each mailbox holds a single character, and the entire collection of boxes is numbered sequentially. (In computer jargon, the mailboxes are called *bytes* and their numbers are known as *memory addresses*.)

Like the CPU chip, memory chips store and transmit information electronically. Sending an instruction from memory to the CPU is therefore a simple matter of transmitting electrical impulses. There is no waiting for a disk to spin or a read/write head to move to the proper position.

Because the CPU can move information in and out of memory so quickly, it uses memory as a kind of electronic desktop—the place it stores whatever it

CPU SPEED VERSUS DISK-DRIVE SPEED

It takes even a fast hard drive 10 to 100 times as long to deliver an instruction as it takes the CPU to execute one.

A TYPICAL PC MOTHERBOARD

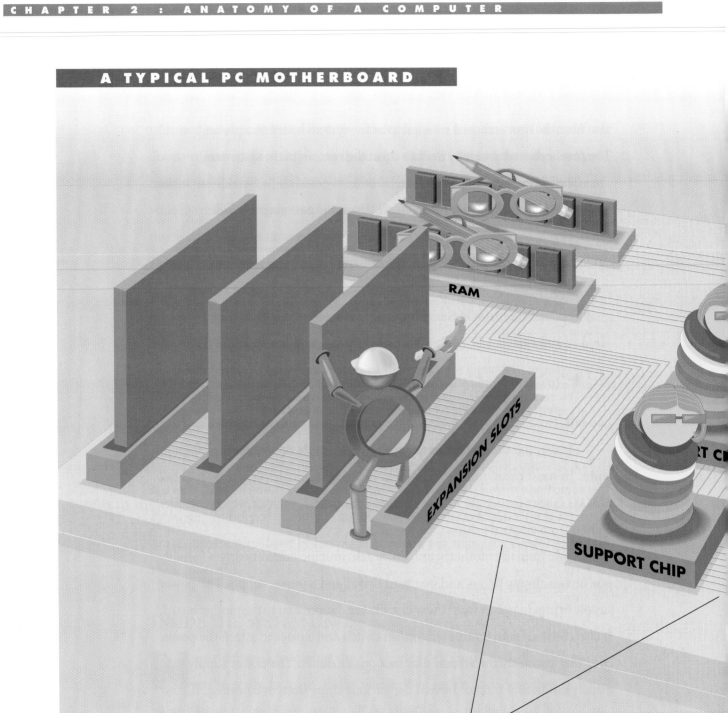

RAM

EXPANSION SLOTS

SUPPORT CHIP

Bus

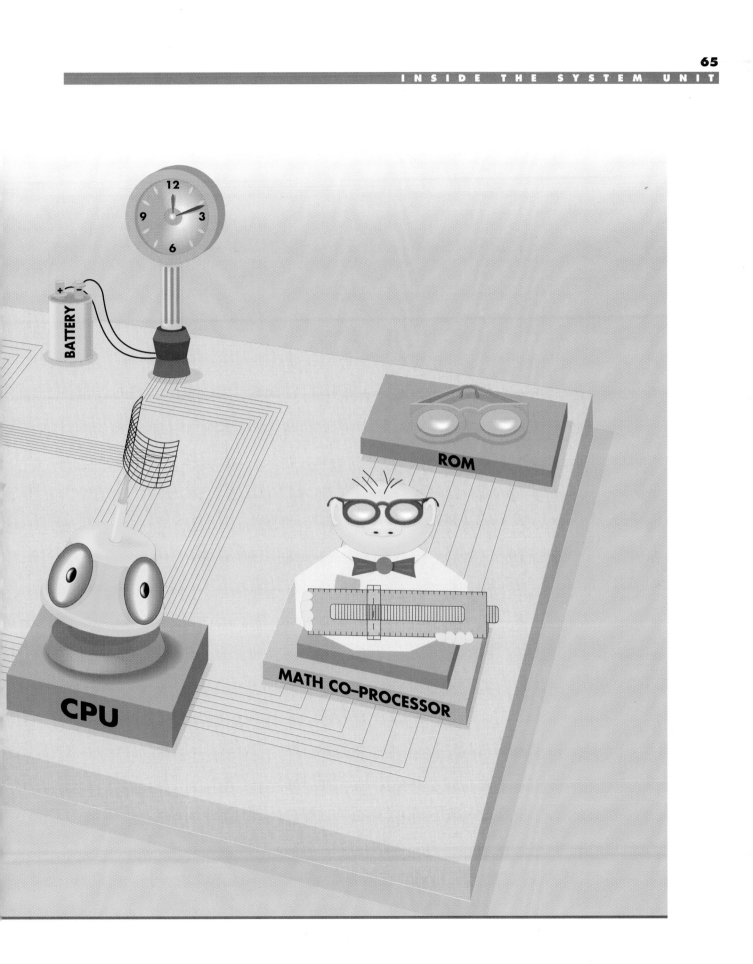

INSIDE THE SYSTEM UNIT

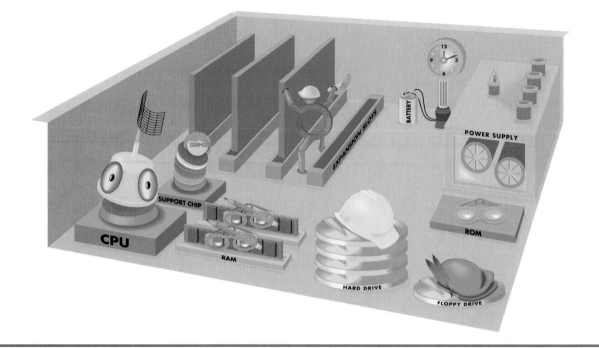

the motherboard itself. The purpose of most expansion boards is to allow an I/O (input/output) device—like a display monitor or a scanner—to communicate with the CPU.

The advantage of this design—a motherboard containing all the standard circuitry of the computer and a set of expansion slots that allow you to plug in additional circuitry as needed—is that it allows you to customize your system. Two people can buy essentially the same computer but add on very different sets of peripherals. This design also allows you to easily add new parts to your computer as your needs change or as new forms of computer paraphernalia are invented.

Expansion boards that are designed to serve as intermediaries between the CPU and some device outside the system unit have *ports* on one end. Ports are sockets that protrude from the back of the system unit. You can think of them as places where you can "dock" various external devices, plugging them into a circuit board that, in turn, connects them to the CPU. (Expansion boards that are designed for components inside the system unit—such as disk drives—do not include ports.)

BUSES

Finally, all motherboards contain a *bus*: a set of circuitry designed to carry data and instructions back and forth between various devices on the board itself. You might think of the bus as a collection of elaborate, high-speed conveyor belts. The bus not only carries data and instructions back and forth between the CPU and memory (both RAM and ROM), it also connects the CPU and memory to any expansion boards that are plugged into the motherboard.

CHAPTER

3

YOUR COMPUTER'S FILING SYSTEM

What Are Files?

▪

File Name Rules

▪

*Saving, Retrieving, and Resaving
Files*

▪

File Formats

▪

*Organizing a Hard Disk:
Folders/Subdirectories*

▪

Working with Floppies

▪

The Care and Feeding of Hard Disks

▪

Computer Viruses

In order to use your computer effectively, you need to understand a bit about its filing system, namely, how it stores and organizes information on disks. This chapter begins by discussing files, the repositories of programs and data on disks and other long-term storage media. You will learn about rules for file names, about file formats used by various application programs, and about the organization of files into groups known as folders or subdirectories. The second half of the chapter delves into detail about the disks themselves—the medium on which files are generally stored. By the time you're through, you will know how to choose the right type of disks for your floppy-disk drive(s), protect floppies from accidental damage, prepare new floppy disks for use, care for your hard disk, and ward off computer viruses.

WHAT ARE FILES?

All data on disks is stored in files. A *file* is simply a named collection of information stored on a disk. There are two basic types of files: *program files,* which contain instructions to your computer, and *data files,* which contain data that you enter through an application program. (In the Macintosh world, data files are generally called documents.)

Unless you delve into programming at some point, most of the files you create will be data files. Every time you enter data in an application program—be it text, numbers, pictures, or anything else—and then save it for the first time, you are creating a new data file. And since all files, by definition, have names, the first thing that happens when you issue the command to save is that the program asks you to assign a file name.

A file is a named collection of information stored on a disk.

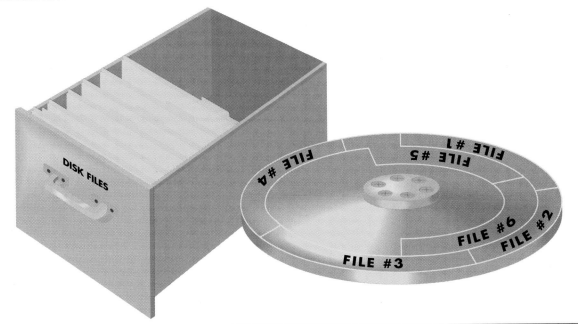

NOTE   *In some programs, data is saved to disk automatically. Many database programs work this way. When you first set up a database, you create a file to hold your data. Then as you enter the information on each customer (or product or order placed or whatever you are storing in your database), that information is automatically saved to disk as soon as you move to the next customer (or product or order).*

FILE NAME RULES

The rules for file names are different on Macs and PCs. On Macintosh computers, file names are all one piece and can contain up to 31 characters. In DOS, file names consist of two parts: a primary file name (often called simply the file name), which can be up to eight characters long, and an optional suffix, called an *extension*, which can be up to three characters long. Macintosh file names can include letters, numbers, spaces, and any punctuation other than a colon (:). DOS file names (and extensions) can include letters, numbers, and the following punctuation characters:

`~ ! @ # $ % ^ & ( ) _ - { } '

Since it's hard to remember which punctuation marks are acceptable, it's often easiest to just stick with letters and numbers. DOS file names *cannot* include spaces.

N O T E   *Because Windows works in tandem with DOS, DOS file name rules apply in the Windows world as well.*

If you elect to add an extension to a DOS file name, you must type a period between the two parts of the file name whenever you refer to the file. If a file has a first name of LETTER and an extension (last name) of DOC, for example, the entire name would be LETTER.DOC.

Sometimes you don't have much choice in the matter of file extensions. Many application programs automatically add a preset extension for you whenever you create a file. If you create a letter in the Ami Pro word processing program, for example, every time you create a new file, Ami Pro assigns it an extension of .SAM.

N O T E   *On Macintosh computers, file names that are entered in different mixtures of upper- and lowercase are considered different file names. You can therefore have files named Memo, memo, and MEMO stored on the same disk. DOS, in contrast, ignores the case of letters, considering Memo, memo, and MEMO to be identical. (DOS actually stores all file names in uppercase, regardless of how you enter them, but it lets you refer to files using any mixture of upper- and lowercase that you like. In other words, DOS may "think" of the file as MEMO, but it understands what you mean if you tell it to copy Memo to another disk.)*

FILE-NAMING CONVENTIONS

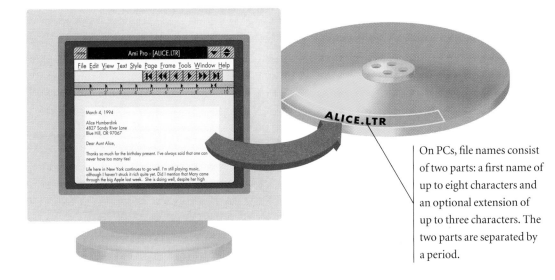

On PCs, file names consist of two parts: a first name of up to eight characters and an optional extension of up to three characters. The two parts are separated by a period.

On Macs, file names are all one piece and can be up to 31 characters.

In general, every file on a particular disk must have a unique name. (We'll explain the qualifications to this rule a little later in this chapter, after you learn about folders/subdirectories.) This way, when you tell your computer to find the file LETTER.DOC and copy it into memory, it knows exactly which file you mean. It doesn't need to determine *which* LETTER.DOC.

You must keep this law of unique file names in mind when copying files. If you copy a file named LETTER.DOC from disk 1 to disk 2, and disk 2 already has a file named LETTER.DOC, the old version of LETTER.DOC is completely and permanently replaced by the new one. If you are using a Macintosh or Windows, you will be asked to confirm that you want to replace the existing file. If you are working directly with DOS, however, you receive no warning at all. The file is simply replaced, and there is nothing you can do to rescue it afterwards.

SAVING, RETRIEVING, AND RESAVING FILES

As you learned in Chapter 2, once something is stored on disk, you can always copy it back into memory when you want to use it again (just as you can fetch a particular document from your file cabinet). This is known as *retrieving* data or *opening* a file.

Just as when you load a program from disk to memory, when you retrieve data, the original copy of that data remains in place and intact on the disk. If you then change the copy in memory, you end up with two different versions: an older version on disk and a newer version in memory. The same situation occurs when you save a new document to disk but continue working on it. You might, for example, get halfway through writing a letter and then save your data to disk. You then have two separate and independent versions of the same letter: one (the older one) on disk and another (the current one) in memory.

COPYING A FILE ONE ON TOP OF ANOTHER

When you copy a file to a disk, that file replaces any existing file with the same file name.

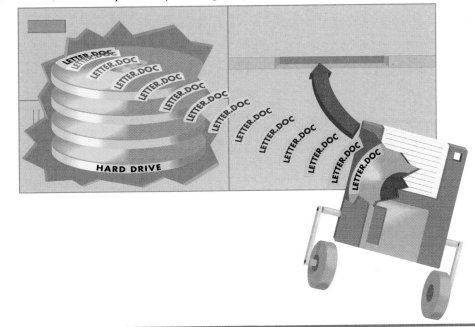

This has a couple of implications:

▶ *First, if you like the new version better than the old one, you must re-member to save it before you leave the application program. Otherwise you'll have only the old version of the document (the one on disk) and your changes will be lost.*

▶ *Second, if you decide that you prefer the older version, you can close the document (remove it from memory) without saving it. When you do so, the version of the document currently in memory is erased. You can then retrieve the old version (the one on disk) and start amending it again. This can be extremely convenient when you completely bungle an edit and want to start all over.*

Whenever you decide to save a file that has already been saved once, you need to decide whether to use the same file name as last time or a new file name. As mentioned, you cannot generally store two files with the same file name on the same disk. In fact, if you copy a file to a particular disk and the disk already contains a file of that name, the new one replaces the old one. The same issue arises when you resave a file. Suppose you create a budget in your spreadsheet program, for example. Halfway through the process, you save your data, then you revise it, and save it again. If you resave it under the same name that you used the first time, the new version will replace the old one on disk. Most of the time, this is exactly what you want. If you want to retain the old version of the file as well as the newly revised one, however, you must assign a different name to the new version.

In Windows and in the Macintosh operating system, there are separate commands for resaving a document under its existing name and for saving it under a new name. (You use the Save As option on the File menu rather than the Save command when you want to save something under a new name.) In some DOS programs, there's only one save command (often called File Save) and you need to remember that saving a file under the same name means replacing the old version. Many application programs also ask for confirmation when you try to save a file under an existing file name.

FILE FORMATS

Most application programs have their own unique format for storing data, a format that only makes sense to that one program. For example, the format in which the Lotus 1-2-3 spreadsheet program stores data is not the same as the format used by the Excel spreadsheet. The format that the Word for Windows word processing program uses is not the same as the format that WordPerfect uses.

In general, if you want to see what's inside a particular data file, you need to look at the file from inside the program in which it was created. For example, if you want to see what's inside an Excel spreadsheet file, you need to look at it from within the Excel program. If you try to look at it from within a word processing program or even from within another spreadsheet program, you will probably just see a lot of nonsense characters on your screen.

Special codes that tell the program how to arrange and format the data distinguish the file format used by one program from that used by another. Each word processing program has its own code for representing italics or page breaks, for example.

Many programs have commands for importing and exporting data in the formats used by other programs. Word for Windows can import WordPerfect files, for example, translating all the WordPerfect formatting codes to their Word for Windows equivalents. In the DOS world, some programs determine which file format is being used by looking at the file extension, and translate the

ASCII AND TEXT-ONLY FILES

Occasionally, a program does not have any tools at all for interpreting the special codes used by another program. In this case, you can save the file in a generic format, without any of the special formatting codes specific to one particular program. The most commonly used generic format is one known as *ASCII* in the PC world and *text-only* in the Mac world. (ASCII stands for American Standard Code for Information Interchange, and is a set of standardized codes used to represent all the characters you can produce on a typewriter, plus a few others.) When you save a file in ASCII or text-only format, your program strips out any proprietary codes—that is, codes that only it knows how to read—leaving you with plain-vanilla text; any special attributes such as underlining or unusual typefaces will be lost in this translation process. Once you have saved a file in ASCII or text-only format, you can open it in almost any other program, although you may need to specify the file format when you open the file or issue a special import command. Consult your program documentation for information on saving and using ASCII text files.

data into the appropriate format automatically. (This saves you the trouble of telling the program about the file format or using a special import command.)

ORGANIZING A HARD DISK: FOLDERS/SUBDIRECTORIES

Hard disks often hold thousands of files. Rather than piling this entire collection of files in a single heap, most people organize their files into groups. These groups are generally known as *folders* in the Mac world and as *subdirectories* in the PC world. You can think of folders/subdirectories as manila folders in a file drawer, each one of which can hold several individual files.

Just as when you set up a manual filing system, when you organize a hard disk you decide for yourself how many folders you need and what to store in each. Often you will place each application program and its associated files in a separate folder (folder/subdirectory). For example, you might have one for your spreadsheet program, another for your word processing program, and a third for your accounting program. Many people prefer to create two separate folders for each application—one to hold the program itself and another to hold the data files created in that program. You might, for example, create one folder to hold your word processing program and another to hold your documents. This makes it easier to find and manipulate the data files. (In most operating systems, it is fairly easy to copy to a floppy disk all the files in a particular folder. Storing your data files (and nothing else) in one folder therefore makes it easy to create a backup copy of your data.)

If you have many different types of data, you might also create separate folders for each type. You might create one folder for business correspondence and another for letters to friends, or one for correspondence, another for reports, and a third for invoices.

FOLDERS AND FILES

On hard disks, files are usually organized into groups known as folders or subdirectories. You can think of these groups as manila folders in a file drawer, each of which can hold several individual files.

You can create additional subgroupings if you like. For example, you might create a folder for word processing that contains your word processing program and then, within that folder, create another folder for the documents you have created and saved.

In short, the filing system you create on a disk is as individual as the one you create in a filing cabinet.

The process of actually creating and manipulating folders/subdirectories varies a bit from one operating system to the next, and is therefore covered in later chapters. For now, just be aware that creating a new folder/subdirectory always involves entering a unique name. The rules for naming folders/subdirectories are the same as the rules for naming individual files: On Macs, you get 31

A FILING SYSTEM WITH FOLDERS/SUBDIRECTORIES

You can create folders/subdirectories within other folders/subdirectories. A word processing
folder, for example, might contain separate folders for reports, memos, and letters.

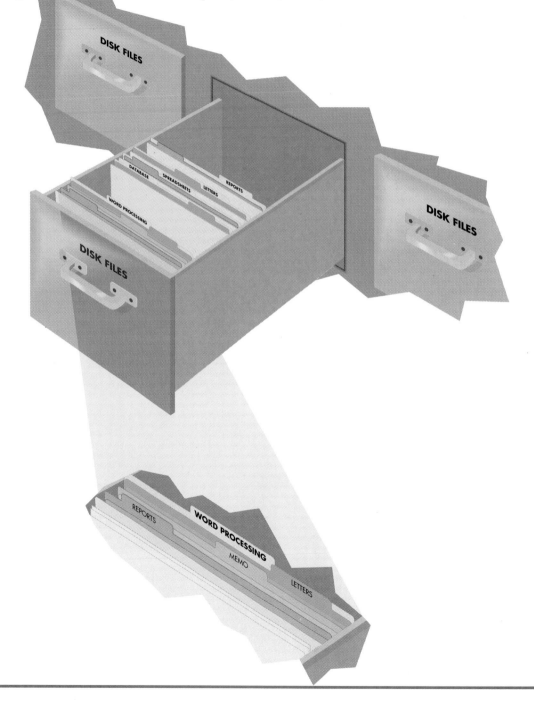

characters to work with, including spaces; on PCs, you get 8 characters and an optional 3-character extension, although the extension is rarely used for subdirectory names.

Now that you know about folders/subdirectories, we can modify an earlier rule: Files in the same subdirectory/folder must have unique names. You can, however, have files of the same name in two different subdirectories/folders on the same disk.

WORKING WITH FLOPPIES

As you learned in Chapter 2, there are two basic types of disks: floppy disks and hard disks. Hard disks serve as the primary repository of data. Floppy disks are mainly used for copying data to and from your hard disk, acting as a kind of gateway between your computer and the outside world.

Floppy disks come in two sizes: 5¼ inch and 3½ inch. Which size of disk you use depends on the type of floppy-disk drive you have in your computer. The floppy-disk drives in Macintosh computers always use 3½-inch disks. On PCs, drives designed to read 5¼-inch disks used to be the norm, but 3½-inch drives are becoming increasingly common and the 5¼-inch variety is gradually becoming obsolete. Some PCs have two floppy-disk drives, in which case one may take 5¼-inch disks and one 3½-inch disks.

As described in the last chapter, the part of the disk that you see and touch is the outside cover—the disk's jacket. Inside this jacket is a flimsy piece of plastic on which data is magnetically recorded. The reason that disks have jackets is that they are extremely sensitive: Scratches and spilled liquids are enough to permanently destroy them, and the oils on your fingers are enough to wreck the magnetic patterns used to record data on their surface.

On 5¼-inch floppies, the jacket contains an oblong read-write hole through which the surface of the disk itself is exposed. When you place the disk in the drive, the drive's read/write head (the part that reads and records data) is positioned right above this hole. When you handle 5¼-inch disks, you therefore need to be careful not to touch this exposed portion of the disk. To be safe, hold the disk jacket by the label. You should also avoid writing on a disk label with a ballpoint pen, since the pressure of the point can damage your data.

You don't need to worry about accidentally touching or scratching the surface of 3½-inch disks, because the disk remains protected until it is actually inserted into the drive. When you insert a 3½-inch disk into a drive, the metal shutter is pushed to the side, exposing the disk's surface so that the read/write heads can read and record information.

With both sizes of disks, you do need to be wary of magnets. Any exposure to magnets can scramble or erase the information recorded on the disk.

Protecting your disk from magnets may take more vigilance than you realize. Magnets lurk in many unsuspected places, including many paper clip holders (that's why the clips stick to the rim of the holder) and various other office accessories, including some document holders. Since the coil for your telephone becomes magnetized every time your phone rings, it's wise to keep disks at least a few inches away from the phone. In addition, metal detectors in airports and government buildings sometimes use magnets to detect the presence of metal in your luggage, so you may want to remove disks from your luggage and show them to the attendant, just as you do with film.

You should also avoid storing both sizes of floppy disks in extreme heat. (Do not, for example, leave a disk on your dashboard on a hot summer day.)

T H E   T W O   T Y P E S   O F   F L O P P Y   D I S K S

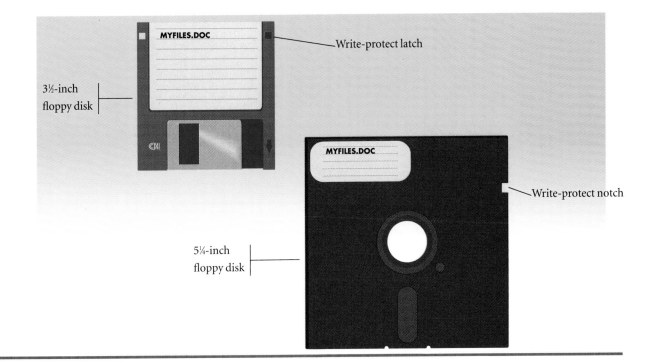

3½-inch floppy disk

Write-protect latch

5¼-inch floppy disk

Write-protect notch

D I S K S   A N D   M A G N E T S

In case you are interested, you need to keep disks away from magnets because of the way in which information is recorded on the surface of the disk. When your computer writes (records) information on a disk, electricity is sent through a coil of wire that is wrapped around a piece of iron within the read/write head. Now as you may remember from grade school science classes, whenever you happen to send electricity through a wire that is wrapped around a piece of iron, the piece of iron becomes magnetized. In effect, the read/write head is temporarily turned into a magnet. This magnet is then used to magnetize tiny particles of iron oxide (in a word, rust) on the disk's surface. As they become magnetized, different sets of particles are aligned in one of two configurations: one configuration represents ones, and the other, zeros. (Remember that computers store all types of information as numbers consisting entirely of zeros and ones.) Now since one magnet—a magnetized read/write head—is used to record the information on a disk, any other magnet has the capacity to realign the iron oxide particles and thereby scramble your computer's record of your data.

INSERTING FLOPPIES

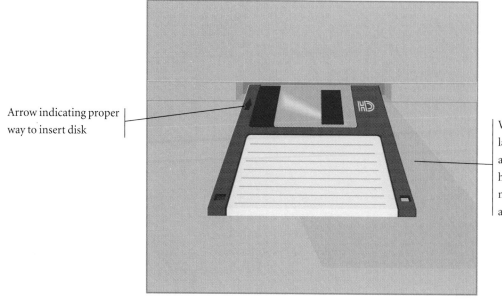

Arrow indicating proper way to insert disk

With 3½-inch disks, the label and HD symbol (if any) should face up in a horizontal drive and, in most cases, to the left in a vertical drive.

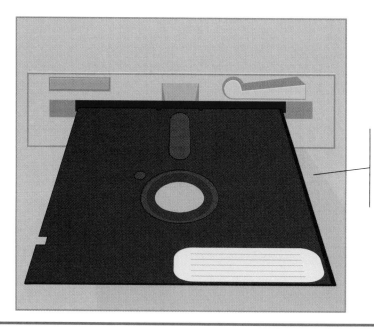

With 5¼-inch disks, the label should face up in a horizontal drive and should usually face left in a vertical drive.

WARNING *When the read/write head is reading or writing to a disk, a small LCD (liquid crystal display) on the front of the drive lights up. Do not remove the disk until the this light goes off, indicating that the process is complete.*

Occasionally, you may want to guard the files on a disk against accidental erasure or overwriting. (You may find this particularly useful for disks that contain programs.) You can do this by *write-protecting* or *locking* the disk— making it impossible for anyone to copy new files onto the disk or erase files already on it. (The term "write-protect" is generally used in the PC world; "lock" is used in the world of Macs.)

The procedure for write-protecting a disk depends on the disk type. 5¼-inch disks contain a notch in the upper-right corner. To write-protect such disks, you simply put something over this hole. When you buy disks, the box includes write-protect tabs (small sticky labels) designed for this purpose. If you don't have any write-protect tabs, just use part of a gummed label to cover up the notch.

3½-inch disks have a tiny latch in the upper-right corner, which is usually closed. To write-protect such disks, turn the disk over and slide the latch downward so that a small window appears in the corner of the disk.

NOTE *Some program disks are permanently write-protected—that is, they do not have a write-protect notch or latch. This prevents you from accidentally erasing the disk; it also keeps you from using it for anything else.*

When you first buy floppy disks, they are essentially blank slates. Before you can store data on them, the surface of the disk needs to be subdivided in some way, so that data can be stored in specific, easily locatable spots. Otherwise, your computer would have an awful time finding files when you needed them. The process of subdividing a disk into sections by embedding magnetic codes on the disk's surface is known as *formatting* or in the Mac world, *initializing.*

A WRITE-PROTECTED DISK

You can guard against accidental overwriting or erasure of data by write-protecting (aka locking) a floppy disk.

N O T E *Hard disks also need to be formatted before use, but they're usually formatted when you buy them. If not, find an expert to do it for you; the process is a bit too complicated for a novice.*

When you format a disk, your computer subdivides the disk in two different ways: drawing concentric circles (known as tracks) around the disk, and drawing straight lines (known as sectors) that divide the disk radially.

You may find it helpful to think of your disk as a stadium. Just as people identify stadium seats by section and row number, your computer identifies where files are "seated" by sector (section) and track (row).

N O T E *The process of formatting a disk is quite simple, but it may take a minute or two. (On Macs, whenever you insert an unformatted disk, a message is displayed asking if you'd like to initialize it. On PCs, formatting requires issuing a*

A FORMATTED DISK

Just as people identify stadium seats by section and row number, computers identify file locations by sector and track numbers.

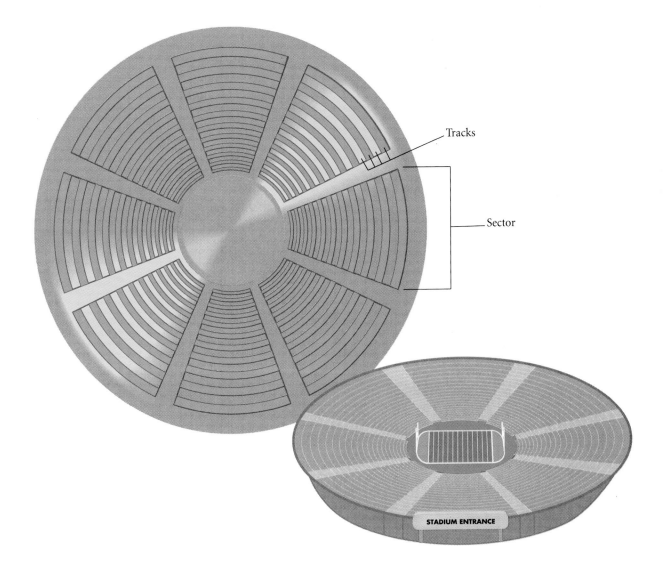

Tracks

Sector

STADIUM ENTRANCE

single command.) In case you're perenially short on time, you can now buy disks that are already formatted for use on PCs. Since they cost a bit more than unformatted disks, you have to decide whether you are willing to pay extra to save yourself the trouble of formatting.

DISK CLUSTERS

To continue with the stadium analogy, when you "seat" data on a disk, you can't always get exactly the number of seats (bytes) you'd like. Instead, you need to "purchase" seats in blocks, usually known as clusters. A *cluster* is the minimum amount of space used to store a file. If the cluster size for your operating system is 256 bytes, even a 1-byte file takes up 256 bytes worth of space. It cannot share its space with other small files. (Remember that a byte is a character's-worth of storage space.) Similarly, if a file is 300 bytes in size (a little more than one cluster), it takes up 512 bytes (2 clusters) on disk. The size (in bytes) of a cluster varies from one operating system to the next, but a cluster always occupies two or more sectors on a particular track. Strictly speaking, your computer keeps track of where files are seated on a disk by storing the starting cluster number for each file. It then uses that cluster number to calculate the corresponding track and sector number.

Different disk drives are designed to read different types of disks. The physical size of the disks is only part of the story. You also have to consider how closely the drive packs data on the disk. Some disk drives, known as high-density drives, store two or more times as much data on the same size disk as other, low-density drives.

You should be able to determine the type of disk drive you have by looking at your computer manual. If you can't find the manual, try getting a list of the files on a high-density disk. (You'll learn to do this in the chapter on your operating system. Chapters 5 through 7 discuss the DOS, Windows, and Macintosh operating systems, respectively.) If your drive can read the disk, it's a high-density drive. If it can't, you'll see an error message.

N O T E   *Most new computers have only high-density drives. The whole issue of disk density is therefore slowly becoming moot as low-density drives become less and less common.*

When you buy disks, you need to be sure to get the right type for your disk drive—not only the right size, but the right density as well. If you have a low-density drive, you should buy low-density disks. (Such disks are generally labeled as double-sided double-density disks since, unlike the disks used in some earlier computers, they can store data on both sides, twice as densely as some older-model disks.) If you have a high-density drive, you should generally buy high-density disks (usually labeled as either double-sided high-density, or simply high-density).

It is possible to use low-density disks in high-density drives. This allows you to trade floppy disks with computers that have low-density drives, even if you only have a high-density drive. However, some older high-density drives are not as well-behaved in handling low-density disks as you would like: While they read low density disks beautifully, once you save any data on the disk, you may no longer be able to read the disk in a low-density drive. (In other words, as soon as you write to the disk using the high-density drive, you can only read it using a high-density drive.) If you have this problem with your high-density disk drive, try to limit your activity with low-density disks to reading rather than writing. Low-density drives cannot read (retrieve information from) or write to (record information on) high-density disks.

THE CARE AND FEEDING OF HARD DISKS

Hard disks are not as vulnerable to dust and liquids as floppies are because they are sealed inside metal cases. They are, however, far from indestructible (as many discovered during the 1989 California earthquake). Knocking a

FLOPPY-DISK DENSITIES

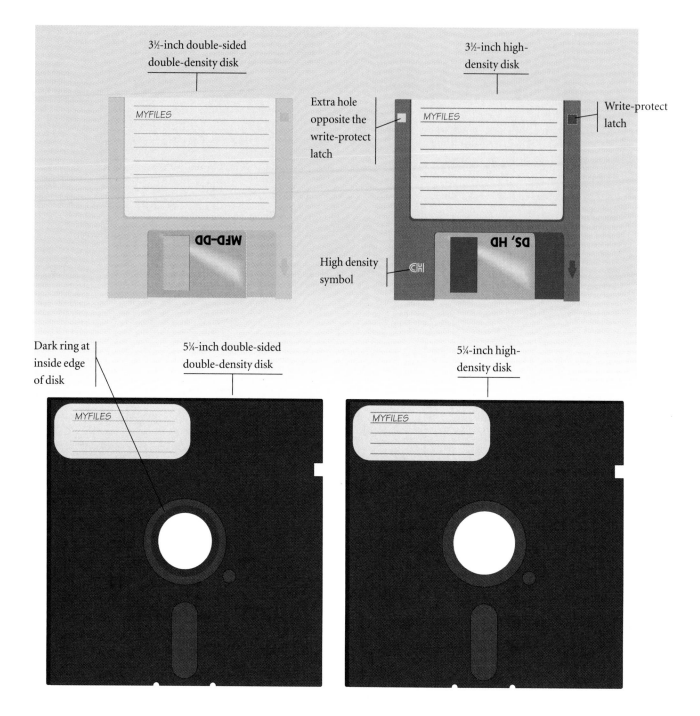

3½-inch double-sided double-density disk

MYFILES

MFD-DD

3½-inch high-density disk

MYFILES

DS, HD

Extra hole opposite the write-protect latch

Write-protect latch

High density symbol

Dark ring at inside edge of disk

5¼-inch double-sided double-density disk

MYFILES

5¼-inch high-density disk

MYFILES

computer off your desk or dropping it on the floor is an almost sure fire way to lose some data if not permanently damage the disk. Some hard disks are more sensitive than others, and may respond poorly to being repeatedly moved from desk to desk.

Hard disks can be especially sensitive to brownouts—dips in electrical power that are common in big cities in summertime. This is because hard disks are designed to spin at a particular speed. If they receive too little current, they spin slower than they're meant to, often with disastrous results.

The basic rules of thumb for caring for a hard disk are

▶ *Don't drop your computer.*

▶ *Unless you have a laptop or other computer designed for travel, don't move it any more often than you have to.*

MORE ABOUT HARD DRIVES

Most hard drives spin at a rate of somewhere between 3600 and 5400 revoluations per minute, generating the equivalent of gale-force winds at the edges of disk platters. While the disk is spinning, the read/write heads on hard disks do not actually touch the surface of the disk. Instead, they hover above or below the disk's surface, at a distance of millionths of an inch. (To make it a little more concrete, the distance between the read/write heads and a spinning disk is less than half the width of a particle of smoke.) When your computer is turned off, the read/write heads do come to rest on the surface of the disk, but only within a specified parking area that is reserved for this purpose and is never used for storing information.

If your hard drive malfunctions for some reason or you drop your computer on the floor, the read/write heads may fall onto the disk, permanently damaging it. This event, which is actually quite rare in modern-day hard drives, is known as a *head crash.* If someone tells you that their hard disk "crashed," they probably mean it underwent a head crash.

The small but essential gap that exists between the surface of the disk and the read/write heads explains why hard disks always live inside sealed containers, safe from such hazards as smoke, dust particles, and soda pop. Since the distance between the disk and the read/write head is half the size of a smoke particle, any encounter with such a particle would be like a high-speed go-cart running into a boulder.

THE READ/WRITE HEAD ENCOUNTERS A DUST PARTICLE

In hard drives, the read/write heads hover only millionths of an inch above or below the disk's surface. A single particle of dust or smoke is therefore enough to block the head's progress.

▶ *If you're relocating to another office or building, try to pack the computer in its original packing materials to cushion it during the move.*

▶ *Most importantly, back up your data regularly. Operate on the assumption that sooner or later, your disk will crash (probably a day or two before some crucial deadline).*

I've been representing each file as occupying a single discrete area of a disk. In reality, files are sometimes stored in segments scattered across the disk. The first part of a file may be wedged in between two other files, for example—perhaps in the space previously occupied by a file that you later deleted. Since not all of the file can fit in that space, your computer simply makes a note of where the next piece is stored (rather like the next clue in a treasure hunt). If there isn't enough room for the rest of the file in that second spot, your computer makes a note of where the third piece is stored, and so on. Files stored in this way are said to be *fragmented.*

Over time, your hard disk will accummulate many of these fragmented files. Every time you load a fragmented file into memory, your computer has to jump from one part of the hard disk to another collecting all the file's different pieces. You can improve your computer's efficiency by periodically *defragmenting* your hard disk—that is, running a special program that rearranges data so that all the parts of each file occupy contiguous clusters on the disk. (You can compare this process to a bunch of people trading seats so a group of friends can sit together.)

COMPUTER VIRUSES

Even people who've never touched a computer have heard ominous tales about computer viruses. A virus is a program, generally designed by a bright but maladjusted computer nerd, that in one way or another interrupts or undermines the normal workings of your computer. Viruses work by copying themselves into legitimate files, called *hosts.* From there, they often branch out, replicating themselves in more and more files on the disk. While some viruses infect almost every file in sight, others are more picky: Some viruses only infect application programs, other infect data files, and still others invade the operating system itself.

The level of destructiveness among viruses varies widely from one program to the next. Some viruses simply display pictures or messages on the screen periodically. Others erase or destroy both programs and data. They also wreak their havoc at very different speeds: for example, some viruses spread

94

FILE FRAGMENTATION AND DEFRAGMENTATION

Over time, files on a hard disk tend to become fragmented (stored in clusters that are scattered across the disk). You can improve your computer's performance by periodically defragmenting the disk—that is, running a program that puts all the parts of each file in adjacent clusters.

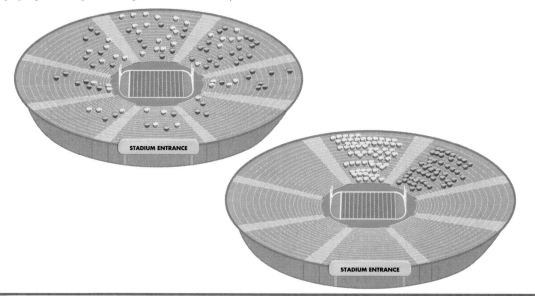

through your system fairly quickly but don't actually do anything for days or even months.

Viruses are usually passed via disk: you buy or are given a disk that already has the virus on it. Some PC viruses are only passed if you boot (start your computer) from an infected disk—meaning you turn your computer on with the disk already in the floppy drive. Others can infect your system when you copy a file from an infected disk or even when you attempt to erase an infected disk. Viruses can also be passed when you use a modem to download (copy) a file from a computer bulletin board or access data or programs on a network.

Before you get too paranoid about viruses, you should know that most computer users never actually encounter one. In my 11 years of working with personal computers, I have yet to contract a virus (although I have a few clients and colleagues who've been less fortunate). The chances of protracting a virus are particularly small if you only install commercially available, shrink-wrapped programs and rarely exchange disks with anyone else. The more computers your system comes in contact with—via modem or via floppy disks—the greater your risk.

There are several steps you can take to protect your system from viruses:

▶ *Back up your data religiously, and don't discard or overwrite all of your older backups. (As mentioned in Chapter 2, you usually back up data by copying it to floppy disks.) It may take you days or weeks to notice and diagnose a virus, and many of your files may be damaged in the meantime. Backing up your data every day may not help in this case—you may just be backing up damaged files. What you need is an older copy of the data, a copy made before your computer was infected.*

▶ *Write-protect floppies whenever possible. Since viruses cannot infect write-protected (locked) disks, you should write-protect any disk that you don't need to copy files to. In particular, always write-protect your original copies of program disks before you insert them into your computer. That way, if you install the program and the copy that resides on your hard disk becomes infected, you can always reinstall from your write-protected floppies.*

▶ *Use antivirus programs. Some antivirus programs only detect and eliminate viruses on command. Others are what is known as "terminate-and-stay-resident" programs, or TSRs, meaning that they remain in memory throughout your work session, automatically hunting down viruses on every disk you insert into your computer. If you're very worried about viruses, you may choose to use the terminate-and-stay-resident type, in which case, the program will check your hard disk for viruses as soon as you turn on your computer, as well as scoping out any floppies you use over the course of the day. If you don't like the idea of waiting for all this virus-checking, you may prefer a less aggressive approach. In this case, simply use a nonresident virus scanning program whenever you suspect that a disk might be infected. One reasonable approach is to use such a program to scan any floppies you get from other people (as opposed to from computer stores) before you insert them into your floppy drive. For good measure, you might also scan your hard disk once a month and then create an infection-free backup copy of everything on that disk. You should create these monthly backups in addition to daily or weekly backups of any new or revised data files. That way if you discover that your hard disk has been infected for a week and that you have been backing up infected files, you will have the older, infection-free backup to fall back on.*

N O T E　*Some terminate-and-stay-resident antivirus programs conflict with some of your application programs. If you install an antivirus program and then start experiencing problems with your other programs, see if uninstalling the antivirus program solves the problem.*

One final note: Now that you know what viruses are, don't start blaming them for everything that goes wrong with your computer. Most of the problems you encounter on computers will be due to hardware problems, program bugs (mistakes within the program), or your typos and other "user errors." If your computer starts displaying messages about being stoned, or if you keep encountering little happy faces in your word processing documents, by all means, investigate virus protection programs. But consider some of the other possibilities first.

NOTE *At best, antivirus programs can prevent or repair damage caused by already known viruses. Since new viruses are invented all the time, however, antivirus programs need to be updated to deal with each new menace to your computer's health. In most cases, you can buy updates to your antivirus program for a fraction of the program's original cost.*

UP AND RUNNING

4

In this chapter, you will learn the proper way to turn on and off your computer, and to communicate with and control your computer via the keyboard and mouse. You'll also learn some tips for arranging the different parts of your computer system for maximum comfort and minimum back, wrist, and eye strain.

STARTING UP YOUR COMPUTER

Many personal computer systems are set up so that all the components, including the system unit and the monitor, are plugged into a single power strip. In this case, you turn on your computer (and everything else in sight) by throwing the switch on the power strip itself. If you don't have a power strip, you'll have to turn on the components one a time.

MAC If you have a Macintosh system with external devices such as an external disk drive or a CD-ROM drive, turn those on first. Then locate the power switch on the system unit. The switch may be a regular looking switch located on the side or back of the machine, or it may be a button—often on the front of the unit—that you press in. Instead of an on/off switch, many Macintosh systems have a power button located either at the top of the keyboard, above all the other keys, or in the upper-right corner of your keyboard. (It is a largish button with a leftward-pointing arrowhead.) Many Macintosh monitors have on/off buttons of their own, so if you turn on the computer and the monitor stays dark, look for a button on the front of the monitor or a switch on the side or back.

PC If you are using a PC with a laser printer, it's a good idea not to turn on the printer at the same time you turn on the computer. Laser printers draw so much electricity that they can cause the power to fluctuate, which can put a particular strain on the computer during its start-up process.

WHAT HAPPENS WHEN YOU TURN ON YOUR COMPUTER

As you learned in Chapter 1, your computer hardware can't do much of anything without instructions from a program. When you turn on a computer, the first thing it does is go searching for a program that can tell it what to do next. (You might think of someone with extremely poor eyesight fumbling around for their glasses in the morning.)

The program the CPU is looking for is a very small part of the operating system known as the *boot program*. This program is stored in ROM (read-only memory) and is known as the boot program because it essentially helps the computer "pull itself up by its own bootstraps," by loading the rest of the operating system into memory. This process is known as *booting*.

Under the direction of this boot program, the CPU performs what is known as a *Power-On Self Test* (POST for short). During this stage, the CPU tests to see whether the various parts of the system are still alive and well.

If you have a PC, you will see a progress report during this phase. At a minimum, you will probably notice the computer counting up its memory. You may also see messages as the CPU checks out various peripherals and you may witness little lights on your keyboard and/or printer turn on and off. Finally, you'll hear a beep, indicating that everything seems to be okay. The same self-testing process occurs on the Macintosh, but with less running commentary.

Once the CPU has finished its internal inventory, it goes hunting for the rest of the operating system: the part that is stored on disk. The first place it looks is in the floppy-disk drive. (If you have a PC with two floppy drives, it looks to the drive named drive A—which is usually the leftmost or uppermost

BOOTING YOUR COMPUTER SYSTEM

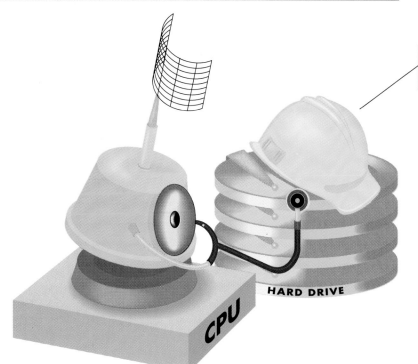

1. The CPU makes sure the disk drives and other components are working.

HARD DRIVE

CPU

MEMORY MAILBOXES

0	1	2	3	4
6	7	8	9	10
12	13			

2. The CPU takes an inventory of memory.

INVENTORY
MEMORY ✓

CPU

3. The read/write head locates the operating system on the hard disk.

4. On a Mac, a happy Macintosh face appears, followed by a Welcome to the Macintosh screen, and then the desktop. On a PC, the DOS prompt appears.

drive. If you have a Macintosh with two drives, it looks on the internal one first and then on the external one).

If the floppy-disk drive is empty, the CPU continues its search on the hard drive. If there is a floppy in the drive, however, your computer checks to see whether it contains the operating system. Now Macintosh computers are a bit smarter about this process than PCs: If the floppy in the floppy drive does not contain the operating system, the Macintosh simply ignores it and looks to the hard drive. On a PC, if there is a floppy without the operating system in the floppy-disk drive, the computer stops and displays the message "Non-system disk or disk error. Replace and strike any key when ready." At this point you have to open the floppy-drive door or eject the disk and press any key on your keyboard. The CPU will then resume its hunt for the operating system and, since it will no longer find a disk in drive A, will look to your hard drive. The moral of this story is that if you plan to work with a floppy disk, postpone inserting it until your system is done booting.

N O T E *The term for a disk that can be used to start up your computer is a* start-up disk, system disk, *or* boot disk. *(The term "boot disk" is almost exclusively used in the PC world.) All of these terms refer to the same thing: namely, a disk that contains the essential operating system files that your computer has to load before it can do anything else. In most cases, the start-up disk you will use is your hard disk. But you might use a floppy start-up disk if something goes wrong on your hard disk.*

As soon as the CPU locates the operating system, it loads it into memory. On a PC, you will then generally see something known as the DOS prompt. On a Macintosh system, you will briefly see the Happy Macintosh Face, followed by a Welcome to the Macintosh screen, and finally the Macintosh Desktop. You may then see icons (pictures) at the bottom of the screen as your computer

A STANDARD PC KEYBOARD

Your keyboard may have a different arrangement of keys. If you are using an older computer or laptop, or a notebook computer, you may have fewer keys altogether.

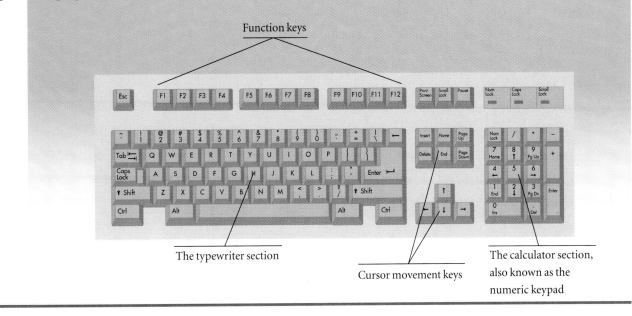

Function keys

The typewriter section

Cursor movement keys

The calculator section, also known as the numeric keypad

to the position of the Shift keys (the keys that let you type capital letters) because they're slightly above the spacebar key rather than directly to the spacebar's left or right. (The spacebar is the long key near the bottom of the keyboard. It is used to enter spaces between words and, less frequently, to select items from a list.) Until you get used to the new layout, you may find yourself pressing the wrong keys—like the ones labeled Ctrl or Alt, or the Command keys on a Macintosh keyboard (the ones with a symbol of an apple, a cloverleaf, or both.)

NOTE *The Caps Lock key on computer keyboards works a bit differently than the Shift Lock key on typewriters. Shift Lock on a typewriter affects punctuation keys and the number keys at the top of the keyboard, as well as letter keys. It allows you to type the character that appears on the top half of the key. Caps Lock on a*

A STANDARD MACINTOSH KEYBOARD

Some of the older models may not have all of these keys.

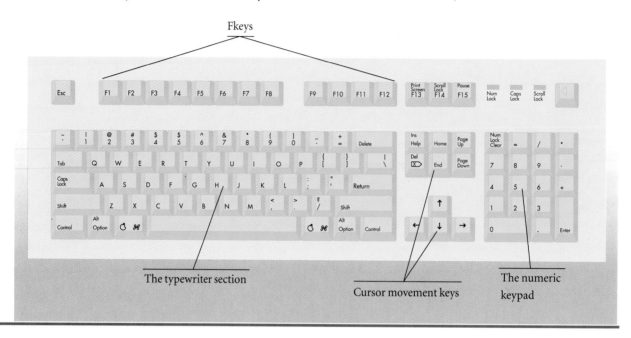

The typewriter section   Cursor movement keys   The numeric keypad

computer keyboard affects letters only. This means that typing a dollar sign requires holding down the Shift key while you press the 4 at the top of your keyboard, even if Caps Lock is on.

Caps Lock is what is known as a toggle key. A *toggle key* is a key that you use to alternately enable and then disable a particular feature. Like the power button on many stereos and TVs, you press it once to turn the feature on and again to turn it off.

The Enter or Return key works something like a carriage return on a typewriter: You press it to move to the next line when you get to the end of a paragraph. (In general, this key is labeled Enter on most PC keyboards and Return on Mac keyboards. Both PC and Mac keyboards may also have an additional Enter key, at the right side of the numeric keypad, to use when you're entering

THE TYPEWRITER KEYS

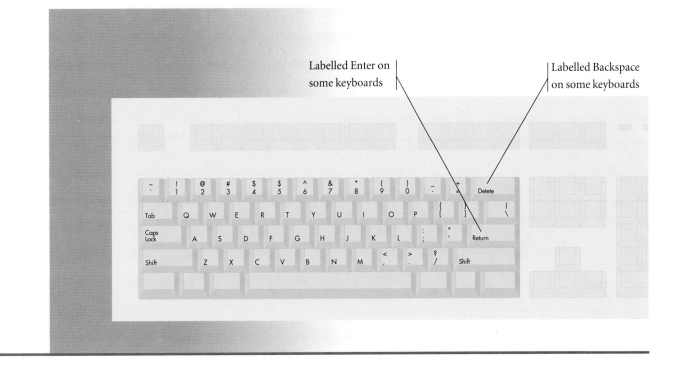

Labelled Enter on some keyboards

Labelled Backspace on some keyboards

numbers.) As you'll learn in Chapter 8, you don't need to press Enter/Return at the end of each line in word processing programs because the program automatically "word wraps" text to the next line when you reach the right margin. You still need to press Enter/Return to force the cursor to a new line before you reach the right margin, however. You also sometimes use Enter/Return to select options from a menu (on-screen list of options) or to indicate that you are done entering instructions or data and want the program to go ahead and respond.

NOTE *On some PC keyboards, the Enter key is labeled with the ⏎ symbol. This symbol is also used to indicate "Press the Enter key now" in many software manuals.*

The Tab key doesn't actually say Tab on some older PC keyboards and many laptops. It just has two arrows pointing in opposite directions, like ⇆ .

On PC keyboards and some of the newer Macintosh keyboards, there are two keys that contain slashes. One of these keys contains a question mark and a slash. The slash on this key is simply called a slash and is occasionally called a forward slash. The other key contains a vertical bar character, which looks like | or ¦. The type of slash on this key is called a backslash. It is rarely used as an actual character; most often it is used to precede a special formatting code, depending on the program. Just remember, if you're told to press slash, press the key with the question mark. If you're told to press the backslash, press the key with the vertical bar character. (The location of the backslash/vertical bar key varies from keyboard to keyboard.)

THE CURSOR MOVEMENT KEYS

In most programs, there is some symbol that indicates where you are on the screen at the moment—kind of like a "you are here" indicator on the map for a park or shopping mall or the bouncing ball that you are supposed to follow in old cartoons. In most cases, the symbol is a little blinking line or rectangle, known as a *cursor*. Sometimes it will be a larger bright rectangle, often referred to as the highlight or cell pointer. When you are entering text in Windows or on a Mac, the "you are here" symbol is a blinking vertical line known as the *insertion point.*

On most keyboards, there are two groups of keys designed to move the cursor around the screen.

The arrow keys move the cursor one character or one unit at a time in the direction of the arrow. To move one character to the left when you are entering text in a word processing program, for example, you press the Left Arrow key. On most keyboards, the arrow keys occupy keys by themselves.

The other cursor movement keys (Home, End, Page Up, and Page Down) let you make larger jumps across the screen. Their effects vary at least slightly from one program to the next. On some older PC keyboards and laptop keyboards, there are no separate cursor movement keys: They are always part of the numeric keypad (the calculator section). You'll discover how to use these dual-purpose keys when you learn about the numeric keypad. (You can also move the cursor using a mouse, if you have one.)

THE SPECIAL KEYS

The special keys include all the keys other than the normal typewriter keys, calculator keys, and function keys. These keys are scattered around the keyboard and are generally used to perform some operation other than displaying a particular character on the screen.

Most keyboards include two keys for erasing. The Backspace key on PC keyboards or the Delete key on Macintosh keyboards deletes the character to the left of your current position. (This key is labeled Backspace on some older Macintosh keyboards. On some PC keyboards, it doesn't say Backspace at all; it simply shows a leftward pointing arrow.)

The key labeled either Delete or Del on PC keyboards and labeled Del on Macintosh keyboards generally deletes the currently selected characters, if any. If no characters are selected, it deletes the character above or immediately just to the right of the cursor. Note that only the extended Macintosh keyboard includes a Del key.

THE BACKSPACE KEY VERSUS THE LEFT ARROW KEY

On PC keyboards, don't confuse the Backspace key and the Left Arrow key. Both of these keys contain leftward pointing arrows. (On older PC keyboards, the word Backspace doesn't even appear on the Backspace key; there's just an arrow.) Although both of these keys move the cursor to the left, the Left Arrow (like all arrow keys) moves the cursor nondestructively; it doesn't change anything. In contrast, the Backspace key moves and erases at the same time. Every time you press the key, the character to the left of the cursor is deleted and the cursor moves left one space to take up the slack. (If you've ever seen or played the game Pac Man, you can think of Backspace as the Pac Man key: it's like a little creature gobbling up the characters in its path.)

THE CURSOR MOVEMENT KEYS

You can move the cursor or insertion point using either the cursor-movement keys or your mouse.

The *insertion point* or *cursor* indicates your current position on the screen.

Untitled

Dear Aunt Alice,

Thanks so much for the birthday prese never too many ties!

Life here York continues to go

YOU ARE HERE

The Home key is often used to move to the beginning of some set of data—such as the top of a document, the beginning of a line, or the upper-left corner of a spreadsheet.

The Page Up key is usually used to move up one page or one screenful of data. (This key is often labeled PgUp.)

The Page Down key is usually used to move down one page or one screenful of data. (This key is often labeled PgDn.)

The End key is often used to move to the end of some set of data—such as the bottom of a document, the end of a line, or the last number or character in a particular block of data in a spreadsheet.

The arrow keys move the cursor one character or one unit at a time in the direction of the arrow.

On PC keyboards without a separate set of cursor movement keys, you use the arrows on the numeric keypad to move the cursor.

DELETING CHARACTERS

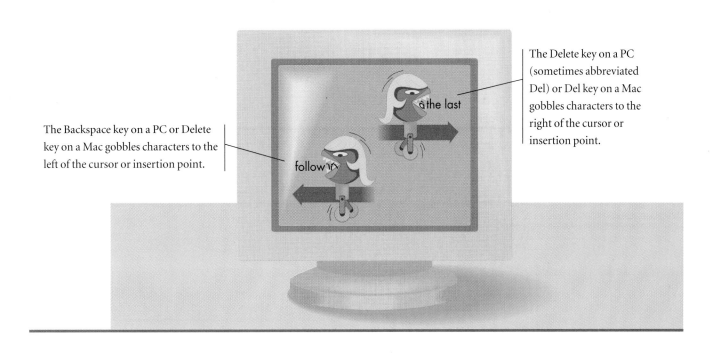

The Backspace key on a PC or Delete key on a Mac gobbles characters to the left of the cursor or insertion point.

The Delete key on a PC (sometimes abbreviated Del) or Del key on a Mac gobbles characters to the right of the cursor or insertion point.

There are a few other special keys on PC keyboards.

The Insert key (often abbreviated as Ins) is a toggle key that determines what happens when you type new characters within existing text. If the Insert feature is on and you type new characters in the middle of a paragraph, for example, the old characters are pushed to the right to make room for the new ones. When the Insert feature is off, the new characters simply replace the old ones. In some programs, the Insert feature is off by default, and pressing Insert the first time turns it on. In other programs, it is on by default, so pressing Insert turns it off. On certain PC keyboards, Insert shares a key with the number 0 on the numeric keypad.

On most PCs, the Print Screen key (often abbreviated to PrtScrn) sends an image of the screen directly to the printer—producing a "hard copy" (that is, a paper copy) of whatever currently appears on your monitor. On some

THE SPECIAL KEYS

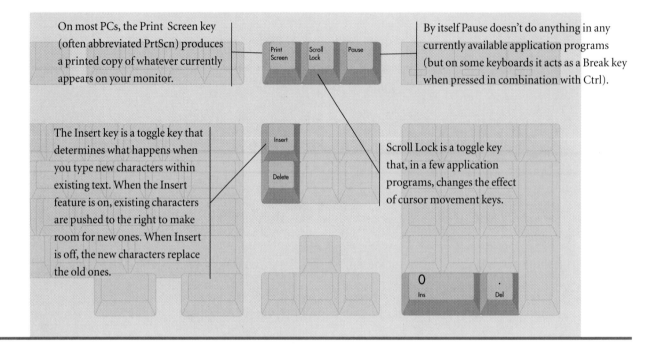

On most PCs, the Print Screen key (often abbreviated PrtScn) produces a printed copy of whatever currently appears on your monitor.

By itself Pause doesn't do anything in any currently available application programs (but on some keyboards it acts as a Break key when pressed in combination with Ctrl).

The Insert key is a toggle key that determines what happens when you type new characters within existing text. When the Insert feature is on, existing characters are pushed to the right to make room for new ones. When Insert is off, the new characters replace the old ones.

Scroll Lock is a toggle key that, in a few application programs, changes the effect of cursor movement keys.

systems, you need to hold Shift while you press the Print Screen key. In Windows, it sends an image of the screen to the Windows Clipboard (which you'll learn about in Chapter 6).

Scroll Lock is a toggle key that, in a few application programs, changes the effect of cursor movement keys. When Scroll Lock is on, pressing the cursor movement keys makes the display appear to scroll while the cursor stays put. Normally, the cursor moves as far as it can and only then does the display start scrolling.

Pause doesn't do anything in any currently available application programs (except on those keyboards where it acts as a Break key when pressed in combination with Ctrl).

THE MODIFIER KEYS

All PC and Macintosh keyboards contain three or more types of special keys that you use almost exclusively in combination with other keys and that don't do anything by themselves. (Many keyboards contain two keys of each type— that is, two Shift keys, two Control keys, and so on.) Since these keys' only function is to modify the effect of other keys, this book will refer to them as *modifier keys.*

PC For those of you who've used typewriters, the Shift key on a type-writer is an example of a modifier key. Pressing the Shift key by itself does nothing. But if you hold down Shift while pressing the letter *A*, you get an uppercase *A* instead of the lowercase *a* you get by pressing the A key by itself. Similarly, on a PC keyboard, nothing happens when you press Shift, Control (often abbreviated as Ctrl), Alt (short for Alternate). But in many application programs, holding down a modifier key while pressing another key is a way of issuing a command. In some word processing programs, for example, holding down the Ctrl key while pressing *U* issues the command to underline any currently selected text (while pressing *U* by itself would simply generate a letter *U* and pressing Ctrl by itself would do nothing).

MAC Macintosh keyboards include three types of modifier keys in addition to the Shift keys.

▶ *Command keys (the ones with the four-leaf clover and, in most cases, an apple) are used in combination with letters to let you issue commands quickly. Once you learn one of these key combination shortcuts, using it is often faster than issuing the same command by selecting options from menus. If you press the Command key by itself, nothing happens.*

KEY COMBINATIONS

When you use a key combination, you always press the modifier key
(in this case Ctrl) first and hold it down while you press the other key.

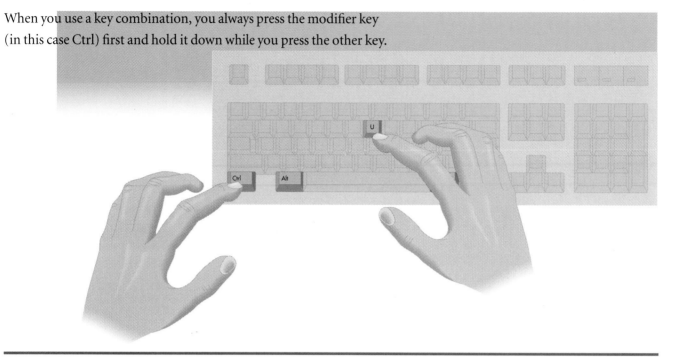

▶ *Option keys (which are generally located next to the command keys)*
  allow you to access special characters like a cent sign or an accent mark.
  They are often used in combination with the Command or Shift key.

▶ *Control keys are used in combination with other keys in a few Macintosh*
  programs. They are included on Mac keyboards largely to let you run
  DOS-based programs on your Mac.

The term *key combination* means a combination of two or more keys (at
least one of which is a modifier key) to perform some operation. Whenever you
use a key combination, you press the modifier key first and hold it down while
you press the other key. Don't try to press both keys at once. (If you do, you'll

often press the second key slightly before you press the modifier key, which has the effect of pressing that second key by itself.)

When computer books or manuals refer to key combinations, they sometimes combine the names of the keys with commas, with dashes, or plus signs. In other words, if you're supposed to hold down Alt while you press the Backspace key, the manual might say Alt,Backspace, Alt-Backspace, or Alt+Backspace.

FUNCTION KEYS

The function keys are the keys labeled F1 through either F10, F12, or F15. They are frequently located at the top of the keyboard, although they sometimes live to the left of the keyboard keys in older PC keyboards.

PC In some PC application programs, function keys are used to issue commands. For example, F1 is frequently used to invoke an application's Help system, which provides you with information on how to use the program. F10 is often used to activate the program's menus.

MAC Function keys are generally known as Fkeys in Macintosh manuals; older Mac keyboards may not have them at all. Although Fkeys rarely serve a set purpose in Macintosh programs, you can purchase special programs, like QuicKeys, that allow you to program those keys to do whatever you like. Fkeys are included on Mac keyboards partly so that you can run PC programs from your Macintosh. (To do this, you must run a special PC-emulation program like Soft PC.)

THE NUMERIC KEYPAD

PC There are currently two basic layouts for PC keyboards: one, often called the *extended keyboard* for desktop PCs, and another layout for laptops. The

THE FUNCTION KEYS OR FKEYS

In some PC application programs, function keys are used to issue commands.

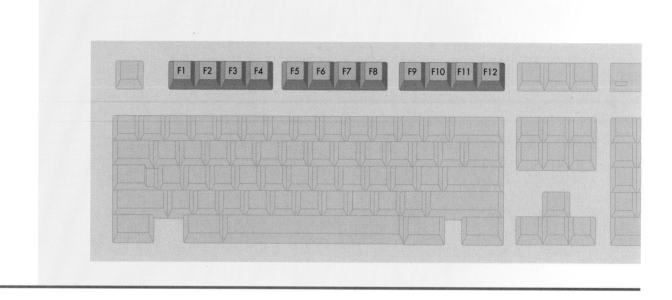

main difference between the two is that desktop keyboards generally have both a numeric keypad and separate groups of cursor movement keys, while laptops usually have a numeric keypad that doubles as a set of cursor movement keys.

PC　On all PC keyboards, you can use the numeric keypad for either of two functions: typing numbers or moving around on the screen. The status of the Num Lock (number lock) setting—which you control by pressing the NumLock key—determines which of these two hats the keypad is currently wearing. Num Lock is a toggle key, like the Caps Lock key (or Shift Lock on a typewriter): Each time you press it, the status of the Num Lock feature changes, from off to on or on to off.

When Num Lock is on, the keys on the numeric keypad generate numbers. When Num Lock is off, they change to cursor movement keys. The 7 key

THE NUMERIC KEYPAD

On PC keyboards, you can use the numeric keypad either for typing numbers or moving around the screen, depending on the current status of the Num Lock setting. On Macs, the numeric keypad is used for typing numbers only.

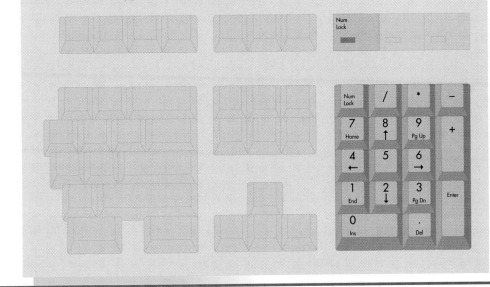

acts like a Home key, for example, and the 8 key serves as an Up Arrow key. The function of the each key is spelled out on the key itself. (The effect of the cursor movement keys was covered earlier in this chapter.)

The gray keys other than the Num Lock key around the outside of the numeric keypad work the same regardless of whether Num Lock is on or off. They let you enter mathematical symbols like + and - (the / symbol is often used to symbolize division and the * symbol is often used to symbolize multiplication). The Enter key works just like the Enter or Return key in the main section of the keyboard.

There are usually several ways to determine whether Num Lock is on or off. On most keyboards, there is a little light on the key itself or a light labeled Num Lock above the key. If the light is on, the feature is on. Many applications programs also display the words Num Lock or Num on the screen when Num

Lock is on. Worse comes to worst, you can just press one of the arrow keys and see whether the cursor moves or a number is generated.

Why, you may wonder, would you want to turn off Num Lock? On older style IBM keyboards and many laptops, there is no separate set of arrow keys. You therefore have to choose between using the cursor movement keys and using the numeric keypad to type numbers. If you don't need to do a lot of moving around at the moment, you might turn Num Lock on temporarily to enter a set of numbers, particularly if you're a wiz at touch-typing on calculators. Otherwise, you leave Num Lock off and use the number keys at the top of the keyboard to enter numbers. The Num Lock key was carried over to the newer keyboards primarily to accommodate all those people who had already grown used to moving around with keys on the numeric keypad (habits are hard to break). The NumLock key also supports older programs not capable of recognizing the new keys. Some people also prefer the layout of arrow keys on the numeric keypad (with the up arrow key above the left arrow and right arrow keys).

Tip: It's a lot easier to type arithmetic operators (like + and *) using keys at the side of the numeric keypad rather than keys at the top of the keyboard. If you use the keys at the top of the keyboard, you always need to remember to hold down the Shift key. If you forget, you get = when you mean + or 8 when you mean *.

MAC Like PCs, most Macintosh keyboards contain a numeric keypad with keys for entering the digits 0 through 9, a decimal point, and the arithmetic operators: + for addition, - for subtraction, / for division, and * for multiplication. On Mac keyboards, unlike PC keyboards, the numeric keypad also includes an = key and a Clear key. In some programs, you can use the Clear key, to clear, or undo, the last number you typed in case you made a mistake, just as you'd use the C or Clear key on many calculators.

WHAT TO DO WHEN YOU GET STUCK

You should never turn off your computer in the middle of an application if you can avoid it. (Turning off your computer is covered later in this chapter.) It can damage data and, at the least, cause you to lose any unsaved data in memory. Occasionally, however, you may just get stuck. There may be a "bug" (glitch) in the program you are using and you may get an error message that won't go away; or the program may stop responding to your commands.

PC Here are some techniques to try if you do get stuck on a PC, listed from the least drastic to the most.

▶ *In many application programs, the Escape key (usually labeled Esc) is a general-purpose "get me out of here" key—used to cancel or back up a step in the current operation.*

▶ *Although there is no key with the word Break on the top, on most PC keyboards, either the Scroll Lock key or the Pause key has the word Break on its front edge. (If you don't find Break on either key, assume that you can use Scroll Lock for this purpose.) Holding down a Ctrl key and pressing this key will interrupt some programs or commands, although not all. This key combination is referred to as Ctrl+Break (pronounced "Control Break").*

▶ *If neither of the preceding techniques works, you can do what is known as rebooting your computer by holding down the Ctrl and Alt keys and then tapping the Del key. Rebooting means erasing memory and then*

GETTING OUT OF TROUBLE ON A PC

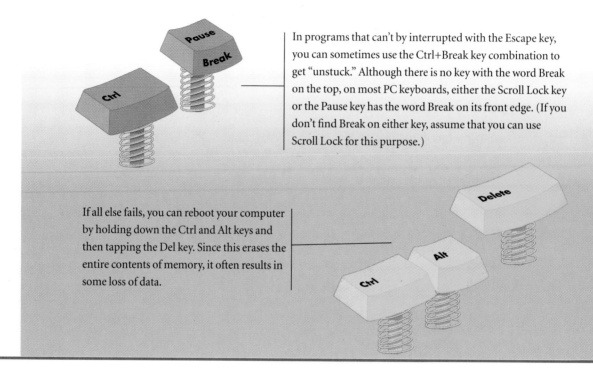

In programs that can't by interrupted with the Escape key, you can sometimes use the Ctrl+Break key combination to get "unstuck." Although there is no key with the word Break on the top, on most PC keyboards, either the Scroll Lock key or the Pause key has the word Break on its front edge. (If you don't find Break on either key, assume that you can use Scroll Lock for this purpose.)

If all else fails, you can reboot your computer by holding down the Ctrl and Alt keys and then tapping the Del key. Since this erases the entire contents of memory, it often results in some loss of data.

reloading the operating system. When you do this, you lose any data currently in memory. In some programs, you may damage data as well, so only use this key combination when you can't think of any other way to get out of your current fix. Although fairly drastic, rebooting is still a bit safer than the next two options.

▶ *Many PCs have a Reset button that lets you restart your computer without actually flicking the power switch. The only practical difference between pressing this button and turning your computer off and on is the main power to the computer's components is not interrupted, resulting in less wear and tear.*

▶ *If all else fails and your computer doesn't have a Reset button, turn the computer off, wait at least ten seconds, and then turn it on again.*

MAC There are also a few different strategies you can try for getting un-stuck on a Mac. Although the Escape (Esc) key is rarely used in Macintosh programs, in a few programs it undoes the last operation or cancels the current one. In some other programs, you can cancel an operation by holding the Command key and pressing the period.

Holding down the Command key and the Option key on a Mac, and then pressing Escape executes what is known as a *forced quit*. This key combination will usually—but not always—get you out of an application program if nothing else will. Assuming it works, you will see a message asking if you really want to quit the program. Select Forced Quit if you do or Cancel if you don't.

USING A MOUSE OR TRACKBALL

Keyboards are only one of the tools available for talking to your computer. The other main tool, and one that's particularly important if you are using a Mac or running Windows, is a mouse or trackball.

A mouse is a hand-held pointing device that lets you point to, select, and manipulate objects on the screen. As you move the mouse around on your desk, a special symbol, known as the mouse pointer, moves in an analogous direction on the screen. If you move the mouse forward and backward, the mouse pointer moves up and down on the screen; if you move the mouse left and right, the mouse pointer moves left and right. Although the mouse pointer most often looks like an arrow, it can assume other shapes, depending on which program you are running and what operation you are performing.

You can hold the mouse in either hand. Most people prefer to use their dominant hand (the right if right-handed or left if left-handed). Make sure that

THE MANY GUISES OF THE MOUSE POINTER

In most programs, the mouse pointer assumes different shapes depending on what you are doing.

the mouse cord is pointing away from you. Then just glide the mouse lightly over the surface of your desk.

If you reach the edge of your desk or your mouse pad before you reach the desired point on the screen, just lift your mouse up and move it. The mouse pointer only moves when the mouse is flat against a surface like a desktop, so that the ball underneath is rolled as you move the device. If you are trying to move the mouse pointer down to the bottom of your screen, for example, and you reach the front edge of your desk when the mouse pointer is still an inch above the desired spot, just lift the mouse, move it back a few inches, and then continue moving it forward.

N O T E   *If you use a mouse often, you may want to purchase a mouse pad: a rectangular piece of nylon-covered rubber that you place on your desktop as a platform for your mouse. Many people find that their mouse gets better traction and* *therefore moves more smoothly on a pad than directly on a desktop, particularly if the surface of the desk is at all uneven.*

A trackball is essentially an upside down mouse. Instead of having a ball on the bottom, it has a ball on the top, set inside a square cradle. Rolling this ball has the same effect as moving the mouse around on your desk.

Many of the operations that you perform using a mouse or trackball involve pushing buttons. Macintosh mice have a single large button. Mice designed for PCs have either two or three buttons: a left button, a right button, and occasionally a third button, known as the middle button. Although there are very few programs that use the middle button, you can often program that button so that pressing it once has the same effect as double-clicking the left mouse button. (For instructions on doing this, see your mouse manual.) When you see instructions to press or click the mouse button, assume that you should use the left mouse button unless explicitly told otherwise. If you are supposed to click the right mouse button, for example, the instructions will say "right-click" or "click the right mouse button" rather than just "click." The button(s) on trackballs are usually positioned at the far end of the device. You can press them using either your thumb or forefinger.

MOUSE SOFTWARE

PC If you are using a PC, you may need to explicitly load your mouse software before you can use the mouse within most programs. If you are running Windows programs in the Windows operating system, you don't need to load mouse software first: Windows has its own program for dealing with the mouse. With most other programs, however, you will need to load the mouse software yourself. If you're not sure whether you need to load your mouse software, you can try starting up the program and seeing whether a mouse pointer

THINGS YOU CAN DO WITH A MOUSE OR TRACKBALL

When you read software manuals, there are five terms you are likely to encounter for the various things you can do with a mouse or trackball.

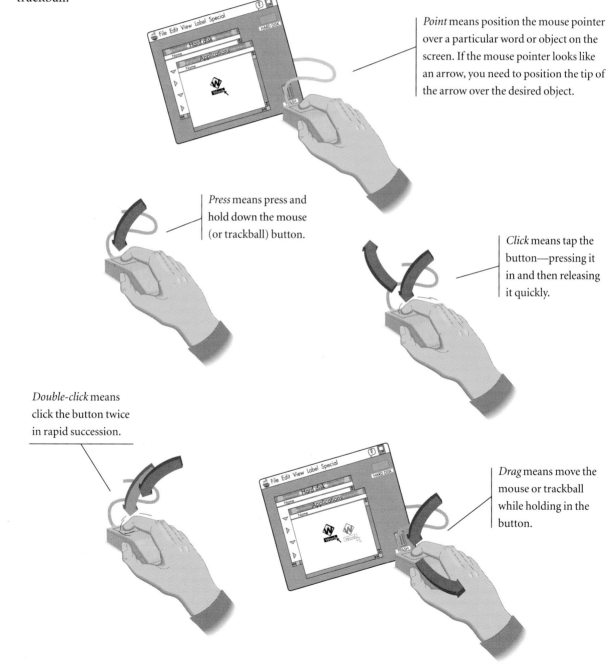

Point means position the mouse pointer over a particular word or object on the screen. If the mouse pointer looks like an arrow, you need to position the tip of the arrow over the desired object.

Press means press and hold down the mouse (or trackball) button.

Click means tap the button—pressing it in and then releasing it quickly.

Double-click means click the button twice in rapid succession.

Drag means move the mouse or trackball while holding in the button.

appears on your screen. (Try moving your mouse around and seeing if anything moves on the screen.) If you do see a mouse pointer, you can assume that either the program has its own tools for communicating with the mouse or that the person who set up your system has directed the computer to load the mouse software automatically as soon as you turn on your computer. If you don't see a mouse pointer, consult your mouse manual for instructions on loading your mouse software. (If you just bought the mouse, you'll probably need to install the software first. Again, see the mouse manual for instructions.)

Cleaning Your Mouse

Turn the mouse upside down and turn the round lid on the underside of the mouse counterclockwise. (On most mice, the open position for the lid is clearly marked.) Once the lid is open, the ball should drop out into your palm. Clean the rollers inside the mouse using a cotton swab dipped in alcohol. Clean the ball using a soft, dry cloth. Then place the ball in one hand, use your other hand to place the mouse part on top of it, and flip your hands over. Replace the lid and rotate it clockwise to the close position.

Turning Off Your Computer

The first thing to know about turning off your computer is that you shouldn't do it too often. In general, you should turn off your computer only when you don't plan on using it again for several hours. If you're simply going to lunch, leaving the computer on for an hour or two causes less wear and tear than turning it off and then on again. As explained in Chapter 9, however, you may want to turn off your monitor temporarily, both to protect the screen and to turn off the electromagnetic radiation.

KEEP YOUR MOUSE CLEAN

Mice should be cleaned occasionally to keep them moving smoothly.

When you are done using your computer for the day, save any unsaved data that you want to be able to use in future work sessions. Then follow this procedure:

PC If you are using a PC, you need to exit any applications programs and exit Windows if necessary before you turn off the computer. You can tell that it's safe to turn off your computer if you see a symbol known as the DOS prompt— usually a capital C followed by one or more characters and then a greater than sign—followed by a cursor (a short blinking line). If you see the words Program Manager on the top line of your screen, you are in Windows. Press and hold down the Alt key and, while Alt is held down, press the letter F to open the File menu. Then type X to select eXit. When you are warned that this will end your

Windows session, press Enter. In a moment, you will be returned to the DOS prompt and can safely turn off the machine.

MAC   With Macs, you must shut down your computer by issuing the Special ShutDown command. To do this, point to the Special option on the menu bar at the top of the screen. Then press the mouse button to open the Special menu. Drag the highlight down to the ShutDown option, and then release the button. The Mac will update its information on the current state of the Desktop (its working environment) and then turn off automatically.

ERGONOMICS: TAKING CARE OF YOUR BODY WHILE YOU USE A COMPUTER

You'll never learn to love (or even tolerate) a computer, if it causes you discomfort or pain. If you're planning to spend hours at the keyboard, it's therefore worth taking time to make the experience as comfortable as possible. Setting up your workstation properly isn't just about feeling good (although that's a worthy goal in itself). It's also a way of preventing painful and potentially debilitating conditions like carpal tunnel syndrome, tendonitis, repetitive motion disorder, or chronic back pain.

The figure "The Ergonomic Workstation" shows how to arrange your computer to cause minimum wear and tear on your body. The basic rules of thumb are as follows:

▶ *The top edge of your monitor should be at eye level or slightly below, so that you're looking down slightly. (You may need to prop up the monitor with a large book or a monitor stand.)*

▶ *Your wrists should never be higher than your elbows. Ideally, your elbows should be bent at a 90 degree angle and your wrists should be straight rather than flexed upward or bent downward. If you can't achieve this position given your desk height, your desk is too high (or your chair seat too low). You may want to get a typing desk or a keyboard drawer that allows the keyboard to sit lower than the desktop.*

▶ *Your feet should touch the floor or a foot rest and the angle between your thighs and spine should be 90 degrees or a bit more.*

One of the worst things you can do to your wrists is lean the heel of your hand on the desk, so that your wrist is flexed backward as you type. Either train yourself to hold your wrists up (like your piano teacher always told you) or buy a wrist rest that raises your wrist to the level of the keyboard. (You can purchase wrist rests in some computer or office supply stores, through office/computer supply catalogs, and often in stores that specialize in back problems.) Some mice—such as the Apple Desktop Bus Mouse II and all mice currently produced by Logitech—are designed to conform to the shape of your hand and may result in less strain.

You can also alleviate wrist strain by adjusting the angle of your keyboard. You can angle most keyboards so that the back is slightly higher than the front. On some Mac keyboards, you adjust the angle by sliding a bar located in the middle of the front side of the keyboard. Most other keyboards have tabs underneath; swinging down these tabs raises the back end of the keyboard.

Part of the problem with most computer keyboards (and typewriters) is that they force you to hold your hands at an unnatural angle to your arms—so that your hands are both more horizontal to the desk than they'd like to be and rotated slightly outward at the wrist. Apple now makes a keyboard—named

THE ERGONOMIC WORKSTATION

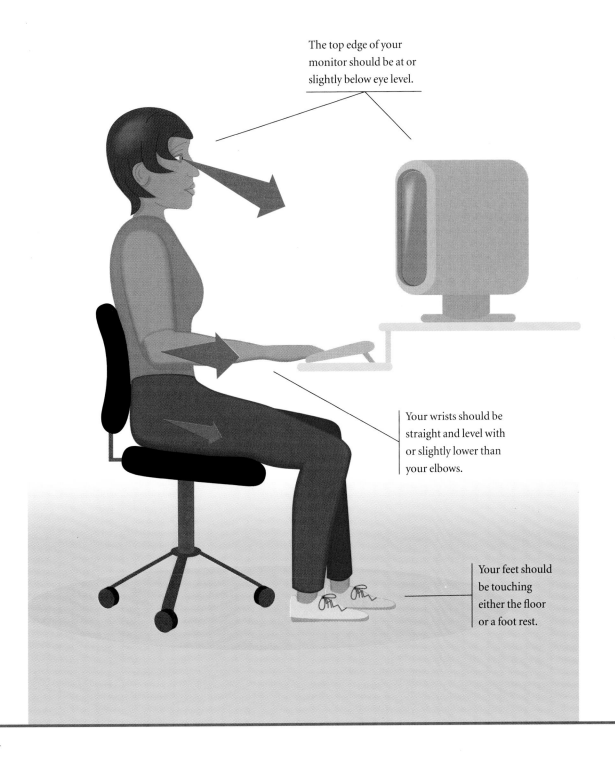

The top edge of your monitor should be at or slightly below eye level.

Your wrists should be straight and level with or slightly lower than your elbows.

Your feet should be touching either the floor or a foot rest.

the Apple Adjustable Keyboard—that is split down the middle, allowing you to move the halves outward as much as 30 degrees. There are similar keyboards available for PCs, although they are not cheap and usually have to be specially ordered.

Many people also experience some eye strain after staring at a computer screen for a few hours. The best approach here is to rest your eyes periodically, by focusing on a distant object once in a while, blinking often, and taking short breaks every hour or two. You should also make sure that you have proper lighting. Avoid overhead lights whenever possible because they almost always reflect off your screen. The best source of lighting is probably a desk or floor lamp or track lights that are not directly aimed at your screen. Beautiful as it is, sunlight streaming in the windows usually leads to glare as well. If your computer resides in a room full of windows, make sure you have shades that you can draw when necessary. For about $20, you can also buy a glare screen, usually made of very fine wire mesh, to fit over the front of your monitor—cutting down on glare and, in many cases, sharpening the contrast between light and dark.

See Chapter 9 for information on the potential health hazards involved in using computer monitors and what you can do about them.

Finally, if you have any back problems (or are determined to avoid them), a good chair is essential. Look for one that provides support for your lower back and that is fully adjustable. (You should be able to change both the height of the seat and the angle of the seat and the back.)

NOTE *Try not to get too paranoid about the health hazards of computers. There are hazards (including boredom) in most lines of work, and pianists and meat packers are about as prone to carpal tunnel syndrome as dedicated computer hackers. What's more, some people work on computers 8 to 10 hours a day, with lousy chairs, poor posture, and no ill effects. (Then again, some people smoke* *two packs a day and live into their 80s.) A good rule of thumb is that you should pay attention to how you feel after a day at your computer. If your neck, back, wrists, arms, or eyes are sore, respond accordingly, doing everything you can to minimize the strain. If all else fails, see a doctor—sooner rather than later.*

You have now learned everything you need to know about hardware in order to get started using your personal computer. You will learn more about hardware—particularly printers, monitors, and networks—in Chapter 9. In the meantime, the focus will move to software—the instructions that tell the hardware what to do.

As you learned in Chapter 1, operating systems are programs that, in effect, allow your computer to operate. They help control the flow of information from one part of the computer to another. They serve as an intermediary between application programs and your hardware. And they allow you to perform disk housekeeping operations like copying, erasing, and renaming files on disks.

Learning at least a little bit about your operating system is an essential step in learning to use your computer. At minimum, you'll need to know enough to start up application programs to erase and copy files. But the more you learn about the operating system, the more you will understand both your hardware and the application programs that use the operating system as their base. The next three chapters cover three different operating systems: DOS, Windows, and the Macintosh operating system. If you are using Windows, start by at least skimming the chapter on DOS. You will need to understand something about how DOS handles files in order to make sense of Windows. Otherwise, just read the chapter on the operating system you will be using.

GETTING TO KNOW DOS

No one has ever accused DOS of being user-friendly. In fact, dozens of programs (including Windows) have been written to shield users from the stark and somewhat intimidating DOS environment.

DOS does have its virtues, however. Despite its gruff manner, DOS is a very efficient vehicle for performing disk housekeeping operations. If you like to get things done with as much speed and little fuss as possible, you may actually prefer DOS to more graphical operating systems. You need to memorize a few commands in order to use DOS, but once you do, you can usually tell the computer exactly what you want it to do with a single command. You don't need to spend a lot of time hunting through menus or windows or other paraphernalia on the screen. In short, DOS is a rather minimalist environment, offering plenty of power if little in the way of assistance or pretty pictures.

As with any operating system, you use DOS to do two things:

▶ *Start up application programs*

▶ *Manipulate and organize files on disks*

Most of this chapter is devoted to what I call "disk housekeeping" commands—that is, commands for managing files. The more you use your computer, the more files you are likely to accumulate. Learning to handle these files—be they word-processing documents, spreadsheets, or other types of data or program files—is an essential part of using your computer well. At a minimum, you'll need to know how to list the contents of a disk, to copy files from one disk to another (like from your hard disk to a floppy or vice versa), to delete files that you no longer need, and to figure out what happened to that file you created last week. You'll learn to do all this and a bit more in the following pages.

THE DOS PROMPT

Working in DOS is a matter of typing in commands next to a special symbol known as the DOS prompt. In most cases, when you first see the DOS prompt it looks like C:\>. I say in most cases because you can customize the DOS prompt to use any characters you like. (Some people change the prompt to display their name or the current date, for example.)

Think of the prompt as DOS's way of saying "Okay, now what?" Any time the last line currently on your screen shows a DOS prompt followed by a cursor (a little blinking line), DOS is ready and waiting for your next instruction.

In general, your interactions with DOS will work like this:

▶ *A DOS prompt appears with the cursor blinking after it.*

▶ *You type one of two things: a DOS command or, if you wish to load an application program, the name of the main program file. (You'll learn more about loading programs later in this chapter.) If you make a mistake while typing, use the Backspace key to back up, erasing as you go, and then type the characters in again. If you want to throw out the entire line, press Esc to display a new DOS prompt.*

▶ *When you finish typing, you press the Enter key to tell DOS "Okay, I'm done typing. Now go ahead and do it."*

▶ *DOS does whatever you asked it to do, often displaying a message or two on the screen to let you know what it's doing.*

▶ *When DOS finishes executing the command, it displays another DOS prompt.*

One thing that people often find confusing at first is that DOS does not clean up after itself: Its responses to previous commands remain on the screen until the screen is full. Once the screen is full, the oldest lines start disappearing off the top of your screen. It might help to imagine the information on your screen as part of an adding machine tape: Even though the results of old calculations may still be visible on the tape, they are no longer relevant to the calculation at hand.

When you use DOS, the only line that's really relevant at the moment is the last one on the screen, the line on which the cursor appears. Everything above that line is simply flotsam and jetsam left over from previous commands.

DOS may be curt, but it's also very forgiving. If you type in a command name that's wrong or invalid, DOS will display the message "Bad command or file name" indicating that it has no idea what you're talking about. (Specifically, the message tells you that DOS knows of no commands or program files with names that match the first word you entered.) Then it immediately displays another DOS prompt, indicating that it is ready to accept another command.

In most cases, the DOS prompt provides you with two critical pieces of information:

▶ *The name of the current disk drive. Remember that on PCs, disk drives are always represented by letters: The first floppy drive is drive A, and the first hard drive is drive C. Whenever you or DOS refers to a particular drive, the drive letter is followed by a colon. Drive C, for example, is represented as C:.*

IN DOS, OLD LINES ARE NOT ERASED FROM THE SCREEN

When you use DOS, the only line that's relevant at the moment is the last one on the screen: the DOS prompt that is followed by a cursor. All the other lines are simply leftovers from previous commands, waiting to be scrolled off screen. A new DOS prompt is DOS's way of saying "What do you want me to do next?"

```
C:\>dir *.sys
   Volume in drive C has no label Volume Serial Number
   is 12E7–0823
   Directory of C:\
HIMEM    SYS   11304  10-31-90    3:00a
CONFIG   SYS     538  04-17-93    3:32p
      2 file(s)   11842 bytes
               76275712 bytes free

C:\>date
Current date is Tue 05-25-93
Enter new date (mm-dd-yy):

C:\>

C:\>delete b:*.*
All files in directory will be deleted!
Are you sure (Y/N)? y
C:\>dir b:
   Volume in drive B has no label
   Directory of B:\
CHAP5    51622  05-24-93   11:18a
      1 file(s)        51622 bytes
                      262144 bytes free

C:\>_
```

▶ *The name of the current directory—that is, the directory that DOS assumes you want to use.*

Returning to the filing analogy introduced in Chapter 3, the DOS prompt tells you which filing cabinet (disk drive) and which part of the file drawer (directory) you are currently in.

When you first turn on your computer, you are looking at the main directory on the disk, which is known as the *root directory*. In the filing analogy, the root directory is the file drawer as a whole. The root directory is always represented by a backslash (the slash that shares a key with the vertical bar character rather than with the question mark). When you see C:\ in either the DOS

WHAT THE DOS PROMPT TELLS YOU

Name of the current disk drive

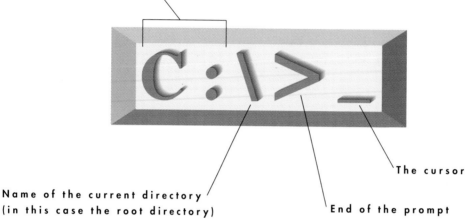

The cursor

Name of the current directory
(in this case the root directory)

End of the prompt

prompt itself or as part of a DOS command, it means "drive C, the root directory" or "the root directory on drive C."

If your disk is organized properly, the majority of files will be stored in subdirectories. When you get a directory listing for your root directory, you should therefore see only a handful of files and several subdirectories. On floppy disks, the situation is a bit different. Since floppy disks contain relatively few files, the entire collection of files usually resides in the root directory: there is no need to group them into subdirectories.

NOTE *Technically, there is only one directory on the hard disk—the root directory; all the subgroupings of files are subdirectories. In practice, the terms are used far more loosely. The root directory is always called a directory, but subdirectories are often called directories, as well.*

If you find that the root directory of your hard disk actually contains dozens of files, copy any files that you recognize as data files—such as word processing documents or spreadsheets—to a floppy disk or to one of the subdirectories on your hard disk. Then you can delete the originals from the root. (You'll learn to copy and delete files later in this chapter.) Be careful not to delete files with the names AUTOEXEC.BAT, CONFIG.SYS, or COMMAND.COM. AUTOEXEC.BAT and CONFIG.SYS are files that DOS looks for in the root directory as soon as you finish booting. COMMAND.COM is the main DOS program file.

As mentioned, DOS always assumes that you want to work with the directory that is named in the DOS prompt. When you first turn on your computer, the DOS prompt probably says C:\>. When you start issuing commands that deal with files on a disk, DOS will therefore assume that you are talking about files stored in the root directory on drive C unless you explicitly tell it otherwise. If you tell DOS to copy a file named LETTER.TXT, for example, and you don't specify where the file is located, DOS assumes that the file is in the drive and directory that appear in the DOS prompt. If DOS can't find the file in that location, it simply says "File not found." It doesn't try to track down the file elsewhere. Later in the chapter, you will learn to change drives and directories, a change that will be reflected in the DOS prompt itself.

Before you start learning individual DOS commands, let's take another quick tour of the keyboard, with an eye toward how various keys work in the DOS environment. The figure called "Keys You Can Use in DOS" explains how certain keys work in DOS.

DETERMINING YOUR DOS VERSION

The first DOS command you will learn is the VER command, which tells you which version of DOS your computer is currently running. All successful programs are periodically updated and, hopefully, improved by their

KEYS YOU CAN USE IN DOS

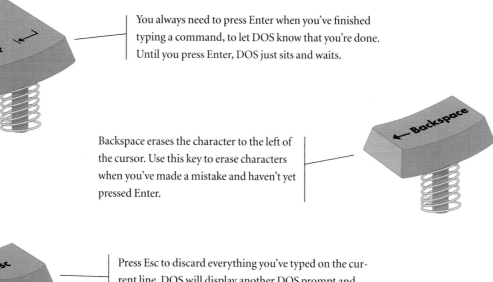

You always need to press Enter when you've finished typing a command, to let DOS know that you're done. Until you press Enter, DOS just sits and waits.

Backspace erases the character to the left of the cursor. Use this key to erase characters when you've made a mistake and haven't yet pressed Enter.

Press Esc to discard everything you've typed on the current line. DOS will display another DOS prompt and you can start again from scratch.

Press Home to move the cursor to the beginning of the current line and End to move back to the end.

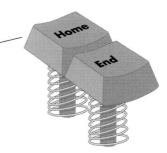

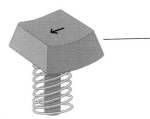

Press the Left Arrow key if you want to back up through the characters you've typed, without erasing as you go. (Press the Right Arrow key or the End key to move back to the right again.)

To interrupt a command that DOS is in the midst of executing, hold down Ctrl and press the key that says Break at the bottom or on its front edge (usually the Pause or Scroll Lock key). If you can't find any key with the word Break, try holding Ctrl and pressing Scroll Lock.

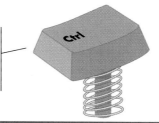

makers. The versions are identified by numbers. You may, for example, be using DOS 6.0 or DOS 3.3. The number to the left of the decimal point indicates a major revision and the number to the right of the decimal point indicates a minor revision. It's helpful to know which version of DOS (or any other program) you are using because the program's newer features will only be available in the most recent versions. In this chapter, I'll point out any features that were only recently added to the program.

You can use the VER command when you sit down at someone else's computer and want to know which of the new DOS features are available.

NOTE *DOS doesn't pay any attention to the case of letters. I'll generally be showing commands in uppercase, but you can enter them in any mixture of upper- and lowercase letters that you like.*

DIR: THE TABLE OF CONTENTS COMMAND

Often the first task in cleaning up a disk or moving files from one location to another is taking stock of the disk's contents. You can do this with the DIR command, which tells DOS to display a *directory* (list) of the files on a disk. You may find it helpful to think of this type of directory as a building directory—the roster of companies displayed in the lobby of many office buildings. You can also think of DIR as the table of contents command. I'm going to spend a bit of time on the DIR command, both because you'll use it fairly often and because it can give you a feel for how DOS commands work in general.

NOTE *You may find it a bit confusing that the word directory has two slightly different meanings in DOS lingo: namely, a group of files on a disk, and a list of files. To help keep things clear, I'll refer to the list displayed when you enter a DIR command as a directory listing.*

By default (meaning, unless you request otherwise), the DIR command produces a list of all the files in the disk and the directory that currently appears in the DOS prompt. At the moment, your DOS prompt probably says C:\>, so if you simply type DIR and press Enter, you will get a list of everything in the root directory on drive C. In most cases, this list will contain a few files and several directories (subdirectories of the root directory). The figure "A Directory Listing for the Root Directory" shows a sample directory listing; yours will undoubtedly look at least a little different.

N O T E *Most hard disks contain a subdirectory named DOS that contains the files for some of the more specialized, less frequently used DOS commands. Most of the other subdirectories of your root directory will probably contain application programs.*

If your computer is on and you are at a DOS prompt, go ahead and try it yourself: Type DIR and press Enter. The resulting list may be too long to fit on the screen, in which case, some text will scroll off the top. (You'll learn how to fix this problem in a moment.)

The figure "Anatomy of a DOS Directory Listing" shows all the different pieces of the directory listing. The centerpiece is a list of files and directories. The directories are the ones that say <DIR> after the name; the others are files (either program files or data files).

The date and time stamps for each file can prove very useful when you find two different versions of a file on two different disks and you want to determine which is the latest version. The number of bytes free displayed at the bottom of the directory makes the DIR command the perfect way to find out how much room is left on a disk. (This will help you determine whether you

The directory listing for the root directory usually contains only a few individual files and several subdirectories.

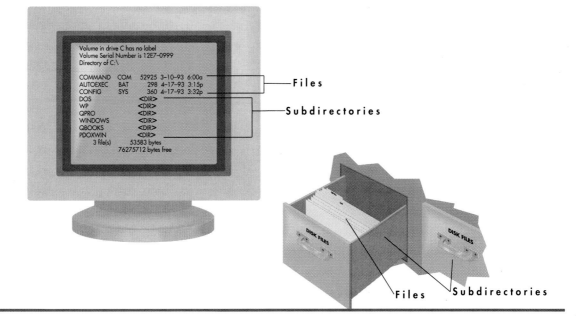

have room to copy a particular file onto a floppy disk, for example, or to install a new program on your hard disk.)

USING COMMAND PARAMETERS

Most DOS commands consist of several parts. There's the command name itself, which always comes first. Then there are usually one or more extra parts, known as *parameters,* that tell DOS what you want it to perform the operation on. For example, if you issue the COPY command, you have to tell DOS what you want to copy and to where. In some cases, as with the DIR command, the parameters are all optional. You only use them when you want DIR command to behave a bit differently than it does without such special instructions.

For example, when you enter DIR and press Enter, DOS assumes you want to see all the files in the current drive and directory (that is, the ones

ANATOMY OF A DOS DIRECTORY LISTING

For files, the size in bytes. For directories, the characters <DIR>. (Remember that directories do not have a fixed size.)

File extensions

Date stamp: The date on which the file was created or last modified. (The date is read from your computer's internal clock. You can reset the date with the DATE command.)

The label assigned to your hard disk, if any

The serial number of your copy of the program

The drive and directory whose contents you are listing. This means that what follows is a directory of the root directory part of drive C.

File/directory names

The number of files in the list

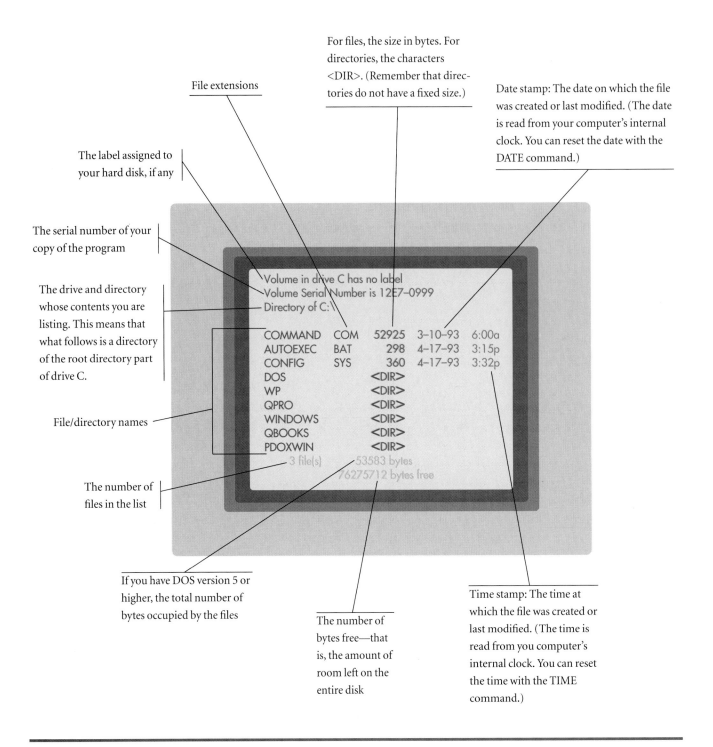

```
Volume in drive C has no label
Volume Serial Number is 12E7-0999
Directory of C:\

COMMAND   COM    52925   3-10-93   6:00a
AUTOEXEC  BAT      298   4-17-93   3:15p
CONFIG    SYS      360   4-17-93   3:32p
DOS             <DIR>
WP              <DIR>
QPRO            <DIR>
WINDOWS         <DIR>
QBOOKS          <DIR>
PDOXWIN         <DIR>
     3 file(s)    53583 bytes
              76275712 bytes free
```

If you have DOS version 5 or higher, the total number of bytes occupied by the files

The number of bytes free—that is, the amount of room left on the entire disk

Time stamp: The time at which the file was created or last modified. (The time is read from you computer's internal clock. You can reset the time with the TIME command.)

displayed in the DOS prompt). But sometimes you'll want to list the files on a different disk or in another directory. You can tell DOS to look in a particular place by including a drive and/or directory parameter in the DIR command. To find out what's on a floppy disk, for example, you could insert the disk in drive A and then enter DIR A: or put it in drive B and enter DIR B:. You'll learn to list the files in another directory near the end of this chapter.

NOTE *If you tell DOS to look on a floppy drive and the drive happens to be empty, you will see a message like "Not ready reading drive A. Abort, Retry, Fail?" If you simply forgot to put a disk in the drive or to close the drive latch, go ahead and do so and then enter R for Retry. If you don't really want to access the floppy drive and prefer to cancel the command, enter A for Abort.*

LOOKING FOR A PARTICULAR FILE

Next, suppose that you don't want to see a list of all the contents of a directory, you just want to know whether a particular file is present. To do this, you add a different parameter to the command: the name of the file you are looking for. To find out whether you have a file named BUDGET.WK1 in the current directory, for example, you would type

```
DIR BUDGET.WK1
```

If DOS finds the specified file, it displays a directory listing that includes only that one file. If it can't find the file, it displays the message "File not found."

You can also look for a particular file on a different disk. To look for BUDGET.WK1 on the disk in drive A, for example, you would enter

```
DIR A:BUDGET.WK1
```

Notice that there is no space between the drive name and the file name. You may find it helpful to think of the drive name as part of the file specification: You are telling DOS to look for a particular file, namely the file on drive A with the name BUDGET.WK1.

USING WILDCARDS

DOS provides two characters—the asterisk and the question mark—to help you manipulate groups of files at once. These characters are called *wildcard characters* because they stand in for other characters, just as wildcards can stand in for any card you like in a poker game. The asterisk stands in for a group of characters of any length. The command DIR *.BAT, for example, would produce a list of all the files in the current drive and directory that have any first name, followed by a period and the characters BAT.

Although the asterisk is often used to represent the entire first names of a group of files, it can be used to represent either the end of the first name, the entire file extension, or the end of the file extension. Here are some examples:

`W*.TXT`

stands for files with names that start with the letter W and have an extension of .TXT. (This would include the files WANNABE.TXT, WILLIE.TXT, and W.TXT.)

`A*.*`

stands for files with names that start with the letter A followed by any other characters in the first name and any file extension.

`LETTER.*`

stands for files with a first name of LETTER and any file extension.

The other wildcard character, the question mark, stands in for any single character. Entering MEMO?.DOC would produce a list of all files with a first name of MEMO followed either by nothing or by a single character and an extension of DOC. File names with more than one character after MEMO would be excluded.

You can use wildcard characters in almost any DOS command that has a file name parameter.

FILE NAMING STRATEGIES

You can take advantage of DOS's wildcard characters by assigning similar names to similar types of files. If the names of all your office memos start with MEM, for example, you can display a list of all your memos with the command

```
DIR MEM*.*
```

As mentioned in Chapter 3, many programs automatically assign their own preferred extension to any data files that you create. If you create a spreadsheet in Lotus 1-2-3, for example, the program automatically adds the extension .WK1 or .WK2, depending on which version you are using. Many word processing programs, particularly DOS-based rather than Windows-based ones, let you assign any extension you like. In this case, you might use the extension to indicate the file type—using MEM for memos, INV for invoices, and LTR for letters, for example—and use the eight-character file name to indicate the file's contents. Then, whenever you want to list, copy, move, or delete all your memos, invoices, or letters as a group, you would just refer to those files as *.MEM, *.INV, or *.LTR when you issue the appropriate DOS command.

BUILDING BLOCKS OF THE DIR COMMAND

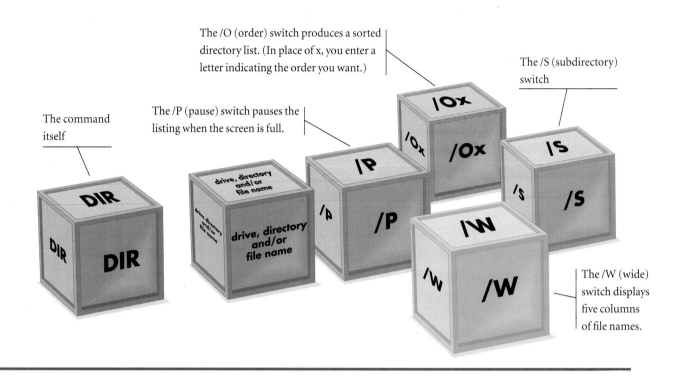

The /O (order) switch produces a sorted directory list. (In place of x, you enter a letter indicating the order you want.)

The /S (subdirectory) switch

The command itself

The /P (pause) switch pauses the listing when the screen is full.

The /W (wide) switch displays five columns of file names.

If you have DOS version 5 or later, you can control the sort order of the directory listing using the /O (for order) switch. When you use this switch, you follow the /O with another letter indicating the order in which you want the files and directories displayed. Your choices include:

▶ */ON, which sorts by file name*

▶ */OD, which sorts by date and time, from oldest to most recent*

▶ */OE, which sorts by extension (last name)*

▶ */OS, which sorts by size, with smallest first*

▶ */OG, which sorts so that directories appear first*

A WIDE DIRECTORY LISTING

Add /W to a DIR command to display a wide directory (five columns of file and directory names without sizes, dates, or times).

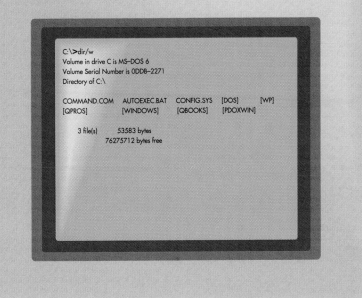

```
C:\>dir/w
Volume in drive C is MS–DOS 6
Volume Serial Number is 0DDB–2271
Directory of C:\

COMMAND.COM    AUTOEXEC.BAT    CONFIG.SYS    [DOS]    [WP]
[QPROS]        [WINDOWS]       [QBOOKS]      [PDOXWIN]

      3 file(s)      53583 bytes
                  76275712 bytes free
```

You can reverse the order of a sort by entering a minus sign between the O and the letter that specifies the sort order. To display a directory in order by date from the latest to the earliest, for example, you would enter DIR /O–D.

COMBINING PARAMETERS

You've now learned several different variations on the DIR command. You've seen what happens when you enter DIR by itself. You've learned to add parameters to specify a drive to look on and a file to look for. You've also learned to control the directory list with various switches (/P, /W, and /O).

You can mix and match these parts, if you like. For example, you could enter

DIR A: /W

to produce a wide listing of the files on drive A, or you could enter

`DIR /P /ON`

to sort your listing by file name, and had DOS pause each time the screen is filled.

You just need to make sure that the command name itself, in this case DIR, comes first.

COPYING FILES

One of the most critical tasks you'll perform with DOS is copying files. The basic form for the COPY command is

`COPY from to`

The *from* parameter refers to the name and possibly the location of the file you want to copy. (You only need to specify a location if the file is somewhere other than the current directory.) The *to* parameter refers to the name and/or location of the duplicate you are about to create. You only need to specify the file name if it differs from the name of the source file (that is, if you want to assign a different name to the copy). You only need to specify the location if the duplicate will be placed somewhere other than the current drive and directory. You can omit this entire part of the command if you are copying from a drive or directory other than the current drive/directory *and* you want the new file to have the same name as the original.

NOTE *Whenever I describe the format of a command, I'll use lowercase for placeholders—that is, parameter names for which you've supposed to substitute a drive directory, and/or file name.*

THE FORMAT FOR THE COPY COMMAND

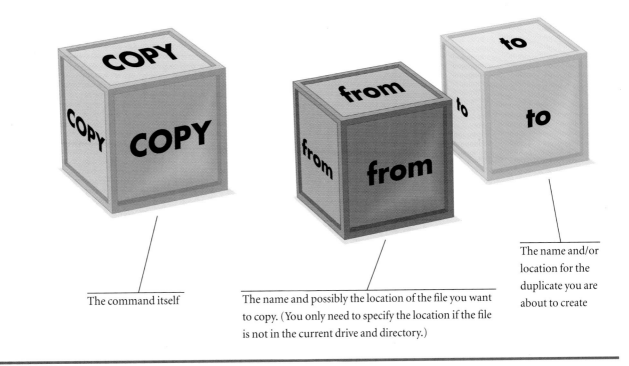

The command itself

The name and possibly the location of the file you want to copy. (You only need to specify the location if the file is not in the current drive and directory.)

The name and/or location for the duplicate you are about to create

The most common purpose of the COPY command is copying from one disk or directory to another. To copy a file from your hard disk to a floppy, for backup purposes, for example, you use the format

COPY *filename* A:

or, if the floppy disk is in drive B rather than drive A,

COPY *filename* B:

To copy a file named DONDUCK from your hard disk to a floppy in drive A, for example, you would enter

COPY DONDUCK A:

COPYING FROM ONE DISK TO ANOTHER

To copy a file from your hard disk to a floppy, you use the format COPY *filename* A: or COPY *filename* B:.

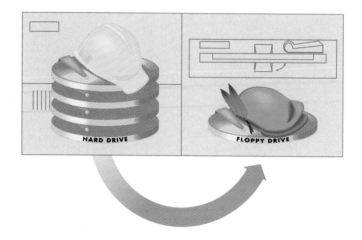

The form for copying from a floppy disk to the currently selected directory (folder) of your hard disk is COPY A: *filename* or COPY B: *filename*.

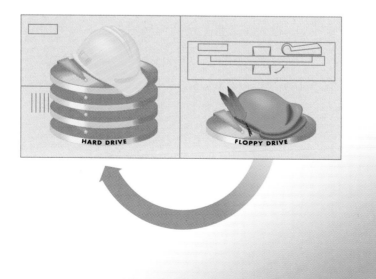

To copy a file named KELLY.LTR from drive A to drive B you would enter COPY A: KELLY.LTR B:. To copy the same file from drive B to drive A, enter COPY B: KELLY.LTR A:.

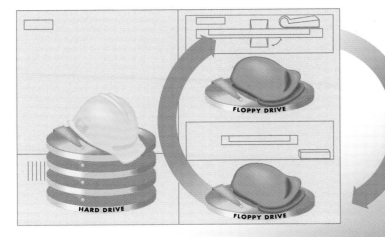

When you make a second copy of a file within a single directory (folder) on a disk, you must assign a different file name to the duplicate. The form you use is COPY *filename newname.*

REPORT.TXT

REPORT1.TXT

You will also often copy files in the other direction: from a floppy disk onto your hard drive. This is what you do when you install new software, for example, or when your co-worker gives you a copy of a letter or spreadsheet to work with and you need to copy it from their floppy to your hard disk. The form for copying from a floppy disk to your hard disk is

```
COPY A:filename
```

or, if the floppy is in drive B

```
COPY B:filename
```

Notice that, in this case, you're actually omitting the third part of the command—the *to* parameter. When you do this, DOS assumes that you want to copy the file to the drive and directory that appear in your DOS prompt and that you want the duplicate file to have the same name as the original.

As with the DIR command, you can use wildcard characters in the file name if you want to copy a group of files that have similar names. To copy all files with an extension of .TXT to drive A, for example, you would enter

```
COPY *.TXT A:
```

To copy everything on drive A to your current drive/directory, you would enter

```
COPY A:*.*
```

To copy all the files in the current drive or directory to drive A, you would enter

```
COPY *.* A:
```

NOTE *The command COPY *.* A: is the simplest way to make a backup copy of all the files in the current directory of your hard disk. It only works, however, if*

the contents of that directory are small enough to fit on a single floppy. See the section entitled "About Backups" at the end of this chapter for info on the commands for backing up larger amounts of data.

You may also occasionally want to copy a file from one floppy disk to another. If you have two floppy drives, you simply include the drive names when specifying the *from* and *to* parameters. To copy a file named KELLY.LTR from a disk in drive A to a disk in drive B, for example, you would enter

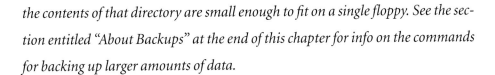

`COPY A:KELLY.LTR B:`

To copy the same file from B to A, you would enter

`COPY B:KELLY.LTR A:`

If you only have one floppy-disk drive, you would use the drive name B: as the destination. DOS will copy the specified file into memory and then ask you to insert a diskette in drive B and press Enter. Go ahead and put the second disk (the one you want to copy to) in the drive, close the latch if necessary, and press Enter. At this point, your computer "thinks" of your floppy drive as drive B. The next time you refer to drive A, it will ask you to put a disk in that drive and press Enter. Assuming the drive already contains a disk, just go ahead and press Enter, so that your computer goes back to thinking of the drive as drive A.

N O T E *Sometimes you'll want to make a copy of a file in the same directory of the same disk. In this case, you need to assign a different name to the duplicate. You might want to do this just to make an extra copy for safekeeping, or because you plan to modify one of the copies and leave the other unchanged. Your command would look something like this: COPY MYFILE.TXT MYFILE.OLD.*

A WARNING ABOUT OVERWRITING FILES

When you copy a file from one disk to another, DOS automatically overwrites any existing file with the same name. Suppose, for example, that you issue the command

`COPY ALFRED.DOC A:`

to copy a file named ALFRED.DOC from the current drive and directory to a disk in drive A. If drive A already contains a file named ALFRED.DOC, the new ALFRED.DOC (the one created by the COPY command) immediately and irrevocably replaces the old one. DOS does not ask if you really mean to replace the file, and doesn't even tell you that a file was replaced. It simply assumes this is what you want and acts accordingly.

Now, if you are simply copying the latest version of your data onto a floppy disk that you use for backup purposes, this doesn't pose a problem: You do, in fact, want to overwrite the old version of the file with the new one. If you are copying from a floppy onto your hard disk, however, you may wind up accidentally overwriting a critical file. Imagine that you copy a little sample file named REPORT.TXT from a floppy onto your hard disk, for example. If your hard disk happens to have a 3 megabyte customer list with exactly the same name, the little file will overwrite the big one and there will be nothing you can do to recover it. (This is when you better hope you have a backup copy of your data.)

The moral of this story is that whenever you copy from one disk to another, make sure that you will not accidentally overwrite existing files. In particular, if you are copying files from a floppy to your hard disk, use the DIR command to check for existing files of the same name before you issue the COPY command. It's particularly important to do this when you are using wildcard characters to copy a group of files from one disk to another. Otherwise you could accidentally overwrite several files at once.

DELETING AND UNDELETING FILES

Just as you need to clean out your filing cabinets or closets periodically, you also need to clear old and unnecessary files from your disks. It's a good idea to perform such spring cleanings fairly often: The longer you wait, the harder it will be to remember what the files contain, and whether you really need to keep them. (Even if you are very diligent in assigning meaningful file names, when you see a file named JONES.LTR a year from now, you may not remember who Jones is, let alone what you had to say to her or him.)

The format for the DEL command is simply

`DEL filename`

To delete a file named MYFILE.TXT from the current drive and directory, you would enter

`DEL MYFILE.TXT`

You can also use wildcards in the file name, to delete a group of files that have common letters in their names. For instance, DEL *.TXT would erase all files with an extension of .TXT. When you include wildcards in the file name parameter, you may also want to add a /P (for Prompt) switch to the command. This tells DOS to prompt you for confirmation on each file. If you enter

`DEL W*.* /P`

for example, DOS will display a message like "C:\WP\WALLY.DOC, Delete (Y/N)?" for each file that begins with the letter W. You can then press Y (for Yes) if you want to delete that particular file or N (for No) if you don't.

To delete everything on a floppy disk, you would enter

or, if the disk were in drive B,

Whenever you tell DOS to delete everything in a particular directory (in this case, the root directory on drive A or drive B), DOS responds with the message "All files in directory will be deleted! Are you sure (Y/N)?" Press Y to confirm the deletion or N if you've changed your mind.

NOTE *The ERASE command does exactly the same thing as the DEL command. Use whichever command name you find easier to remember.*

When you erase a file in DOS, the data is not physically removed from the disk. Instead, DOS simply makes a note that the area occupied by that file is now available for reuse. It does this by erasing the first character of the file name in its internal table on files and their whereabouts. (This table is known as the File Allocation Table.) This method of handling deletions makes it possible for you to "undelete" a file, as long (and only as long) as DOS has not reused part or all of the file's disk space for another file.

The command for undeleting a file is UNDELETE, and its format is

UNDELETE *filename*

You can include wildcards in the file name parameter if you want to undelete files that have common characters in their file names.

When you issue the UNDELETE command, DOS tells you how many files it has that match your specifications, and how many of those can be recovered.

DELETING AND UNDELETING FILES

DEL REPORT.DOC

When you delete a file in DOS, the data is not physically removed from the disk. Instead, DOS simply makes a note that the area occupied by that file is now available for reuse. It does this by deleting the first character of the file name in its File Allocation Table.

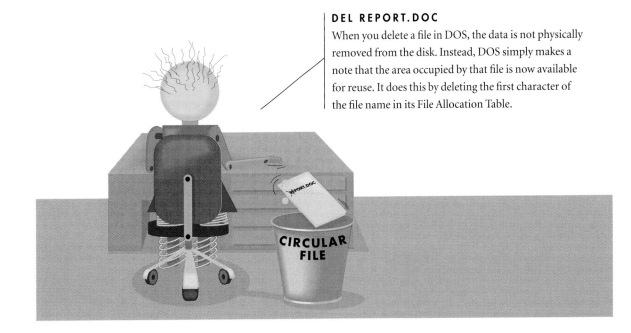

UNDELETE REPORT.DOC

You can use the UNDELETE command to undelete a file (assuming DOS has not already reused its disk space). When you do, DOS will ask you to fill in the first character of the file name.

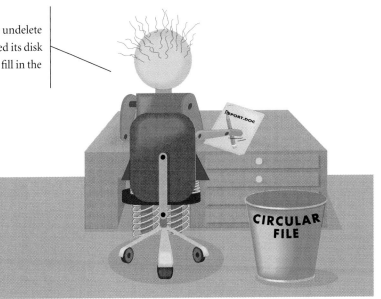

(DOS can only recover files that have not already been overwritten.) Then it displays the name of the first file, with a ? where the first character would normally appear, and asks you to confirm that you want to undelete it. If you are undeleting a file named LETTER.SAM, for example, you will see ?ETTER.SAM, followed by the file's size, date, and time (as in a directory listing) and then "Undelete (Y/N)?" If you type Y (for Yes) to confirm the undeletion, DOS asks you to supply the first letter of the file name. Once you enter a letter, the file is undeleted.

N O T E *DOS has no way of knowing whether the letter you enter as the first name of the file is correct. It will accept any letter you enter.*

RENAMING FILES

As you know, you always assign a name to a file when you first create it. If you are creating the file by saving data in an application program, you supply a file name when you issue the save command. If you create a file by copying an existing file, DOS uses either the name of the original file or a name that you specify as part of the COPY command itself.

Occasionally, you'll need to change a file's name later. You might have accidentally entered LETTET instead of LETTER when saving a file, for example. Or you may name a file BUDGET.WK2 only to realize next year that you should have named it BUDGET94.WK2, to distinguish it from the next year's budget.

You can change the name of a file using the RENAME or REN command. (The commands work the same: RENAME may be easier to remember; REN's a little quicker to type.) The form for the command is

```
REN oldname newname
```

RENAMING A FILE

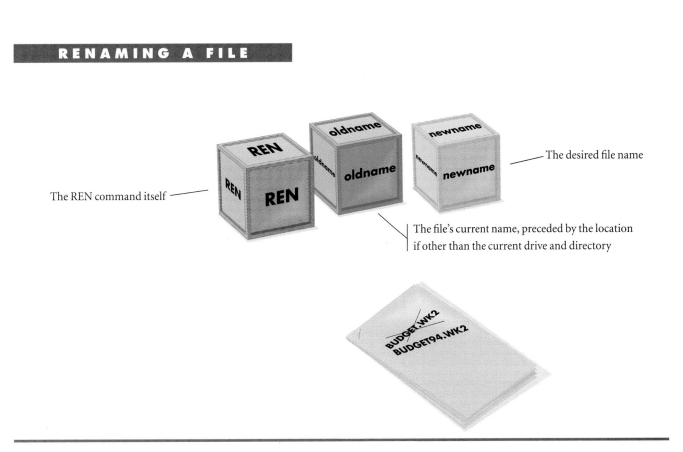

The REN command itself

The desired file name

The file's current name, preceded by the location if other than the current drive and directory

To change the name of a file in the current directory from ARDVARK to AARDVARK, for example, you would enter

REN ARDVARK AARDVARK

If the file is located somewhere other than the current disk or directory, specify the location as part of the *oldname* parameter. The command

REN A:MEMO MEMO64

would change the name of a file called MEMO, which is located on drive A, to MEMO64. You never include a location as part of the *newname* parameter, because at that point you're only specifying a name for a file. DOS already knows which file you mean and where it's located.

FORMATTING DISKS

As discussed in Chapter 3, when you buy brand-new floppy disks, they are usually unformatted—meaning that they are blank slates without the track or sector lines that allow your computer to "seat" your data in an organized fashion. Before you can use such disks, you need to format them, directing your computer to draw the track and sector lines. If you format a disk that already contains data, that data is erased when you reformat the disk.

To format a disk using DOS, you use the FORMAT command. Assuming that you want to format a disk in drive A, you would issue the FORMAT command by typing

```
FORMAT A:
```

and pressing Enter. If you want to format a disk in drive B, you would type

```
FORMAT B:
```

and press Enter.

NOTE *Never tell your computer to format drive C (the hard disk) unless you are specifically directed to do so by an expert. Doing so will erase all the data and programs on the disk.*

As soon as you issue the FORMAT command, DOS will display a message like "Insert new diskette for drive A: and press ENTER when ready." (The message varies slightly from one version of DOS to another.) If you have not already placed your floppy disk in drive A, do so now. If the drive has a drive latch, go ahead and close it. Then press Enter to initiate the formatting process.

FORMATTING A DISK

When you format a floppy disk, the read/write head draws in track and sector lines so that DOS can "seat" data in an organized fashion.

NOTE   *If you change your mind at this point and decide that you don't really want to format a disk, press Ctrl+Break to interrupt the command.*

The formatting process takes a minute or more. While it's happening, DOS displays messages about what it's doing. Again, these messages vary a bit by DOS version. When the formatting process is complete, you may be given a chance to assign a name to the disk. The message will be something like "Volume label (11 characters, ENTER for none)?" If you want to assign a name to the disk, type it in at this point. You can use up to 11 characters, no spaces. (Most people just note the disk's contents on a sticky label attached to the disk jacket, rather than naming the disk itself.) Finally, you will see the message "Format another (Y/N)?" Press Y for Yes if you do want to format another disk; press N for No if you don't.

DIRECTORIES AND PATHS

As you learned in Chapter 3, most hard disks contain several directories, or groups of files. When you first turn on your computer, the current directory is the root directory. If you think of a disk as a file drawer, the root directory is the drawer as a whole, within which there are multiple folders (subdirectories). When it comes to envisioning the many subdirectories on a hard disk, some people find it easier to think in terms of a tree rather than a file drawer. At the base of the tree is the root directory, out of which branch various subdirectories, some of which have branches (subdirectories) of their own.

Many programs, including DOS, represent directory structures in more or less this fashion, displaying diagrams known as directory trees or tree diagrams. (You'll learn to display a DOS directory tree shortly.) In most such directory trees, the root directory is shown either at the top of the diagram or in its upper-left corner, with the branches (subdirectories) extending downward or to the right. (Think of a tree turned on its side.)

As you have seen, whenever you issue a DOS command that involves files (like DIR, COPY, DEL, UNDELETE, and RENAME), DOS assumes that you are referring to files in the current directory. If you want to work with files in a directory other than the current directory, you have two choices:

▶ *You can specify the location of the other directory in the command.*

▶ *You can change the current directory.*

Let's start with the first alternative. You've already learned how to specify a disk drive in a DOS command. To get a list of files on the disk in drive A, for example, you enter

DIR A:

VISUALIZING A DIRECTORY TREE

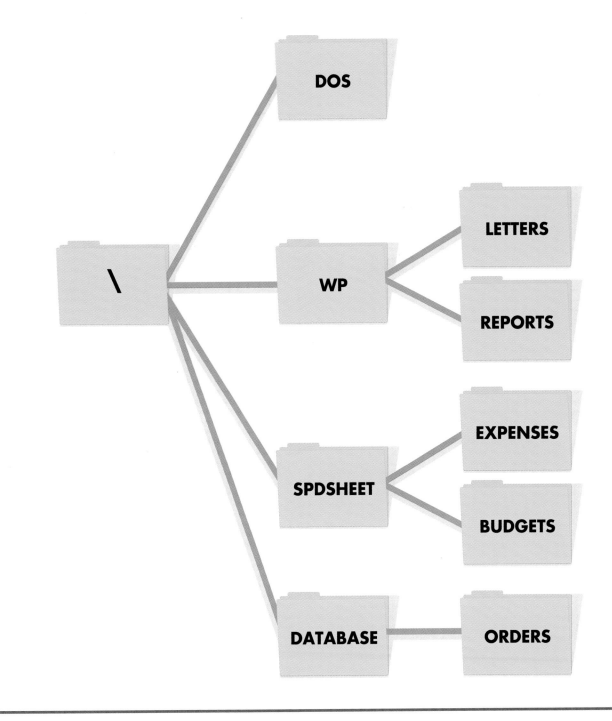

To copy a file from the current directory to drive A, you enter

```
COPY filename A:
```

To delete a file on drive A, you use

```
DEL A:filename
```

You use a similar form when you want to tell DOS to manipulate files in another directory rather than (or in addition to) another disk drive. But instead of naming a drive, you state the location of a directory.

Note that I said the location of a directory, rather than the name of the directory. In order to tell DOS to look in a particular directory on the disk, you need to give it a set of instructions on how to get there. This set of instructions is known as a *path*. Although you can sometimes give directions starting from the current directory, it's usually safest to give instructions starting from the root directory. (DOS always knows how to get back to the root.)

As an example, suppose all your word-processing files are stored in a directory named WP which is a subdirectory of the root directory. The most generic instructions you can give DOS for finding this directory are "Wherever you are now, go back to the root directory and then look for a directory named WP." The way you say this in DOS-speak is \WP.

To tell DOS to look for files in the WP directory, you would enter

```
DIR \WP
```

(This is very much like telling DOS to display a list of files on drive A by entering DIR A:, only instead of specifying a drive, you specify the directory path.) To tell DOS to copy a file named MYLETTER to the WP directory, you would enter

```
COPY MYLETTER \WP
```

To tell DOS to copy all the files in the WP directory to a disk in drive A, you would enter

```
COPY \WP\*.* A:
```

Let's take a slightly more complex example. The path for a directory named LETTERS, which is a subdirectory of the WP subdirectory, which is a subdirectory of the root, would be \WP\LETTERS. This means start at the root directory, then look for the WP directory, and, once you get to the WP directory, look for the LETTERS directory. (It's a little confusing, but you use a backslash both to represent the root directory and to separate the names of subdirectories in case there are more than one in a path. In the latter case, it serves as a kind of punctuation mark, separating one directory from the next.)

When you want to refer to a file that is located in a particular directory, you enter the directory's path, followed by an extra backslash and then the name of the file. If you want to tell DOS to copy a file named SALES.WK1 to drive A from a directory whose path is \LOTUS, for example, you would enter

```
COPY \LOTUS\SALES.WK1 A:
```

If you think of the second part of this command, \LOTUS\SALES.WK1, as a set of directions for finding the source file, you have the following:

▶ *Start at the root directory.*

▶ *Within that directory, look for a subdirectory named LOTUS.*

▶ *Within that subdirectory, look for a file named SALES.WK1.*

Whenever a DOS command has a file name parameter, you can include a directory path as part of that parameter. This is known as specifying a file's *path name.* (The path name for a file named SALES.WK1 located in the LOTUS directory is \LOTUS\SALES.WK1.)

FINDING MISPLACED FILES

It is all too easy to misplace files on a hard disk—either by neglecting to specify the desired directory when you save a file from inside an application file, or by specifying the wrong one in a COPY command. If you know that you have a file with a particular name, but you can't remember where you put it, you can use the command DIR *filename* /S to tell DOS to start looking in the root directory and then search through all its subdirectories as well. (It's the /S switch that tells it to include subdirectories in the search.) In effect, this tells DOS to search through every directory on the current drive. (If you want to search a different drive, just enter the drive name right before the backslash.)

The second means of getting to and manipulating files in other directories is by actually changing the current directory. You do this by means of the CD (change directory) command. You can think of this command as a way of moving to a different part of your file cabinet or, if you prefer to think of the directory structure as a tree, as moving from one branch to another. The format for the CD command is simply

`CD path`

If your hard disk contains a directory named WP, for example, you can change to that directory (open up that hanging folder) by entering

`CD \WP`

(The space immediately after CD is actually optional; CD\WP has the same effect as CD \WP.) As soon as you press Enter, the DOS prompt will change to reflect your new location. If you changed to the WP directory, for example, you will see C:\WP> instead of C:\>. Since DOS always assumes that you want to manipulate files in the current directory (that is, the directory named in the

PATHS AND PATH NAMES

To specify a file in a directory other than the current directory, you include the file's "path" in the file-name specification. The path is essentially a set of directions to the file. In this case, the path \WP\LETTERS tells DOS to start at the root directory, look for a subdirectory named WP, and then look for a subdirectory named LETTERS.

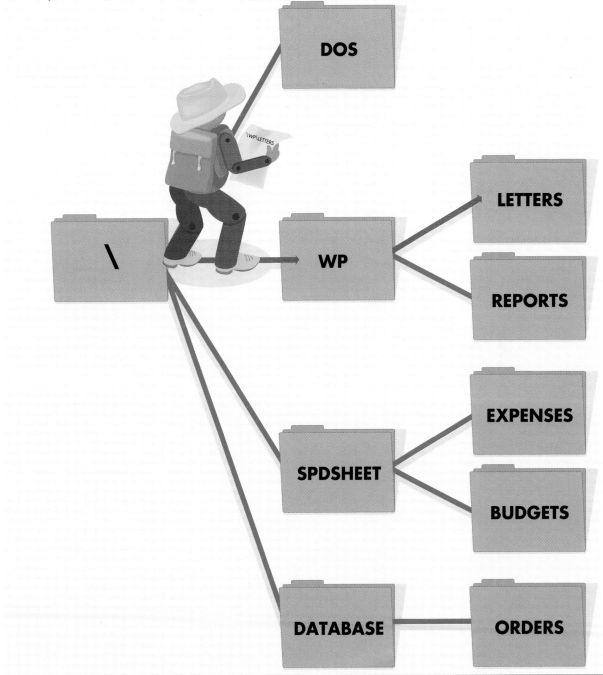

DOS prompt), you will get a list of files in the WP directory if you enter DIR at this point. Similarly, if you issue a COPY, DEL, or REN command, DOS will assume that you mean to copy, erase, or rename a file in the WP directory, unless you specify otherwise. (If you want to try this yourself, you need to change to one of the directories on your own hard disk. You may or may not have a directory named WP.)

To change back to the root directory, you enter CD \ or CD\.

N O T E *Just because the DOS prompt changes to display the name of a particular application program does not mean that you've left DOS. If your DOS prompt says C:\LOTUS>, for example, it means that you're on drive C, in the LOTUS directory—that is, the place where the Lotus files are stored. This is not the same thing as being "in" the LOTUS program itself. (You'll learn how to load programs in a moment.) It just means that you're looking at the LOTUS "folder." You might find it helpful to think of this as being at the Lotus program's front door, with the DOS prompt as a kind of signpost indicating that Lotus "lives here."*

There are two reasons to change directories. If you want to work with the files in a particular directory for a while, changing directories can save you the trouble of specifying the directory path in every command. Suppose, for example, that you want to get rid of some of your old word processing files and the directory in which they are stored is named \WP60\DATA. Instead of entering commands like this

```
DIR \WP60\DATA\*.* /ON
DEL \WP60\DATA\JONES.*
DEL \WP60\DATA\SMITH.TXT
DEL \WP60\DATA\STOCK.DOC
DEL \WP60\DATA\TODO.LST
```

you could enter commands like this:

```
CD \WP60\DATA
DIR *.*/ON
DEL JONES.*
DEL SMITH.TXT
DEL STOCK.DOC
DEL TODO.LST
```

You may also want to change directories to load a program that is stored in a different directory. You'll learn more about this in the next section.

DISPLAYING A DIRECTORY TREE

As mentioned, many programs, including DOS itself, represent directory structures as trees rather than file drawers. You can display a directory tree for your own hard disk using the DOS TREE command. Unless you add a path parameter to the command, the resulting tree diagram will start with the directory that appears in the DOS prompt. In other words, you will see a diagram that includes the current directory and any subdirectories of that directory. If you want to display the directory structure of the entire disk and you're not currently in the root directory, enter

```
TREE \
```

meaning "display a directory tree starting with the root directory." On many hard disks, the directory structure is too complex to fit on a single screen. If you find that the tree scrolls by too fast for you to read, enter

```
TREE | MORE
```

THE DOS DIRECTORY TREE LISTING

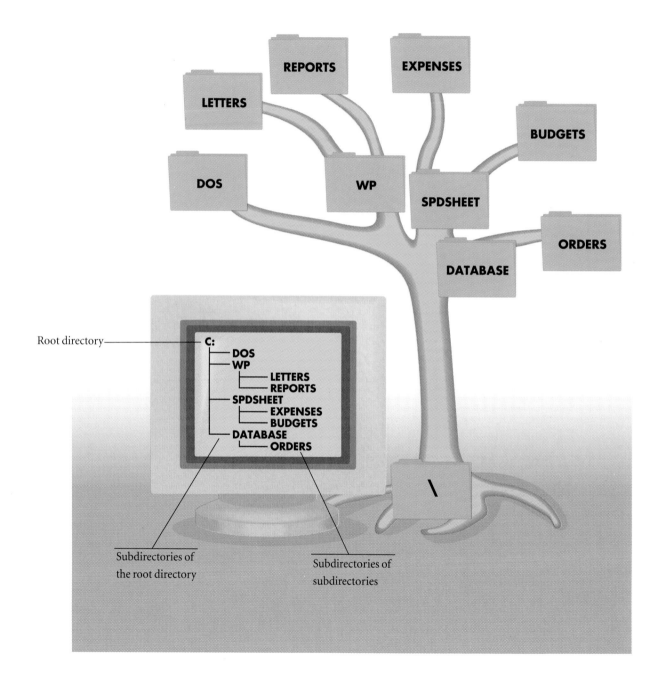

Root directory

C:
DOS
WP
LETTERS
REPORTS
SPDSHEET
EXPENSES
BUDGETS
DATABASE
ORDERS

\

Subdirectories of
the root directory

Subdirectories of
subdirectories

The | MORE part of this command is somewhat complex, but it is known as a *piping*. Its effect is to make the listing pause when the screen is full, similar to the /P switch on a DIR command.

If you want to print a copy of the tree diagram, make sure that your printer is turned on and then enter

`TREE > PRN`

You will probably need to eject the last page from the printer manually. (If you don't know how to do this, see the section on printers in Chapter 9.)

LOADING A PROGRAM

As mentioned, there are basically two things that you use DOS for: performing disk housekeeping operations and loading application programs. Whenever you want to load an application program, you must state your request to DOS. You might find it helpful to think of DOS as a waiter or waitress—that is, as the "person" who "serves" you various application programs. Whenever you want to use a particular program, you place your order with DOS. Alternatively, you can think of DOS as a reference librarian who, in most cases, only lets you check out one reference book at a time. Whenever you want to use a program, you ask the librarian (DOS). Whenever you "turn in" (exit) a book (program), you are back at the librarian.

NOTE *A few special programs, including Windows, allow you to "check out" multiple application programs at once. Unless you are running one of those special programs, however, you can only use applications one at a time on a PC.*

In most cases, the first step in loading an application program is changing to the directory in which the program is stored. (This is like saying "Go to

CHECKING ONE APPLICATION PROGRAM

You can think of DOS as a reference librarian who finds and hands you programs. Whenever you want to use a program, you ask the librarian.

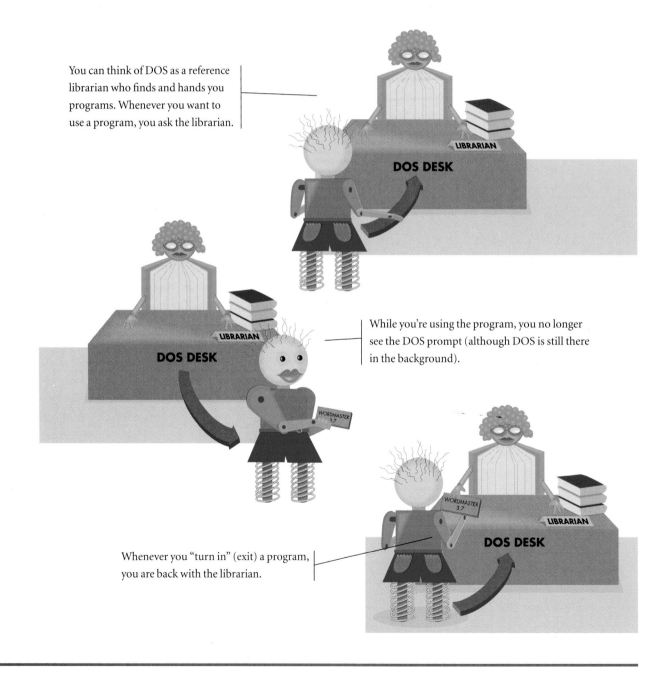

While you're using the program, you no longer see the DOS prompt (although DOS is still there in the background).

Whenever you "turn in" (exit) a program, you are back with the librarian.

where the x program is stored" or "Move to the x program folder.") Once you have moved to the proper directory, you enter the first name of the program's main program file. If the name of the main program file is QPRO.EXE, for example, you type QPRO and press Enter.

Most programs consist of many different disk files. Some of them are program files (that is, sets of instructions). Some are supplementary files. For example, word processing programs that allow you to check for spelling errors need dictionary files that contain the proper spellings of words. Programs that perform fancy printing operations need files called printer drivers that contain the data that your computer needs in order to "talk to" various printers.

Every program has one main program file, the file that you must load into memory to start the program. If you forget the name of a program's main program file, here's a tip: Its extension is either .EXE, .COM, or .BAT. (EXE stands for executable, COM for command, and BAT for batch, as in a whole batch of commands.) So to determine the name of the program file, first change to the directory that contains the program's files. Then try entering DIR *.EXE and see if the list contains any likely candidates. If not, try entering DIR *.COM, and finally DIR *.BAT.

LOGGING ONTO ANOTHER DISK

You've already learned how to change the current directory—so that a different directory path appears in the DOS prompt. You can also change the current disk drive. To do this, simply enter the name of the drive (don't forget the colon after the drive letter) and press Enter. This is known as logging onto a different drive. To log onto drive A, for example, you would type A: and press Enter.

As with changing directories, changing drives can occasionally save you some typing. If you plan to issue several commands involving files on drive A, for example, logging onto that drive will eliminate the need to type A: before every file name. The other reason for logging onto drive A is to load a program that is stored on a floppy disk. You will often need to do this when installing new programs on your computer. In many cases, the instructions for installing will tell you to first log onto drive A, and then enter INSTALL. This tells DOS to load the program named INSTALL into memory. Since you are already logged onto drive A, DOS automatically looks for the INSTALL program on your floppy disk.

You can always log back onto drive C by typing C: and pressing Enter.

LEARNING ABOUT YOUR SYSTEM WITH CHKDSK

The CHKDSK command (pronounced "check disk") serves two functions:

▶ *It provides you with information about your system, including the amount of disk space and memory you have. This can be extremely useful when you sit down at an unfamiliar computer and want some information about the equipment you are using.*

▶ *It looks for and, if instructed, fixes certain types of problems on the disk. It's a good idea to issue the CHKDSK command as a precautionary measure any time you lose power or crash when you're in the middle of running an application program.*

When you issue the CHKDSK command, DOS checks your disk for unreadable areas or misplaced data. In general, DOS is very good at filing data in an orderly fashion. If you leave a program in the wrong way—by accidentally turn off the computer without leaving your application program, for example—

A TYPICAL CHKDSK REPORT

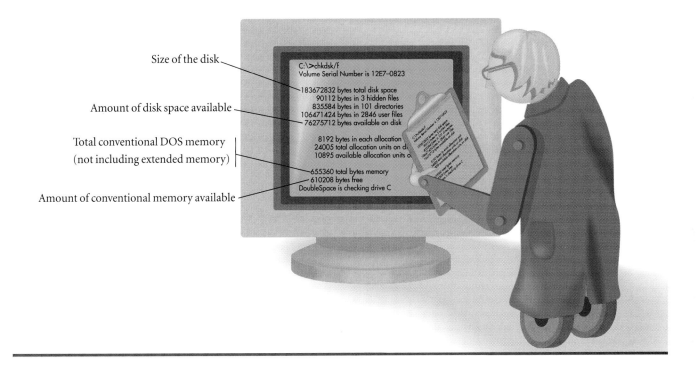

Size of the disk

Amount of disk space available

Total conventional DOS memory
(not including extended memory)

Amount of conventional memory available

```
C:\>chkdsk/f
Volume Serial Number is 12E7-0823

183672832 bytes total disk space
    90112 bytes in 3 hidden files
   835584 bytes in 101 directories
106471424 bytes in 2846 user files
 76275712 bytes available on disk

     8192 bytes in each allocation
    24005 total allocation units on di
    10895 available allocation units o

   655360 total bytes memory
   610208 bytes free
DoubleSpace is checking drive C
```

DOS may not get a chance to store everything where it belongs. In this case, you may end up with lost clusters: chunks of data that are not stored in any particular file on the disk. (Think of papers accidentally misfiled, so that they're in between the file folders. Or, if you're a Star Trek fan, think of a transporter malfunction, scattering some unfortunate soul's molecules across the galaxy.)

If you include the /F switch when you issue the CHKDSK command (so the whole command is CHKDSK /F), DOS groups all such misplaced data into new files. You can then either attempt to edit those files or, more likely, simply erase them from the disk. All files created by CHKDSK are located in the root directory and have names starting with the letters FILE and extensions of .CHK. You can therefore delete all of them at once with the command

`DEL \*.CHK`

VARIETIES OF MEMORY

In PCs, RAM is typically divided into three basic types:

▶ *Conventional memory (sometimes known as normal memory) means the first 640K of RAM in your computer. DOS itself only knows how to run programs and store data within this area of memory.*

▶ *Upper memory (also known as high memory) is the area between 640K and 1MB of memory. Upper memory is generally reserved by DOS for managing various input and output devices, and other operating system functions.*

▶ *Extended memory is memory beyond the first megabyte. If your PC has four megabytes of RAM, for example, you have 640K of conventional memory, 384K of upper memory (for a total of 1,024K or exactly 1MB) and three megabytes of extended memory. DOS itself cannot directly access extended memory, but other programs including Windows can. However, in some cases those programs require the assistance of a special additional program known as an* extended memory manager.

If you have DOS 5 or DOS 6, you can find out how much of each type of memory your computer has by issuing the MEM command. (Just type MEM at the DOS prompt and press Enter.) DOS will respond by listing each of the types of memory, noting how much is installed in your system, how much is currently in use, and how much remains available. (In this listing, the upper memory category is broken down into two parts, identified as upper memory and adapter RAM/ROM.)

There is one last type of memory—called *expanded memory*—that you should know about. In contrast to the other types of memory mentioned, expanded memory is not so much a region of memory as a particular strategy for accessing memory, using an expanded memory manager. The CPUs in the first PCs—namely the 8088 and 80286—were only capable of using up to a single megabyte of memory. Expanded memory was developed as a strategy for breaking this one-megabyte barrier. The expanded memory manager loads programs and data to the extended memory area and then reserves a region within the first megabyte of memory as a special swap region. Whenever you need to access the programs or data in the extended memory area, the memory manager temporarily "swaps" (moves) it into the swap region—the area that DOS knows how to use.

As more and more programs become capable of directly accessing extended memory, expanded memory is becoming obsolete. There are, however, some DOS programs that can only utilize extended memory if it's treated as expanded memory—that is, if it's swapped in and out of a region inside the first megabyte.

ABOUT BACKUPS

Creating regular backup copies of your data is one of the most important habits you can develop (right up there with flossing your teeth). Sooner or later, something bad will probably happen to your computer. The hard disk will fail, a power surge will damage some of your data, your office will fall prey to thieves, or your computer will come down with a virus. With luck, such a disaster will only happen to you once in a lifetime's worth of computer use. But given Murphy's Law, it's most likely to strike at the worst possible moment. When it does, having a backup copy of your data can keep an inconvenience from becoming a disaster.

The COPY command is fine for backing up small amounts of data. If you need to back up more data than will fit on a single floppy disk, however, you will need a different tool for the task. If you are using DOS version 5.0 or earlier, you use the BACKUP command. If you are using DOS 6.0 or later, you use a command named MSBACKUP. Rather than simply copying data to a disk, both BACKUP and MSBACKUP store the data in a special backup format. If something happens to the original copies of your data and you need to use your backup copy, you can't simply copy the contents of the backup disk back onto your hard disk. In the case of BACKUP, you need to use a RESTORE command. In the case of MSBACKUP, you need to select the Restore option on the main MSBACKUP screen.

MSBACKUP is significantly more sophisticated than the BACKUP command provided with earlier versions of DOS. It not only creates a backup copy of your data, it compresses it in the process—meaning that it shrinks it down considerably in size by removing blank spaces. (Don't worry, the spaces are put back in when you restore the files.) This both speeds up the backup process and allows you to fit more data on your floppy disks. MSBACKUP also allows you to perform what are known as *incremental backups*—backing up only those files that have changed since the last time you performed a full backup. If you perform a full backup of 20 files one day and then change two of them the next day, for example, the incremental backup will copy only the two that have changed.

The BACKUP, RESTORE, and MSBACKUP commands are beyond the scope of this book. (MSBACKUP, in particular, is easy to use, but it leads to a menu-driven program in itself, that takes a little time to set up and get used to.) Refer to your DOS manual or a book on DOS for information on how to use them.

OTHER COMMANDS TO EXPLORE

Although the material in this chapter will give you a good start with DOS, sooner or later you will probably want to buy a book on the subject. (For a thorough, easy-to-follow introduction, try *PC Learning Labs Teaches DOS 6.0*, published by Ziff-Davis Press.) In particular, you may want to explore the following commands:

▶ *XCOPY copies files in a way that is often more efficient than the COPY command and supports several additonal switches (including one that lets you copy files that changed on or after a specified date).*

▶ *MOVE lets you both move files and rename directories.*

▶ *MD (make directory) lets you create new directories on a disk.*

▶ *RD (remove directory) lets you eliminate empty directories from a disk.*

▶ *DELDIR (delete directory) lets you erase the contents of a directory and then remove the directory from the disk.*

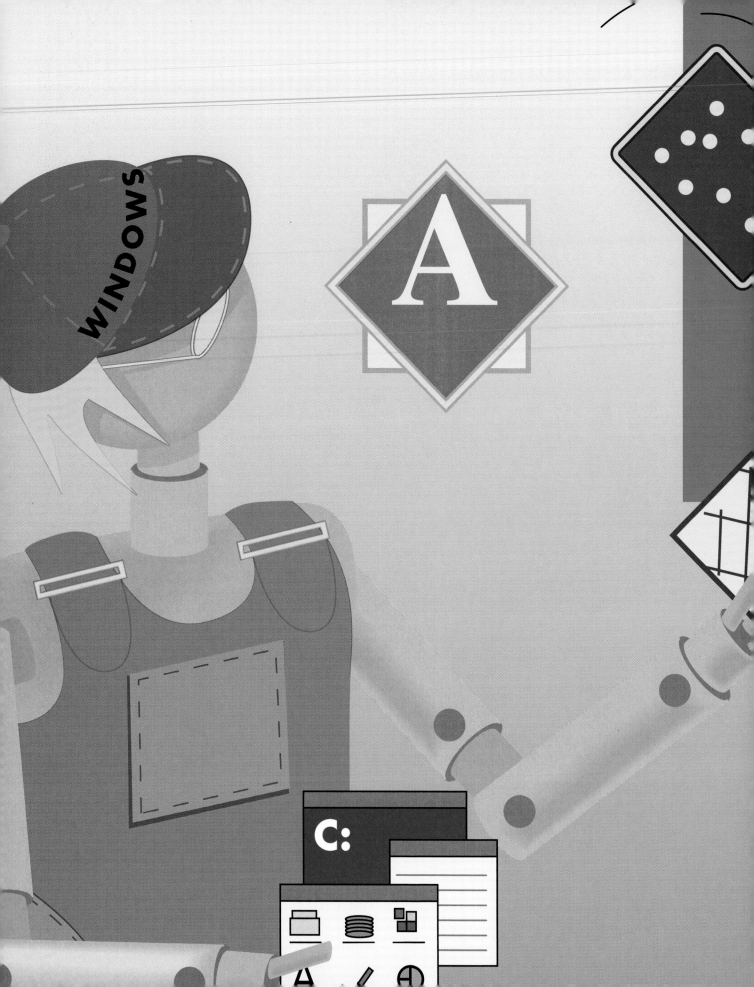

USING WINDOWS

As you learned in Chapter 1, Windows is an operating system that works hand-in-hand with DOS, providing a more graphically oriented alternative to the DOS command line. This chapter introduces the Windows environment including how you start and exit Windows, how you load application programs within Windows, and how you use Windows to perform disk housekeeping operations like copying and deleting files. It also explores many of the features common to all Windows application programs as well as Windows itself—things like windows, dialog boxes, and menu bars. Since installing Windows is no task for a beginner, it is beyond the scope of this book. I will therefore assume that Windows has already been properly installed on your computer. (Many computers are now sold with Windows already installed.)

NOTE *In order to run Windows, you need a fairly powerful PC, one with both a reasonably fast CPU (an 80286 is the minimum, an 80386 or 80486 is better) and a substantial amount of memory (preferably at least 4 megabytes). You also need a monitor and video adapter card capable of displaying graphics. (A video card is an expansion board that lets your computer "talk to" your monitor. You'll learn more about monitors and video adapter cards in Chapter 9.)*

WHAT'S SO GREAT ABOUT WINDOWS?

For the uninitiated, Windows is an operating environment created by Microsoft. It provides users of DOS-based personal computers with the kind of "graphical user interface" (GUI) long cherished by Macintosh users. In other words, the Windows environment is organized primarily around pictures rather than around text. While issuing orders in DOS is a matter of typing in commands, in Windows programs it's a matter of clicking pictures on the screen or making selections from menus (on-screen lists of options). The advantage of this way of interacting with the computer is that it's less intimidating to new users and there is less memorization required. If you forget how to perform a particular task, you can often refresh your memory simply by poking around on the screen, seeing which menu options and icons are available.

Another advantage of using Windows is that most programs designed to run within Windows look and behave similarly. Most Windows application programs are populated with entities such as icons (pictures that represent data files, programs, or groups of programs), dialog boxes (frames that display information and/or ask you questions) and, as you might guess, windows (rectangular frames in which programs and data are displayed). Almost all Windows programs also feature similar menu systems and at least a few of the same commands. To leave any Windows application, for example, you choose the Exit option from a menu named File. Once you have mastered one Windows program, it's fairly easy to learn the next because Windows programs have so much in common.

Windows also allows you to run multiple programs at once. If you're just getting started with computers, this feature may seem of limited value: Why would you want to run two programs at once when you're still feeling overwhelmed by the first one? Once you get a little more comfortable with your system, however, you may find this feature invaluable. Imagine getting a phone call about your latest sales figures when you're in the middle of typing a letter in your word processing program, for example. If you are using Windows, you can easily open your spreadsheet program and find the necessary information without leaving your word processing program. When you're done, a single

THE WINDOWS CAST OF CHARACTERS

File Manager   Clipboard   Print Manager   ATM Control Panel

Icons are pictures that represent programs, groups of programs, or data files.

Print   ?

Number of copies: ↓ 1 ↑

Page range:
- ● All
- ○ Current page
- ○ From: ↓ 1 ↑   To: ↓ 9999 ↑

including:
- ○ Even pages
- ○ Odd pages
- ● Both

Printer: HP LaserJet Series II on LPT1:

OK
Cancel
Options
Setup

Dialog boxes are used to display information, ask questions, and/or allow you to change settings.

Paintbrush - (Untitled)

File   Edit   View   Text   Pick   Options   Help

Windows are rectangular frames in which programs and/or data are displayed. (This is the window for the Paintbrush program which comes with Windows.)

keystroke will take you back to your word processing document, and you can pick up exactly where you left off. Windows also includes a feature known as the Clipboard that lets you easily copy or move data from one program to another. This means that you can copy those sales figures directly from your spreadsheet into your word processing document without having to use any special importing or exporting commands, as you would in DOS.

Windows not only allows you to open two (or more) programs at once, it also allows you to carry out work in both programs simultaneously. If you need to perform a time-consuming task in one program, you can simply start the process and then switch to a different program. The task you started in the first program will continue unattended while you continue working in the second one. People refer to this ability to work on two things at once as *multitasking*. It's the computer equivalent of patting your head while you rub your stomach.

STARTING WINDOWS

If your computer has been set up to run Windows automatically, you will probably see a screen with the words "Program Manager" at the top shortly after you turn on your computer. (It may take a few moments for the program to load, so be patient). If you know your computer has been set up to run Windows, but you see a DOS prompt (something like C:\> followed by a blinking cursor) rather than the Program Manager screen, you'll need to start Windows yourself. To do this, type WIN and press the Enter key.

If DOS responds with an error message, you need to switch to the subdirectory of your hard disk that contains the Windows files first, by typing CD \WINDOWS and pressing Enter. With luck, the last line on your screen will now read C:\WINDOWS>. Next, go ahead and type WIN and press Enter. You will briefly see a Windows sign-on screen. Then the screen will clear and you

MULTITASKING

Multitasking means doing two or more things at once. You can multitask in Windows by starting an operation in one program and then switching to another program while that operation continues in the background. In this case, a word processing program runs in the foreground while a database program prints a report in the background.

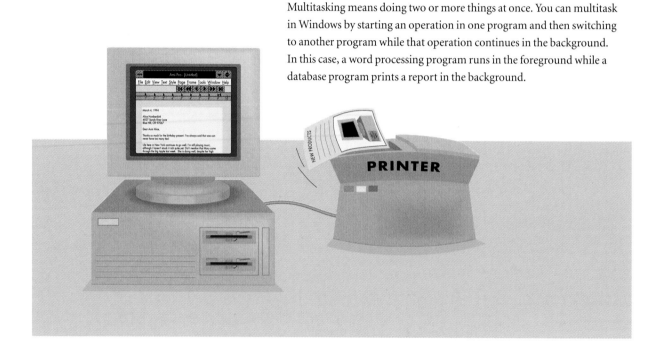

People multitask all the time— reading while watching television, talking on the phone while cooking dinner, chewing gum while jogging.

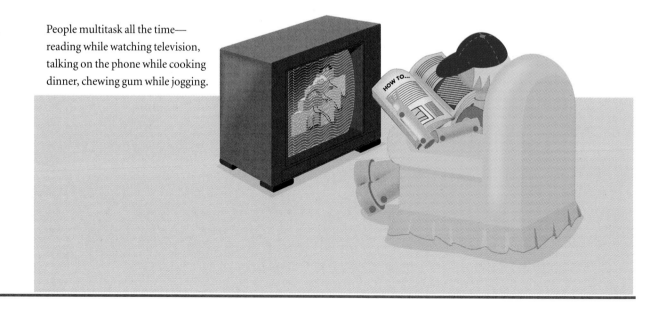

will probably see the Windows Program Manager. Once you see the Program Manager screen, you know that Windows is up and running.

N O T E   *If none of these strategies work, you'll need to check with the person who set up the computer or with some other accessible computer expert to make sure that Windows has been installed on your computer and, if so, where.*

WHAT ARE WINDOWS?

The Windows program gets its name from its most ubiquitous feature: the rectangular frames, called *windows,* that you encounter at every turn. Just about everything that happens in the Windows environment takes place inside a window.

When you first start Windows, you usually land in a window known as the Program Manager. The reason I say that you "usually" land in the Program Manager is that the Program Manager is actually one of two possible *shells* (master programs) available in Windows. The other is the File Manager, which you'll learn about later in this chapter. You can designate the File Manager as your shell program; if you do, you will see the File Manager window when you first start Windows and you will launch application programs from there.

The Program Manager is the Windows control center: the place from which you launch (start) other programs. Not only is it the first screen you see when you start Windows (after the Windows sign-on screen), it's also the last window you see before you exit. And it's the place from which you install new programs or remove old ones.

There are two types of windows in the Windows environment. An *application window* is a window that houses a program. A *document window* is a window that you open inside an application window. It contains data specific to that program. If you load the word processing program Word for Windows, for example, a Word for Windows application window appears on the screen. Then, every time you open or create a document, it is displayed in its own document window within this main window. Document windows always reside inside of application windows and cannot exist without them. If you close an application window, any document windows it contains are closed as well.

NOTE *In case you're wondering where the two types of windows get their names, in Windows-speak, programs are usually called applications, and document means any set of data, regardless of whether it contains text, pictures, numbers, or anything else. The term "document" is therefore roughly equivalent to "file," except that a document has not necessarily been named and saved to disk. If you are using a spreadsheet program, each spreadsheet is a document. If you are using a drawing program, each drawing is a document.*

Both Windows itself and most Windows applications let you arrange your electronic desktop in any way you like. You can work with one window at a time or several. You can move the windows around, shrink them, expand them, arrange them side by side, pile them on top of each other, and so on. In short, you can keep your electronic desktop as spartan or as cluttered as your other desk. (As with a normal desk, however, the more chaotic your Windows desktop, the harder it becomes to find what you need when you need it.)

THE PROGRAM MANAGER

As mentioned, the first window you are likely to encounter when you load Windows is the Program Manager window. This window remains open as long as you stay in Windows, even if it is completely obscured by other

OPENING TWO APPLICATION WINDOWS AT ONCE

In Windows, you can run two (or more) applications at once, and arrange them in any way you like on the screen.

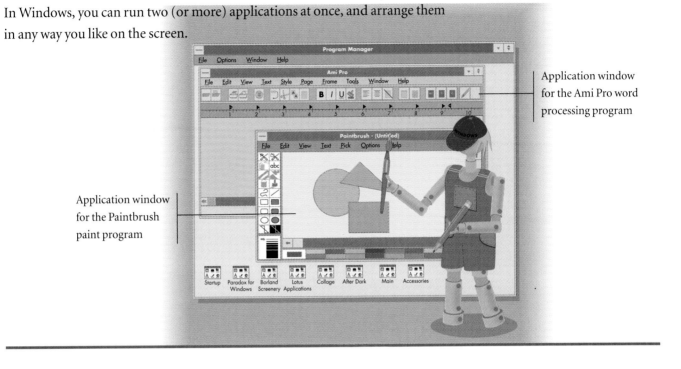

Application window for the Ami Pro word processing program

Application window for the Paintbrush paint program

application windows. As soon as you close the application windows, the Program Manager window will emerge from the background.

It's difficult to say what, exactly, your Program Manager window will look like because this depends on which programs have been installed and how you (or whoever set up Windows for you) chose to arrange elements on the screen. But it will probably contain a handful of items known as *program groups.*

You can think of program groups as little baskets used to organize program icons. As you'll learn later in this chapter, you use these icons to launch application programs. It's entirely up to you how many program groups you have and which icons they contain. Program groups can either appear as windows with one or more icons inside or as icons themselves.

At a minimum, you probably have program groups entitled Main, Accessories, and Games. (Again, I say probably because this, too, can be customized.

APPLICATION WINDOW WITH TWO DOCUMENT WINDOWS

Most Windows programs allow you to open two or more document
windows at one time.

The application window
for Paradox for Windows
(a database program)

Two Paradox document
windows

Paradox for Windows

File   Edit   Table   Record   Properties   Window   Help

Table : CLIENTS.DB

CLIENTS	Client I.D.	Name	Address
1	ALLEN	Reggie Allen	934 Cornell Str.
2	ALLEN1	Emile Allen	6471 Morega Drive
3	BRENNER	Barbara Brenner	4313 Salem Ave
4	EPLER	G	
5	FRANKEL	D	
6	FRANKLIN	M	
7	KERN	E	
8	LANSING	P	
9	ROMERO	S	
10	WESTON	A	
11	WILLIAMS	A	
12	WONG	J	

Table : PETS.DB

Client I.D.	Pet's Name	Species	Type
ALLEN	Aurora	Cat	Abyssinian
ALLEN1	Moki	Dog	Gray shepherd mix
BRENNER	Idgie	Cat	Calico
BRENNER	Rose	Dog	Yellow Labrador
BRENNER	Ruth	Cat	Tabby
FRANKLIN	Cole	Dog	Springer Spaniel
FRANKLIN	Fem	Rabbit	Angora
FRANKLIN	Peter	Rabbit	Angora
FRANKLIN	Selene	Cat	Calico OSH
KERN	Joss	Dog	Australian Shepherd

Record 2 of 17

If some grinch in your office set up Windows and didn't want you to waste
company time having fun, she or he may have deleted the Games program
group, for example.)

Each icon inside a program group represents an individual application.
For instance, the Main program group contains icons for the Control Panel and
File Manager, among others, which are little application programs that are
built into Windows. The Games program group generally contains icons for
the games Solitaire, Reversi, and Minesweeper.

All windows contain several common elements, which are shown in the
figure "Anatomy of a Window."

THE PROGRAM MANAGER

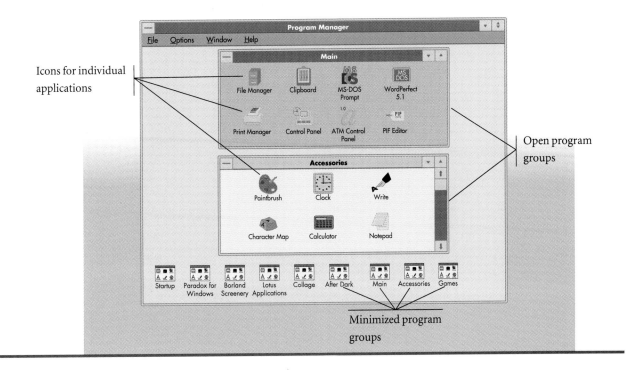

Icons for individual applications

Open program groups

Minimized program groups

HAVING YOUR WAY WITH WINDOWS

All the windows you'll encounter in Windows are very malleable: You can expand, shrink, push, pull, and rearrange them to your heart's content. When you first open a window, it may occupy less than the entire screen or, in the case of a document window, less than its entire application window. If you want more room to work in, you can expand the window as far as possible by either clicking its Maximize button or opening its Control menu and selecting Maximize. (You can open the Control menu either by clicking the Control menu box or by holding Alt while you press the spacebar in an application window or holding Alt while you press the hyphen in a document window.) Bear in mind that even when you maximize an application window, other application windows, including the Program Manager, remain open on the Desktop; they

ANATOMY OF A WINDOW

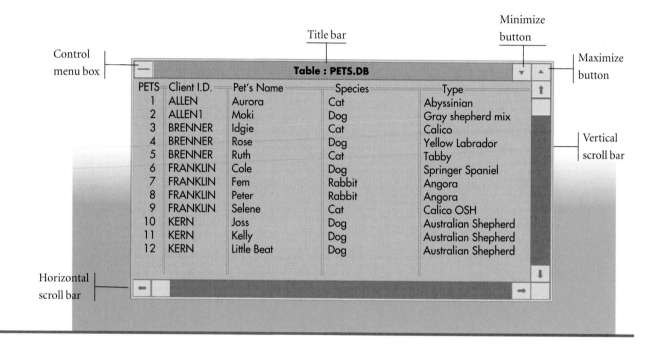

Control menu box

Title bar

Minimize button

Maximize button

Vertical scroll bar

Horizontal scroll bar

are just not visible at the moment. (You will learn to switch from one application window to another later in this chapter.)

NOTE *When you maximize a document window, you get two sets of Control menu boxes and sizing buttons, which can be a little confusing. The Control menu box and sizing buttons at opposite ends of the title bar affect the application window. The ones on the next row control the document window.*

Once you have maximized a window, the Maximize button itself is replaced by a Restore button, which contains one arrowhead pointing up and another pointing down. Clicking on this button restores the window to its previous size—that is, the size it was just before you maximized it.

You can also maximize and restore windows by double-clicking their title bars. If the window is not maximized, double-clicking the title bar expands it to full screen; if it is already maximized, double-clicking the title bar restores it to its previous size.

To minimize a window (temporarily reduce it to an icon), you click its Minimize button. When you minimize a window, it disappears from the screen and is replaced by an icon, usually at the bottom of the screen. Minimizing a window is rather like placing it in a corner of your desk, somewhere in your "to do" pile. You're not putting it away completely; you're just removing it from the center of your attention, with the aim of returning to it later. (In more technical terms, when you minimize a window, you shrink it on the screen but leave it in memory.) You can restore a minimized window in an instant just by double-clicking its icon.

If you prefer using your keyboard, you can also maximize, restore, and minimize a window by opening the window's Control menu and selecting the appropriate option.

NOTE *When you're first getting used to Windows, it's sometimes hard to distinguish between the types of icons. Any icon that's "loose" in the Program Manager window, rather than enclosed in a program group window, represents an entire program group rather than an individual program. In addition, program group icons always look like little windows with icons inside. (Some people say they look a bit like waffles.) The icons for individual application programs are less standardized.*

MOVING, RESIZING, AND CLOSING WINDOWS

You can move a window (assuming it is not maximized) by dragging its title bar with the mouse. If you prefer using your keyboard, open the Control menu, select Move, and then press the appropriate arrow keys. Press Enter when you reach the desired spot.

MAXIMIZING, MINIMIZING, AND RESTORING WINDOWS

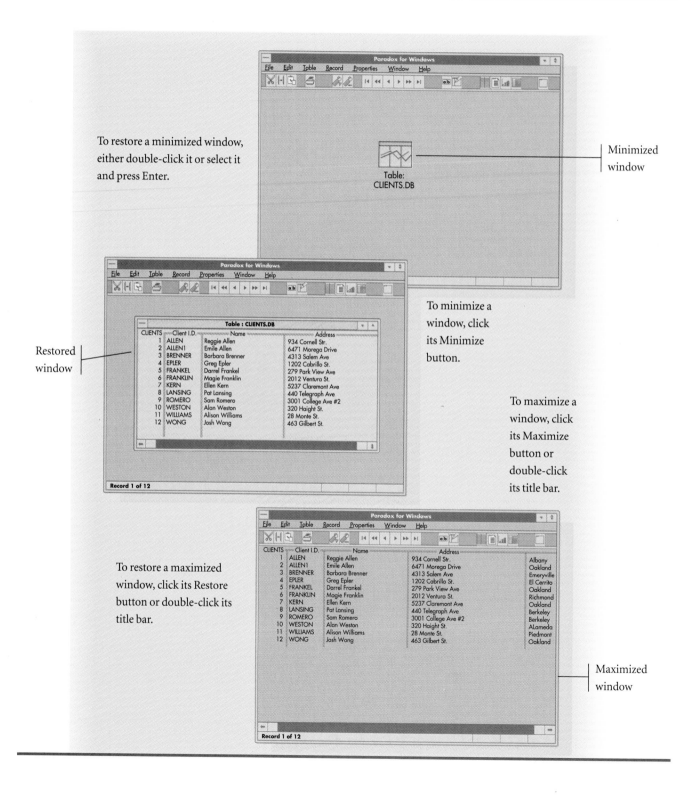

To restore a minimized window, either double-click it or select it and press Enter.

Minimized window

To minimize a window, click its Minimize button.

To maximize a window, click its Maximize button or double-click its title bar.

Restored window

To restore a maximized window, click its Restore button or double-click its title bar.

Maximized window

To resize a window, simply drag its borders with your mouse. Start by slowly moving the mouse pointer across the border until you see the pointer change to a double-headed arrow. Then press the left mouse button, drag the border until the window is the desired size, and release the mouse button. If you want to change both the height and width of a window, drag one of the window's corners. To resize a window using the keyboard, open the Control menu and select Size. Then use your arrow keys to move the window's borders, and press Enter when you're done.

There are four ways to close a window:

▶ *You can double-click the Control menu box in the window's upper-left corner.*

▶ *You can make sure the window is active and press Ctrl+F4. (This only works in document windows.)*

▶ *You can open the window's Control menu and select Close.*

▶ *You can open the File menu and select Exit. (This only works for application windows and closes the application itself.)*

Bear in mind that closing a window means removing its contents from memory. In the case of document windows, this just means removing data from memory. In the case of application windows, it means leaving the program.

USING WINDOWS'S MENU SYSTEMS

As you have seen, there are many operations that you can perform in Windows just by clicking, double-clicking, or dragging with your mouse. But others require you to work with menus, telling the computer what you want it to do by selecting options from on-screen lists.

RESIZING AND MOVING WINDOWS

To resize a window, simply drag one of its borders or its corners using your mouse.

To move a window, drag its title bar.

There are three main types of menus in Windows and in most Windows applications: menu bars, pull-down menus, and cascading menus. Some applications also feature what are called *pop-up menus,* which pop up from the bottom of the screen and only remain on screen as long as you hold down the mouse button. And a few feature *object menus,* which appear whenever you point to an object on the screen and press the right mouse button.

In many cases, selecting an option from one menu evokes another menu with a more specific set of options. For example, in most Windows programs, selecting File displays a pull-down menu of options related to managing files on your disk, including options for creating new files and opening existing ones. Many of the options on the File menu lead to cascading menus that contain more detailed sets of options. In some cases, you may need to select options from three or four menus before anything actually happens. When you have to select options from more than one menu to issue a command, the command's full name consists of all the various options. The command for leaving an application, for example, is File, Exit—meaning first select File and then select Exit. (You may also sometimes see the options separated by vertical bar characters, as in File|Exit.)

To select an option from a menu bar, you can either:

▶ *Click the option with your mouse. For example, to select File and thereby open the File menu, you simply click on the word "File."*

▶ *Hold down the Alt key and press the underlined letter in the option name. To select File, for example, you would press Alt+F. You can also press F10 to activate the menu bar and then press either the Right Arrow or Left Arrow key until the desired option is highlighted and press Enter, or type the underlined letter in the option name.*

THE THREE MAIN TYPES OF MENUS

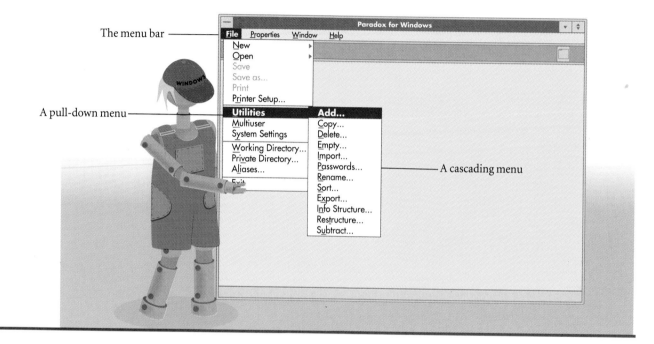

The menu bar

A pull-down menu

A cascading menu

Once a pull-down or cascading menu is open, you can select options in one of three ways:

▶ *You can click on the option with your mouse.*

▶ *You can use the Up Arrow or Down Arrow key to highlight the option and then press Enter.*

▶ *You can type the underlined letter in the option name.*

To close a menu, simply click anywhere outside the menu or press Esc.

LOADING AN APPLICATION PROGRAM

Windows's main purpose is to serve as a platform for applications software, a launch pad for more goal-specific database, spreadsheet, and/or word processing programs. The first step in loading an application program is finding and, if necessary, opening its program group. (Most programs belong to program groups that bear either the program's or manufacturer's name.) If you don't see the program group you are looking for, select the Window option on the menu bar at the top of the Program Manager window either by clicking the option or pressing Alt+W. A complete list of program groups will appear at the bottom of the menu and you can select the one you want.

If you see the program's program group but it is minimized (appears as an icon), open the group either by double-clicking the icon or clicking the icon once and then selecting Restore from the resulting Control menu. Once the desired program group is open, you can start the program itself by double-clicking on its icon or by selecting the icon and pressing Enter.

A program does not need to be designed for Windows in order to run inside the Windows environment. You can run regular DOS programs under Windows as well. (The main reason for doing this is to run more than one program at once, and switch back and forth between them.)

To launch a DOS application from inside of Windows, open a DOS window by double-clicking the MS-DOS icon (usually located in the Main program group) or by selecting the MS-DOS icon and pressing Enter. Then, when you see the DOS prompt, follow the usual procedure for starting up the program. It's also possible to create an icon for a DOS application so that you can launch it directly from the Program Manager, but it's a little early to learn the specifics here. (Once you get comfortable with Windows, refer to your Windows documentation for instructions on creating a new program item.)

When you first open a DOS window, it occupies the full screen. If you prefer to display it inside a window on the Desktop, press Alt+Enter. (You can press Alt+Enter again if you want to switch back to full-screen mode.)

SWITCHING APPLICATIONS

As mentioned, one of the benefits of using Windows is that you can run several applications at once. In fact, whenever you are working with an application program in Windows, you are always running at least two programs: the application itself and the Program Manager.

No matter how many applications you open at once, however, only one of them is active at one time. That program is sometimes called the *foreground application*, because it always sits on top of the stack of application windows—"in front" of all the others. (Depending on whether the window is maximized, you may or may not be able to see part of the other application windows underneath.) The foreground application is also the one that receives most of your CPU's attention. Other open applications are said to be running *in the background*, meaning that they continue to plod along at any tasks you have assigned to them, but they do so slowly, since they are receiving a relatively small part of your CPU's "brain power."

There are several methods of switching from one program to another while inside Windows:

▶ *If any part of the other program's application window is visible, click in that window.*

▶ *If the desired application has been minimized and its icon is visible, double-click on the icon.*

▶ *Hold Alt and press Tab to switch from one application to the next. As you cycle through the programs, Windows displays only the border of each application window, including the title bar. When you reach the application you want, release both keys. The Alt+Esc key combination works in almost the same way, but automatically switches you to a full-sized window rather than displaying just the window title.*

▶ *Hold Ctrl and press Esc to open the application window's Control menu. Then select Switch To to display the Task List, which shows all the programs that are currently running. Choose the desired program from the list and then select the Switch To button, or else double-click on the appropriate program name.*

NOTE *Bear in mind that if you open too many programs at one time, your system may slow to a crawl. The more programs you are running, the more time your computer needs to spend swapping things into and out of memory, and the less attention each program receives from your CPU.*

USING THE CLIPBOARD

Windows has a feature, known as the Clipboard, that allows you to copy or to "cut and paste" (move) data from one place to another. Think of the Clipboard as a temporary holding pen, a place that you place data that you want to transport from one spot to another.

You can use the Clipboard to:

▶ *Move or copy data to another location within the same data file. You might copy a paragraph from the third page to the fifth page of a report, for example, or move a set of numbers from one part of your spreadsheet to another.*

▶ *Move or copy data to a different data file within the same application, copying a sentence or two from one letter to another, for instance.*

A WINDOWS TASK LIST

One way to switch windows is to hold Ctrl and press Esc to display a Task List which shows all the programs that are currently running. Then you either double-click the desired program from the list, or highlight it using your mouse or the keyboard and select Switch To.

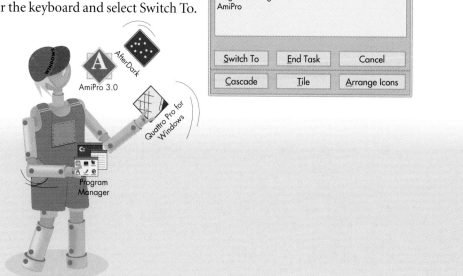

▶ *Move or copy data to a data file in another application. You might copy part of a spreadsheet into a report you are creating in your word processing program, or copy a picture from a graphics program to a newsletter you are creating in a desktop publishing program.*

Bear in mind that you can only copy or move the data into a file or area that suits it—that is, in which that type of information makes sense. You can't just drop a photograph into the middle of a word processing document, for example, although if your word processing program supports graphics, you can create a special graphic box and place the picture inside of that.

Moving or copying data via the Clipboard involves four steps:

▶ *First you must select the data that you want to move or copy. (More on this in a moment.)*

U S I N G   T H E   C L I P B O A R D

You can use the Clipboard to copy blocks of text between different types of applications. In this case, data from a spreadsheet has been copied from a spreadsheet to a quarterly report in a word processing program.

CHOCOLATE SALES

	Units Sold	Unit Price	Total Sales	Average Sale	Units Sold
Chocolate Cigars	537	.90	528.30	1.49	537
Truffles	451	1.50	676.50	3.80	451
Fudge Sauce	67	6.00	536.00	9.93	67
TOTALS	1,105	1.56	1740.80	2.97	1,105

Quarterly Sales Figures

As you know, sales for the first quarter have been particularly good. The figures for 3 months through March are as follows:

	Units Sold	Unit Price	Total Sales	Average Sale	Units Sold
Chocolate Cigars	537	.90	528.30	1.49	537
Truffles	451	1.50	676.50	3.80	451
Fudge Sauce	67	6.00	536.00	9.93	67
TOTALS	1,105	1.56	1740.80	2.97	1,105

▶ *Then you either copy or "cut" (move) that data to the Clipboard, using the Edit, Copy or Edit, Cut command. (To do this, open the Edit menu by either clicking the word Edit on the menu bar or by holding Alt and pressing E. Then select either Cut or Copy.) If you have trouble figuring out whether to cut or copy, think about what you want to happen to your original copy of the data. If you want the original to remain where it is, use Copy. If you want the original to be erased, use Cut. In either case, the data will be copied to the Clipboard for pasting somewhere else.*

▶ *Next, you move to the desired location—be it in the same file, a different file, or a file in another application.*

▶ *Finally, you paste the data from the Clipboard using the Edit, Paste command.*

NOTE *When you paste data from the Clipboard, you do not erase it from the Clipboard. You simply copy it to a designated spot. Anything you place in the Clipboard remains there until you either place something else in the Clipboard or leave Windows. This means that you can easily paste the same set of data into several different locations. (If you have a very long company name, for example, you might type it once, copy it to the Clipboard, and then paste it in from the Clipboard every time you want to use it again.)*

SELECTING DATA FOR THE CLIPBOARD

As mentioned, the first step in copying or cutting data to the Clipboard is selecting the data that you want to manipulate. In most Windows programs, you can select data by dragging across it with your mouse. You can also often select data by clicking at one end of the set of data you want to select and then holding Shift while you click on the other end. To select discrete items on the screen, you select one by clicking, and then hold Ctrl while you click others. If you prefer to select data using your keyboard, try any of the following:

▶ *Shift+End selects from the insertion point to the end of a line*

▶ *Shift+one of the arrow keys selects from the current position of the insertion point to wherever you move the insertion point. If you hold Shift while you press the Down Arrow key three times, for example, you'll select from your original spot to a spot three lines down.*

KEYBOARD SHORTCUTS

Most Windows programs let you issue commands using key combinations (often known as keyboard shortcuts or menu command shortcuts). To determine the shortcuts for the cut, copy, and paste commands in a particular program, open the Edit menu (by clicking on Edit or pressing Alt+E) and then see which shortcut is listed to the right of the option name. The ∧ character is used to represent Ctrl, so ∧C, for example, means hold Ctrl and press C.) The shortcut for Edit, Copy is usually either Ctrl+C (meaning hold Ctrl while you press C) or Ctrl+Ins (hold Ctrl while you press Ins). The shortcut for Edit, Cut is either Ctrl+V or Shift+Del. The shortcut for Edit, Paste is either Ctrl+V or Shift+Ins.

COPYING FROM DOS APPLICATIONS

If you are running a DOS application under Windows, you can copy data from that program to the Windows Clipboard, but the procedure's a little different. (You cannot cut data from a DOS application to the Clipboard.) If you are running the application "full screen" rather than inside a window on the Desktop, press Alt+Enter to switch to a window. Then open the window's Control menu, select Edit, and then choose Mark. Next, press the arrow keys while you hold Shift to highlight the data that you wish to copy to the Clipboard. Finally, open the Control menu again, and choose Edit and then Copy to copy the data to the Clipboard. Then you follow the usual procedure for switching to another application and pasting in the data.

MANAGING FILES WITH THE FILE MANAGER

Chapter 5 explained how to use DOS to perform disk housekeeping operations like copying and deleting files. In Windows, you can perform these same operations using a program named File Manager.

You start the File Manager just as you would any application program. First you need to find the appropriate program icon. (In most cases, the File Manager icon resides in the Main program group.) Once you find it, either double-click it, or select it and press Enter.

The File Manager window always contains at least one document window, which I'll refer to as a *directory window,* that displays information about the contents of a particular disk. At the top of the directory window, just below

FILE MANAGER WITH A DIRECTORY WINDOW

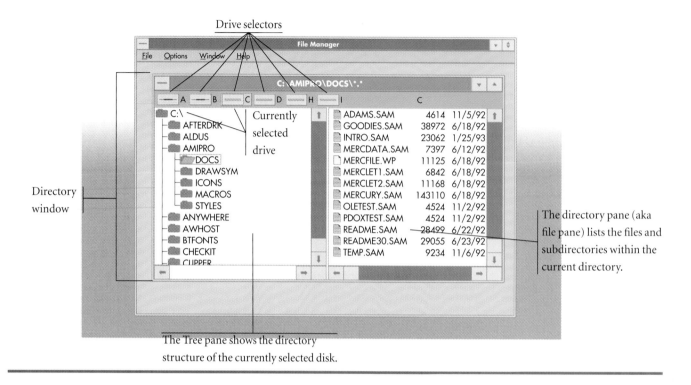

Drive selectors

Currently
selected
drive

Directory
window

The directory pane (aka
file pane) lists the files and
subdirectories within the
current directory.

The Tree pane shows the directory
structure of the currently selected disk.

the title bar, are a set of buttons representing various disk drives, with a box around the drive that is currently selected. (Recall that A and B represent floppy drives, C and higher are hard drives or other mass storage devices like CD-ROM drives.) To view the contents of a different drive, just click the appropriate drive letter.

Unlike the other windows you encounter in Windows programs, directory windows are divided into two sections, known as *panes.* The left pane, called the *tree pane,* contains a graphic representation of the directory structure of the currently selected disk. (As mentioned in Chapter 5, such representations are commonly known as *directory trees.*) At the top of the directory tree is a folder representing the root directory (the main directory on the disk). Below and to the right of that folder are folders representing the subdirectories of the root directory. By default, the directory tree includes only the root directory and its subdirectories; it does not include another level of subdirectories. To display the subdirectories of a particular subdirectory (if any), either double-click its folder icon, or select it by clicking or moving to it using the arrow keys. Then press the plus sign (+). To display all the levels of subdirectories below a particular subdirectory, select the subdirectory and press the asterisk (*). To display all the levels of subdirectories on the entire disk, hold down the Ctrl key and press the asterisk. To hide all levels below a particular subdirectory, either double-click its folder icon or select the subdirectory and press the minus sign (–).

The right pane of the directory window is known as the *directory pane* or *file pane*. It displays a list of the files and subdirectories in the currently selected directory. To select a different directory, click the directory's name in the tree pane. The contents of the directory pane will immediately change to reflect the contents of that directory. Whenever you select a directory, its name is highlighted and its icon changes to an open file folder. (The folders for all the other directories are closed.) The current directory's name also appears in the directory window's title bar.

You can use the scroll bars to scroll through either the tree pane or the directory pane, and you can move down and up a windowful at a time by pressing the PgDn and PgUp keys. The End key takes you to the bottom of the list and Home takes you back to the top.

The first step in manipulating (copying, moving, renaming, or deleting) a file is selecting its name in the list of files within the directory pane. There are a few techniques you can use to select files.

▶ *To select one file, just highlight its name by clicking or using the arrow keys.*

▶ *To select multiple files, highlight the first one's name and then hold down Ctrl while you click on others.*

▶ *If the files you want to select happen to be contiguous, highlight the first (highest) one you want to select and then hold down Shift while you highlight the last (lowest). (You can also highlight the last file and hold down the Shift key while you click the first file.)*

▶ *If the group of files that you want to manipulate can be specified using DOS wildcard characters, issue the File, Select Files command (select File from the menu bar and then choose Select Files). Windows will display a little dialog box in which you can enter your file name specification. (If you want to select all files with an extension of .TXT, for example, enter *.TXT. To select files with a name that starts with Z, enter Z*.*.) Next, click on Select to select the specified files. (You will see lines above and below the names of all the files that match your specifications.) Finally, click on Close to close the dialog box and highlight the files.*

To deselect a group of files, click the mouse anywhere else, without holding down Ctrl or Shift.

Once you have selected one or more files, you can use one of two strategies to copy or move them: You can drag one of the selected files icons to the icon representing the destination, or you can issue a copy or move command, using either the menus or menu command shortcuts. Let's start with the dragging techniques.

To copy file(s) from your hard disk to a floppy, simply drag any one of the selected file names over to the button representing that drive and then release the mouse button. To move a file or files to a floppy disk, press the Shift key and hold it down while you drag.

SELECTING MULTIPLE FILES

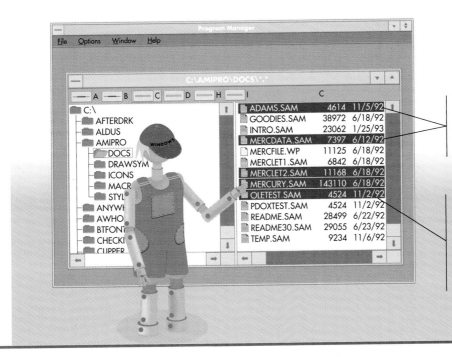

To select file names that are not contiguous, click one, and then hold down Ctrl while you click the others.

To select contiguous file names, click the file name at one end of the group (either the first file or the last) and then hold down Shift while you click the file name at the other end.

To copy or move files from a floppy to your hard drive:

▶ *In the directory tree at the left side of the File Manager window, select the directory on the hard drive into which you want to copy or move the files.*

▶ *Click the icon for the floppy drive that contains the file(s) you want to manipulate.*

▶ *To copy, just drag the icon for any one of the selected file(s) from the directory pane to the icon for drive C. To move, hold down the Shift key while you drag.*

To copy or move files from one directory on your hard disk to another:

▶ *In the directory tree at the left side of the File Manager window, select the directory on the hard drive into which you want to copy or move the files.*

▶ *Click the icon for the drive that contains the file(s) you want to manipulate.*

▶ *To move, just drag the icon for any one of the selected file(s) from the directory pane to the folder in the tree pane that represents the desired directory. To copy, hold down the Ctrl key while you drag.*

In each case, when asked whether you're sure you want to copy or move the selected files or directories, select Yes.

As mentioned, you can also copy or move files using menu commands or menu shortcuts. To copy files, issue the File, Copy command (select File from the menu bar and then choose Copy) or press F8. To move files, issue the File, Move command, or press F7. Regardless of which command you choose or how you initiate it, Windows will display a dialog box in which you can specify the destination. If you want to copy or move files to a different directory, be sure to include the path when you enter the file name. (Paths were explained near the end of Chapter 5.) For example, to copy or move a file to LOTUS, which is a subdirectory of the root directory, you would enter \LOTUS.

To delete one or more files, start by selecting the files and then either press Del or issue the File, Delete command. Windows will display a dialog box entitled Delete that names the file(s) to be deleted. Click OK to proceed, or click Cancel if you've had a change of heart. Next, another dialog box asks you to confirm the deletion of the first file you selected. Click Yes if you want to delete that particular file and then be asked about the others. Click Yes to All to delete all the selected files. Click No if you've decided not to delete that particular file. Click Cancel to cancel the entire delete operation.

If you want to undelete a file that you've deleted by accident, select the file and then issue the File, Undelete command.

To rename one or more files, select their file names and then issue the File, Rename command. When Windows displays a Rename dialog box, enter the new name you want to use in the box labeled "To" and click on OK.

To format a floppy disk, place it in the drive and, if necessary, close the drive latch. Windows will display a Format Disk dialog box. If you want to format a disk in drive B rather than drive A, click the little arrow at the right side of the Drive A box. This will drop down a list of floppy drives. Click on Drive B. Leave all the other options as is and select OK to initiate the formatting process.

GETTING HELP

Windows features a very extensive and easy to use Help system—a series of informational screens and a set of tools for navigating them and finding the information you need. When you are in an application program, the Help system provides information on that particular program. When you are at the Program Manager, the Help system provides information on Windows itself.

There are two ways into the Windows Help system:

▶ *You can open the Help menu on the menu bar by clicking it or pressing Alt, H and then select the desired option.*

▶ *You can press the function key F1, which is usually located in the upper-left corner of the keyboard, to the right of the Esc key.*

The options on the Help menu depend on which application you are in. The first option is always Contents, which leads to a kind of table of contents for that program's help screens. The last option is always named either About or About *x* (with *x* being the name of the program), and usually displays the program's serial number and the name of the person to whom it is registered. In the case of the Program Manager, this option also provides information on the available memory and system resources (meaning both memory and processor power). The other options on the Help menu vary from one program to the next.

The F1 key usually leads to what is known as *context-sensitive help*, meaning a screen with information about whatever operation you are performing or object you are manipulating at the moment. If you open a menu, highlight an option, and then press F1, for example, you will see a screen with information about that menu option.

The figure "The Program Manager Help Screen" shows the window displayed when you select Contents from the Help menu option in the Program Manager. In all help screens, words or pictures that are underlined are called *keywords*. (On color monitors, keywords appear in a contrasting color, such as green.)

There are two types of keywords:

▶ *Topics, which have solid underlines, are links to additional help screens on the specified subject.*

▶ *Terms, which have dotted underlines, invoke dialog boxes with definitions of the underlined word(s).*

Whenever the mouse pointer moves across either type of keyword, it changes from an arrow to a hand. To select a keyword, you either click it, or press Tab until it is highlighted and then press Enter. (You can move backwards through the keywords on a screen by holding down Shift and pressing Tab.)

All the screens in the Help system contain both a menu bar and, in most cases, a bar of mouse buttons. To use one of the buttons, click it or type the

Windows features an extensive, easy-to-use Help system. To get in, either select Help from the menu bar at the top of the screen or press F1.

Keywords

underlined letter in the option name. The Program Manager's Help screen includes these buttons:

▶ *Contents always takes you back to the Contents screen.*

▶ *Search leads to a Search dialog box that you can use to locate information on particular topics. (Sometime the Help menu itself contains a Search option that opens the same dialog box.) To use this dialog box, you can select the list of topics by clicking it or tabbing to it, and then move down to the topic you are interested in, using either the arrow keys or the scroll bar. Alternatively, you can type in a word or words and, as you type, the highlight will move to the item that is closest alphabetically to the word or words you typed. Once you have an interesting item highlighted, click the Show Topics button to display a more specific list of topics, highlight one of those, and then click the Go To button.*

▶ *Back takes you back to the last help screen you viewed.*

▶ *History displays a list of help screens you have viewed. To return to one of those screens, either double-click that option in the list or tab to it and press Enter.*

▶ *Glossary (only available in the Program Manager) displays a list of terms for which help screens exist. These are all defined terms, so you can just click them or tab to them and press Enter to display a definition.*

Help is really its own little program. It runs in its own application window, and can be minimized like other application windows. When you are learning a new application, you may want to keep the Help system running but minimized so that you can easily access it when you need it. (Remember that you can restore a minimized application by double-clicking its icon.)

When you are done using the Help window, close it just as you would any other application window. (It's usually easiest to double-click the Control menu box or use the File, Exit command.)

For more information on using the Help system, open the Program Manager's Help menu and select How to Use Help. The Help menu also includes an extremely useful option entitled Windows Tutorial. Select this option for an interactive tour of Windows in which you'll get a chance to practice your mouse skills and manipulate windows.

LEAVING WINDOWS

You should always leave Windows and return to the DOS prompt before you turn off your computer. To leave Windows, simply return to the Program Manager and then close the Program Manager window, using any of the usual window-closing techniques. (Double-click the Control menu box, issue the File, Exit command, or click the Control menu box once and choose Close.) You will see a dialog box informing you that this will end your Windows session. Press Enter or click OK to proceed. If you have any open application windows with open and unsaved documents, Windows will ask if you want to save your data. Once you have either saved or discarded any unsaved documents, you will be returned to the DOS prompt.

NOTE *If you are running any DOS (non-Windows) applications within Windows, you will need to close them before you can leave Windows. Otherwise, you will see a dialog box informing you that an application is still active.*

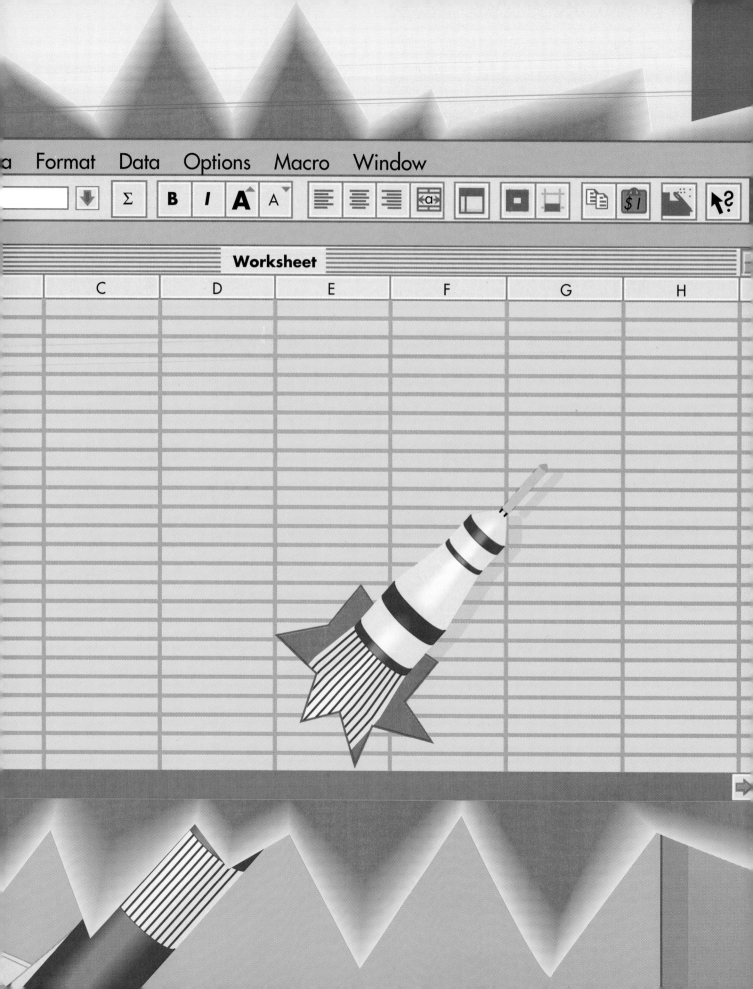

C H A P T E R

7

THE MACINTOSH OPERATING SYSTEM

The Macintosh's main claim to fame is its operating system.

Compared to almost any other operating system in existence, it is extremely unintimidating to the new user, easy to learn, and even fun. It is also a very "intuitive interface," meaning that once you understand the basics, almost everything is pretty much the way you expect it or want it to be.

While some of the Mac's features—like the pictures of happy faces and trash cans—may strike serious DOS types as frivolous, the Macintosh operating system is actually extremely powerful. It provides multitasking abilities (the capacity to run two programs at once) and multimedia (picture- and sound-handling) talents that rival or surpass anything in the DOS world.

N O T E   *The latest version of the Macintosh operating system is known as System 7. I assume that you are using this version. If you are using an earlier version, a few of the features (like Balloon Help) and menu options (like the Find option on the File menu) described in this chapter may not be available.*

THE FINDER AND THE DESKTOP

The Macintosh operating system actually consists of two parts: the system software itself and a program known as the Finder, which acts as the intermediary between you and the system software. The Finder is the first piece of software you encounter when you start up your computer. It is also the program that you use to:

▶ *Start other programs*

▶ *Install programs*

▶ *Find, list, delete, copy, and rename files, and organize them into groups known as folders*

▶ *Initialize, erase, and eject floppy disks*

You use the Finder to tell the Macintosh what to do—which disks you want to use, which programs you want to run, where you want to store your files, and so on. At its most basic level, learning to use a Macintosh involves learning about the Finder. The Finder is so called because one of its main roles is to help you find (and then utilize) programs and data. It does this by providing you with a graphic representation of the contents of disks and other storage media—that is, by displaying icons and windows you can use to view and manipulate your files.

The Finder is responsible for displaying and managing something known as the Macintosh desktop. The *desktop* is the gray or patterned background that appears behind all the other elements on the screen. Like its wooden or metal counterparts, the Macintosh desktop serves as a work space, a surface on which you spread whatever tools and documents you plan to use. Aside from the menu bar that stretches across the top of the screen, the main residents of the desktop are icons (little pictures) and windows (rectangular frames that serve as portholes, letting you view the contents of both disks and data files).

The desktop is only the first metaphor you will encounter in the Macintosh environment. In a sense, the entire Macintosh operating system is built around such analogies. Not only is the screen like a desktop, disks are also like file drawers filled with folders, which in turn contain programs and documents (data files).

The linchpins of the Macintosh filing system are folders. As described in Chapter 3, folders are repositories for files. Like paper folders in file cabinets, folders in the Macintosh world are used to organize information. A typical hard disk might contain folders for Work, Games, and Utility Programs. Within each of those folders, you might have additional folders for individual

THE MACINTOSH DESKTOP

The desktop serves as your workspace, a surface on which you spread the tools and documents you plan to use.

The Finder menu bar

Hard Disk

Trash

The desktop

applications, and within those folders you might have folders for different types of data. Alternatively, you might have one folder for all your application programs and then separate folders for your word processing documents, spreadsheets, and graphics. Or, if the whole family is sharing one Mac, you might give everyone a folder of his or her own. The number of levels in your filing system is entirely up to you, and individual files can be stored at any level in disks, in folders, in folders that live within other folders, and so on.

As shown in the figure "Mac Iconography," there are different types of icons for the various elements in the Macintosh filing system. At a minimum, the desktop contains icons for your hard disk and any other storage device that is currently in use. (If you have a disk in your floppy drive, for example, you will see an icon representing that disk. If you put a CD into a CD-ROM drive, you will see an icon representing that CD.)

THE MAC'S FILING SYSTEM HIERARCHY

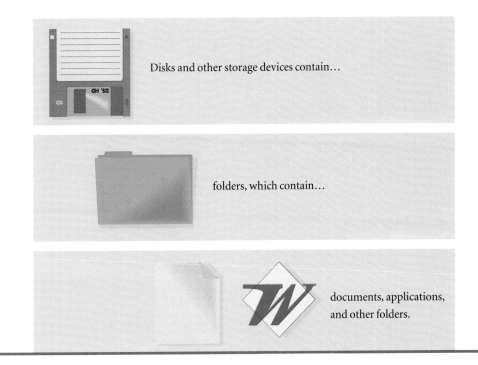

Disks and other storage devices contain...

folders, which contain...

documents, applications, and other folders.

STARTUP OR BOOT DISKS

Almost all hard disks contain a folder entitled System Folder. This folder contains the parts of the Mac operating system software, including the Finder, that are loaded from disk when you start up your computer (as opposed to the part that is stored in read-only memory). In other words, this folder contains the software that your computer needs in order to function. At this stage, all you really need to know about the System Folder is that you shouldn't delete it or even change it unless you know what you are doing.

You may find it helpful to think of icons as containers. Disk and folder icons contain other icons. File icons contain either programs or data. To find out what's inside an icon, you double-click it with your mouse. The results will depend on the icon type:

▶ *When you double-click a disk or folder icon, the icon opens up into a window with a set of icons representing the disk's or folder's contents.*

MAC ICONOGRAPHY

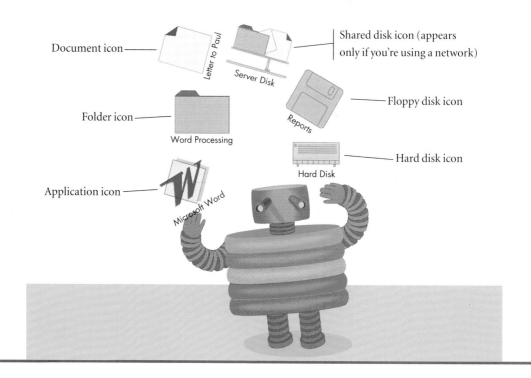

Document icon

Letter to Paul

Server Disk

Shared disk icon (appears only if you're using a network)

Folder icon

Word Processing

Reports

Floppy disk icon

Hard Disk

Hard disk icon

Application icon

Microsoft Word

▶ *When you double-click an application (program file) icon, the Macintosh starts up the program. (In some programs, an empty window immediately appears on the screen, waiting to be filled with data. In others, the only thing that changes is the menu bar.)*

▶ *When you double-click a document icon, the Macintosh starts up the program in which the document was created, and then loads the document.*

NOTE *The Trash icon (the picture of a trash can that usually resides in the lower-right corner of the desktop) is like a special kind of folder that contains objects you are planning to delete. As with other folder icons, double-clicking the Trash icon opens a window containing folders and file icons. You will learn to use the Trash icon later in this chapter.*

ICONS OPEN UP INTO WINDOWS

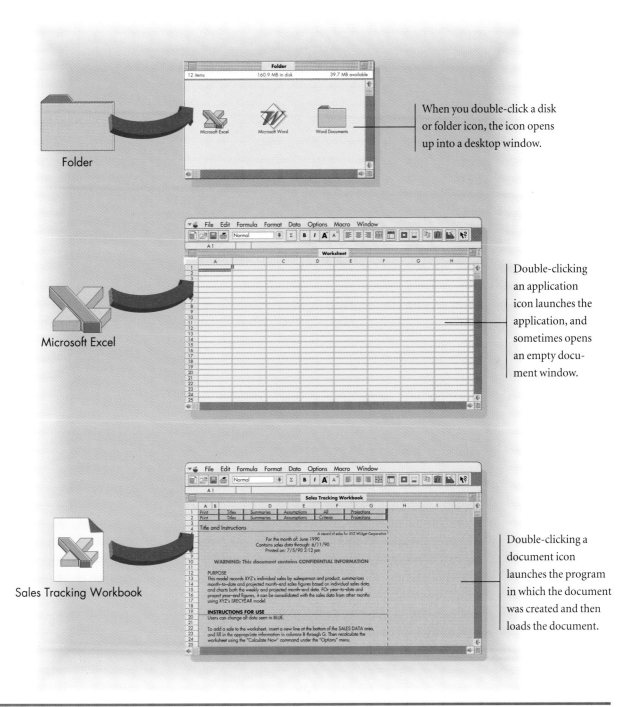

When you double-click a disk or folder icon, the icon opens up into a desktop window.

Folder

Double-clicking an application icon launches the application, and sometimes opens an empty document window.

Microsoft Excel

Double-clicking a document icon launches the program in which the document was created and then loads the document.

Sales Tracking Workbook

In the Macintosh world, you can place the icons for both files and folders directly on the desktop rather than inside a disk or folder, just as you might move files and folders from a file drawer onto your wooden desk. You might do this on occasion to make it especially easy to find a file or folder that you intend to use again. Whenever you move an icon to the desktop, the file or folder itself retains information on where it belongs as if it had a built-in homing device. To return the file to its folder, simply click its icon to select it and then choose the Put Away option on the File menu. (Now if only paper files and folders knew their own way back to their proper spots in your file drawer.)

CONTROL PANELS

You can use the Control Panels option on the Apple menu to customize the Macintosh environment to your own tastes. (I like to think of it as the interior decorating option.) You can also use the General Controls panel to reset the date and time (something you'll want to do at least twice a year, as you reach and then leave daylight savings time). The details of using the control panels are beyond the scope of this book. The only reason I mention it is that if you are using a Mac already customized by someone else, your screen may look a little different than the ones shown in this chapter. For basic instructions on using control panels, see your *Macintosh User's Guide.*

USING THE MENU SYSTEM

Just about every Mac program displays a menu bar (a list of menu titles) at the top of the screen. When you point to any one of these menu titles and press down the mouse button, a pull-down menu appears. (Pull-down menus are so called because they pull down from the menu bar, almost like window shades.)

To issue a command, you generally point to a menu title on the menu bar, and then press and hold down the mouse button to open the associated pull-down menu. (You need to keep the mouse button pressed down or the pull-down menu disappears.) Then, you drag the mouse pointer downward until the desired option is highlighted. Finally, you release the mouse button, to select the highlighted option.

MAC MENUS

In the Finder and most Mac programs, you issue commands by selecting options from menus.

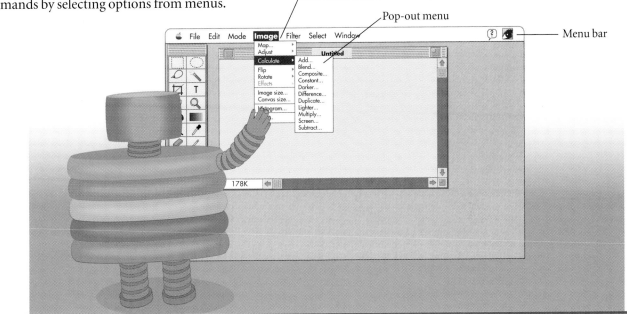

Pull-down menu

Pop-out menu

Menu bar

Occasionally options on pull-down menus lead to *pop-out menus* (also known as *submenus*), which appear slightly lower and to the right of the pull-down menu. Whenever you highlight an option that has an associated pop-out menu, the pop-out menu will appear and you need to keep holding the mouse button while you drag to the desired option on that menu. Then you can release the button. (Pop-out menus are especially prevalent in the PageMaker desktop publishing program.)

Menu titles or options that are gray rather than black are currently unavailable, usually because they don't make sense in the current context. For example, the Eject Disk option on the Special menu is only available if you have a disk in your floppy-disk drive.

To the right of many commands in the pull-down menus are little codes like ⌘C. These are known as *keyboard shortcuts*: key combinations that you can use as an alternative to selecting the menu option. For example, ⌘C is the keyboard shortcut for the Copy option on the Edit menu. Holding down the Command key (the one that has the cloverleaf and/or Apple symbol) while you press C therefore has exactly the same effect as opening the Edit pull-down menu and selecting Copy. (As detailed later in this chapter, this command happens to copy whatever data is highlighted at the moment to a special area of memory known as the Clipboard.)

Any menu option that has three dots after its name leads to a dialog box: a rectangular frame in which you set options or express preferences. (Think of it as a tool for holding a dialog—that is, exchanging information with—the program.) Almost all dialog boxes contain a Cancel option. This makes it safe to wander into dialog boxes as you explore the menu system, because you can always click on Cancel to leave the box without actually doing anything.

The other type of menus that you will encounter in Macintosh programs are pop-up menus, which sometimes appear in dialog boxes. Pop-up menus usually look just like text boxes (little rectangular frames with words inside) except that they have shadows along their bottom and right edges and small solid triangles to the right of their names. To display the list of choices, just point to the menu name and hold down the mouse button. To select an option, drag to it with your mouse before you release the mouse button.

The menus available on the menu bar depend on which program is currently active. When you first turn on your Macintosh, the Finder is active, and the menu bar contains the titles of menus specific to that program. (You can always tell when the Finder is active because the word Special appears in the menu bar.) If an application program is active, the menu titles will change to reflect the menus available in that application.

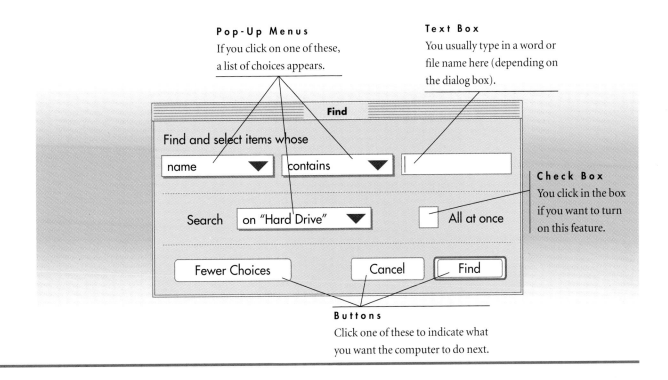

Pop-Up Menus
If you click on one of these,
a list of choices appears.

Text Box
You usually type in a word or
file name here (depending on
the dialog box).

Check Box
You click in the box
if you want to turn
on this feature.

Buttons
Click one of these to indicate what
you want the computer to do next.

NOTE *As mentioned in Chapter 4, the proper way to turn off your Mac is to se-lect the Shut Down option on the Special menu. (Remember that the Finder is active.) On older Macs, you can then flick the on/off switch. On newer Macs, which have a Power On key rather than an on/off switch, the system shuts down automatically.*

WORKING WITH WINDOWS

As mentioned, all Macintosh icons lead to windows—either windows full of icons or windows full of data. The windows that open when you double-click a disk or folder icon are called *desktop windows* or *directory windows.* The windows that open when you double-click a program or document icon are called *document windows.*

THE FINDER MENU BAR

This is the menu that appears whenever the Finder is active.

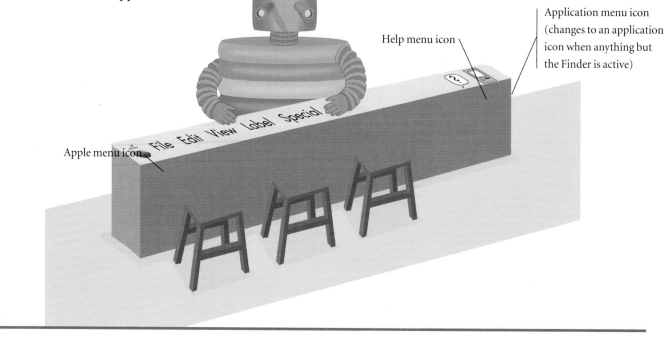

Apple menu icon

Help menu icon

Application menu icon (changes to an application icon when anything but the Finder is active)

As shown in the figure "Anatomy of a Mac Window," all Macintosh windows have several features in common. These features allow you to move, resize, scroll, and close the window using only your mouse. They include

▶ **Title bar.** *Displays the name of the window. Drag this bar to move the window to a different location. If you see horizontal stripes within the title bar, the window is active.*

▶ **Close box.** *Click here to close the window.*

▶ **Information bar.** *This bar appears only in active desktop windows. It contains information on the number of items in the window, the amount of space used, and the amount of space available on the disk.*

ANATOMY OF A MAC WINDOW

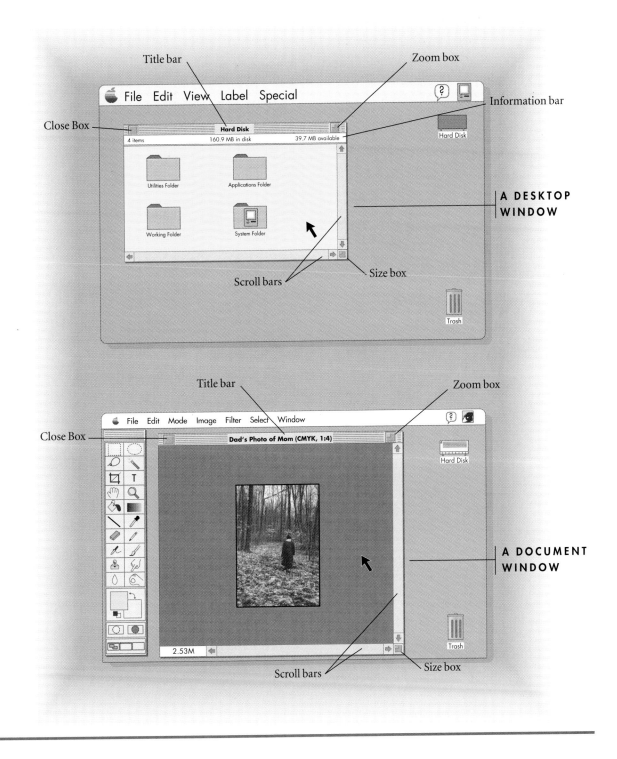

Title bar

Zoom box

Information bar

Close Box

Hard Disk

A DESKTOP WINDOW

Scroll bars

Size box

Title bar

Zoom box

Close Box

A DOCUMENT WINDOW

Scroll bars

Size box

▶ **Zoom box.** *Zooms (expands) or unzooms (shrinks) the window. When you zoom a disk or folder window, it expands only as much as necessary to display all the files and folders it contains. When you zoom a document window, it expands to fill the whole screen.*

▶ **Size box.** *Drag this box to resize the window. To make the window taller, for example, drag the size box downward. To make the window narrower, drag the size box to the left.*

▶ **Scroll bars.** *The color of the scroll bars indicates whether there is more data or more items than can fit within the window. When a scroll bar is gray rather than white, there are additional items or data in that dimension (that is, if the scroll bar is horizontal, there are other items to the left or right; if the scroll bar is vertical, there are other items up or down). To scroll one windowful at a time, click within the bar, somewhere in between the scroll box and the edge of the scroll bar that you want to move toward. If you want to move upwards, for example, click somewhere above the vertical scroll box. You can also scroll by dragging the scroll boxes or clicking the scroll arrows.*

▶ **Scroll boxes.** *You can scroll the contents of the window by dragging the scroll boxes in the desired direction. If you drag a scroll box all the way to the bottom of the vertical scroll bar, for example, you'll see whatever's at the very bottom of the document or collection of icons (in the case of desktop windows). Drag the scroll box to the middle of the scroll bar to see the middle of the icons or document.*

▶ **Scroll arrows.** *Clicking these arrows moves you in small increments in the direction of the arrow. In a word processing document, for example,* *clicking the up scroll arrow moves you up one line and clicking the down scroll arrow moves you down one line.*

As soon as you start working with your Mac, your screen tends to fill with windows. You may start by peeking inside your hard disk by double-clicking the hard disk icon. From there, you may open the window for a folder. Next you may open a window for another folder, which is contained within the first folder. Then you might open a document window by double-clicking a document icon. (This gives you four open windows already.)

FINDING FILES

Working your way down through the filing system hierarchy is not the only way to locate a particular program or document. You can also use the Find option on the File menu. When you issue this command, the Macintosh displays a dialog box in which you can enter the name of the file you are looking for. As soon as you select Find, the Macintosh locates the folder that contains that file, opens the folder on the desktop, and selects the file's icon. If you have a file that is located in a folder within a folder on your hard disk, this can save you the trouble of opening several different windows in order to select it. Note that if you have multiple files with the specified name stored in various folders, the Find command normally finds only the first one. Use the Find Again option on the File menu to find others.

Only one window can be active at any given time. The active window is easy to locate because it has horizontal lines in its title bar and tools like the close, zoom, and resize boxes along its border. If you have several windows stacked on top of each other, the active window is also the one at the top. If no windows are currently active, the desktop itself is considered active.

To activate a particular window, just click anywhere inside its borders. To activate the desktop itself, click a spot outside of all the windows, or hold down the Option and Shift keys and press Up Arrow. You can also activate a window via the associated icon. Whenever you open a disk or folder icon, the icon itself turns dark gray or fills with dots. (Whenever you see such an icon, you know that a window for that icon is already open somewhere on the desktop.) If you double-click a grayed or dot-filled icon, the associated window becomes active and moves in front of any windows that are currently hiding it from view. (You will learn other means of activating document windows under "Launching and Switching Applications" later in this chapter.)

Given how easy it is to clutter the desktop, some of the first things you'll want to know about windows is how to move them around for better viewing, and how to close them. You can move a window simply by dragging its title bar. To close a window, click the close box in its upper-left corner. To close all open windows, hold the Option key while you click the close box in any one of the open windows.

As you create documents, install programs, and move icons from one place to another, your windows can grow both cluttered and disorganized. If you're the type who loves to straighten bookshelves or rearrange file cabinets, you'll love the Clean Up Window option on the Special menu. This option neatly arranges all the icons within an active desktop window. As soon as you select Clean Up Window, the icons in the active window snap to the nearest spot on an invisible grid that underlies the desktop. If an icon's name is particularly long, the adjacent storage spot will be left empty to keep the names from overlapping. (This is a good reason to stick with fairly short names for your files and folders.) You'll learn to sort icons as you straighten up in the next section.

To straighten up icons on the desktop itself, click any icon on the desktop, so that no windows are selected, and then choose Clean Up Desktop from the Special menu. All the icons on the desktop will fly to the nearest spot on the invisible grid.

When you shut down your Mac, the Finder remembers which windows were open when you left and where they were positioned on the desktop. When you turn your computer back on, the Finder automatically opens those same windows in the same spots. This is great when you want to pick up exactly where you left off, or if you always work with the same sets of windows. In some cases, however, you may prefer to start with an empty desktop. To do this, just hold down the Option key while you start your computer. (Don't release it until you see the desktop.)

CHANGING YOUR VIEW OF A WINDOW

By default, the Finder is set up to represent the contents of disks and folders as icons (pictures) on the screen. If you prefer, you can use various options on the View menu to have it display lists of file names instead. The figure "Different Views of a Window" shows the various possibilities. Two of the options (by Small Icon and by Icon) represent files and folders as pictures. The others (by Name, by Size, by Kind, by Label, and by Date) represent them as a list of file names with sizes, file type, label, and the date and time the file was last modified (much like a DOS directory listing). Labels, in the Mac world, are like little tags that you can attach to files or folders to organize them into groups by project or level of priority. If you have a color monitor, you can use them to control the color of file and folder icons.

NOTE *If you see less than seven options on the View menu, it means that someone has limited your options using the Views Control Panel.*

The View menu is only available when a desktop window is active, and the option you select only affects the active window. The option that is currently in effect is preceded by a check on the menu itself.

To sort icons, first select a view that sorts files and folders the way you want. (If you want to sort them by name, for example, select by Name from the

DIFFERENT VIEWS OF A WINDOW

When the view is set to by Icon or by Small Icon, the contents of desktop windows are represented by free-floating labeled icons.

When the view is set to by Name, by Size, by Kind, by Label, or by Date, the content of the desktop windows is represented as a list of items arranged in the specified order.

View menu.) Then switch the View setting back to by Icons, and finally, hold down the Option key while you select the first option on the Special menu. The option will be something like Clean Up by Name or Clean Up by Size, depending on which View you used right before switching back to icons.

MANIPULATING FILES AND FOLDERS

The first step in copying, deleting, or renaming files or folders is selecting their icons. Once an icon is selected, it changes color and its name turns from black on white to white on black. You can always select a single icon by clicking on it once with your mouse, and if your plan is to drag that icon somewhere else, there's actually no need to click it first. (The moment you move the pointer to the icon and press the mouse button in preparation for dragging, the icon becomes selected.) If you are trying to select an icon in a crowded window, however, you may find it easier to use your keyboard: If you type the first character of the icon's name, the Finder will highlight the first icon in the active window that starts with that character. If that's not actually the icon you're looking for, press Tab to move to the icon that falls next in alphabetical order. Press Tab again to move to the next icon, and so on.

You can select a set of adjacent icons by drawing a rectangle around the entire group. To do this, move your mouse pointer to a spot just above and to the left of the first icon you want to include. Then press down the mouse button and drag to a spot below and to the right of the last icon. As you drag, you will see a dotted outline, known as a *marquee,* around the icons. (It's called a marquee because it's supposed to resemble the lights around the edge of a movie marquee.) When you release the mouse button, all icons inside the marquee remain highlighted.

SELECTING MULTIPLE ICONS

You can select a set of adjacent icons by drawing a rectangle around the entire group using your mouse. Usually the easiest way to do this is to drag from a spot above and to the left of the group to a spot below and to the right of the group. As you drag, a flashing dotted line, called *a marquee*, appears around the group.

A marquee

To move one or more selected icons from one folder to another, you simply drag them with your mouse. As you drag, an outline of the icon(s) appears on the screen. As soon as you release the mouse button, the icon(s) themselves move, taking the place of the outline. Bear in mind that you can drag icons to other icons as well as to desktop windows or the desktop itself. If you want to move a file from one folder to another, for example, you can simply drag it to the other folder's icon. You don't need to open a window for that folder first. When you drag to an icon, you need to place the tip of the mouse pointer on top of the icon. (You can ignore the outline of the icon you are dragging.) As soon as the pointer crosses your destination, its icon name becomes highlighted. You can then release the mouse button.

If you want to copy rather than move one or more icons from one folder to another, simply hold down the Option key while you drag. (As always, you can drag to a window, an icon, or the desktop itself.) To create a copy of a file or folder within a particular disk or folder window, first select its icon and then choose Duplicate from the File menu. The object will be copied and the word Copy will be appended to its name.

To copy files or folders from one disk to another, you just select the icons of the desired files or folders and drag them to an icon or window that represents either the disk you want to copy them to or one of the folders on that disk. You don't need to hold down the Option key while dragging. To copy files from a floppy disk to your hard disk, for example, you open a window for the floppy disk, select the icons for the items you want to copy, and then drag to the icon or window representing either the hard disk itself or, more commonly, a folder on your hard disk. (You'll learn to copy entire floppy disks under "Handling Floppies.") To copy from your hard disk to a floppy, select the appropriate icons and then drag them to either a window or icon representing the floppy disk.

To rename an icon, click the icon name rather than the icon itself. (When the name is selected, it is both highlighted and enclosed in a box.) Then either type a new name or click within the existing name and edit it as much as you like. (Use the Delete or Del keys to erase characters. New characters you enter will be inserted into the text.) When you're done replacing or editing the icon name, press Return or click somewhere else.

To create a new folder, start by selecting the container in which you want the new folder to reside. (You can select either a disk icon, a disk window, or a folder window.) Next, select the New Folder option from the File menu. A folder will appear with the name "untitled folder" and the name will be selected. Finally, type in a new name for the folder. (If you accidentally select some other element on the screen before you type in a new name, just click on the folder's name to select it again, and then type in a new name.)

MANIPULATING ICONS

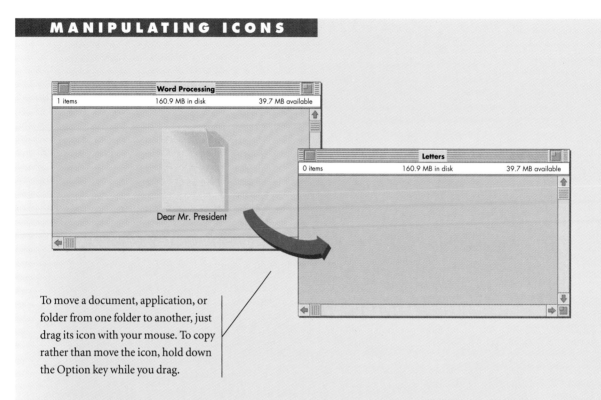

To move a document, application, or folder from one folder to another, just drag its icon with your mouse. To copy rather than move the icon, hold down the Option key while you drag.

If you are copying from one disk to another, just drag to the floppy disk icon or window to copy, or hold down the Option key while you drag to move.

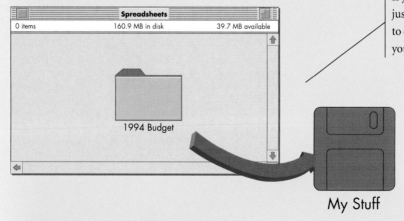

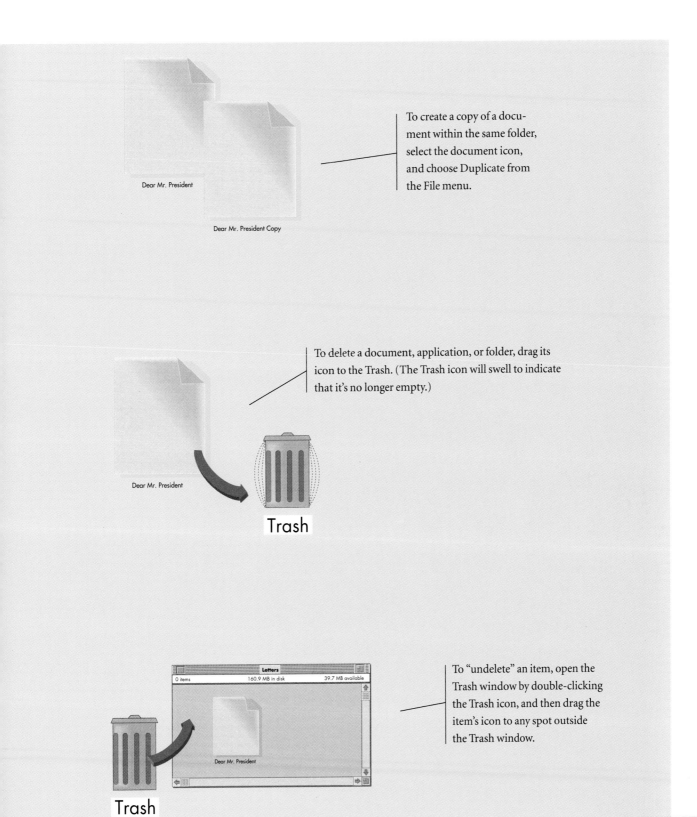

To create a copy of a document within the same folder, select the document icon, and choose Duplicate from the File menu.

Dear Mr. President

Dear Mr. President Copy

To delete a document, application, or folder, drag its icon to the Trash. (The Trash icon will swell to indicate that it's no longer empty.)

Dear Mr. President

Trash

To "undelete" an item, open the Trash window by double-clicking the Trash icon, and then drag the item's icon to any spot outside the Trash window.

Letters
0 items · 160.9 MB in disk · 39.7 MB available

Dear Mr. President

Trash

DELETING ICONS

Deleting files or folders on a Macintosh is a two-step process. The first step is to drag the file or folder icon(s) to the Trash icon (usually located in the lower-right corner of the screen). When the tip of the mouse pointer reaches the Trash icon, the icon itself will darken. You can then release the mouse button. The selected icon(s) will disappear into the Trash and the Trash icon will bulge to indicate that it is no longer empty. (If you delete a folder—that is, place it in the Trash and then empty the Trash—everything inside that folder is deleted as well.)

The second step in deleting is to "empty the trash" by choosing the Empty Trash option from the Special menu. When you do this, you will probably see a warning box asking if you really want to discard the items in the Trash. Select OK to proceed with the deletion or Cancel if you've had a change of heart. Once you have emptied the Trash, its contents are actually deleted from disk.

N O T E   *If you get tired of being asked for confirmation every time you empty the trash, you can disable the warning box by selecting the Trash icon, choosing Get Info from the File menu, clicking the checkbox labeled Warn Before Emptying so that it no longer contains a check, and then closing the Get Info dialog box by clicking its close box.*

Any items that you place in the Trash remain there until you explicitly empty the Trash, even if you turn off your computer. Up until that point, you are free to go through the Trash and rescue any items you've decided to keep. As with any other icon, you examine the contents of the Trash icon by double-clicking it. To remove something from the Trash, either drag it out of the Trash window to another window or icon or to the desktop itself, or click the item once to select it and then choose the Put Away option from the File menu to direct the Finder to put it back where it was right before you dragged it to the Trash.

Handling Floppies

As mentioned in Chapter 3, to insert a floppy disk on a Mac, you simply push it into the drive. When it's all the way in, it clicks into place. In a moment, an icon representing that disk will appear on the desktop. As with the hard disk, you can view the contents of the floppy disk by double-clicking its disk icon.

There are several ways to eject a floppy disk:

▶ *Drag it to the Trash icon.*

▶ *Select the disk icon and then choose the Put Away option on the File menu. (The keyboard shortcut for this command is ⌘Y.)*

▶ *Select the Eject Disk option from the Special menu. (The keyboard shortcut is ⌘E.)*

Floppy disks are ejected automatically when you shut down the system.

You already know how to copy individual files and folders between disks. You'll also occasionally need to copy the entire contents of a floppy to a different disk—to make backup copies of data or programs or to install new programs.

To copy the entire contents of a floppy disk to another disk, drag its icon to another floppy-disk icon or to the hard-disk icon. If you copy the contents of a floppy onto your hard disk, the Finder automatically stores them in a folder that has the same name as the floppy. You can always rename that folder or move its contents afterwards.

EJECTING A FLOPPY DISK

There are several ways to eject a floppy disk. The easiest way is to drag the floppy disk's icon over to the Trash.

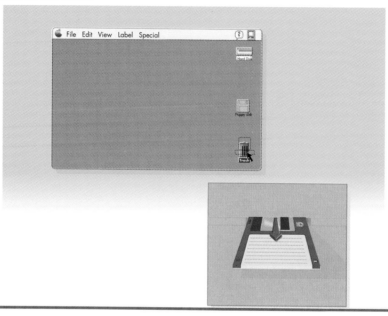

ABOUT BACKUPS

As on PCs, there are several approaches that you can take to back up data on a Mac. If most of your work involves creating word processing documents, spreadsheets, and other files that are relatively small, you can simply copy those files to floppy disks whenever you create and change them. If your files are too big to fit on floppies or if you prefer to have one big backup of all your files, however, you will need a different strategy. Either you will need to copy data to a medium other than floppies—such as cassette tape—or you'll need to use a special backup program that's capable of splitting a file or group of files across two or more floppy disks. Like DOS, the Macintosh operating system has its own built-in backup program, which is called HD Backup. See your Macintosh documentation for information on how to use it. You can also buy fancier backup programs at any computer store. Both HD Backup and most other backup programs allow you to perform both full backups (which involve backing up all the files on your hard disk) or incremental ones (which back up only those files that have changed since the last full backup).

In any case, you should decide on *some* method of backing up your data before you accumulate too many files. And whatever strategy you choose, be sure to follow it. Any hard-disk crash is unfortunate. A hard-disk crash when you don't have a backup of your data is a disaster.

A   W A R N I N G   A B O U T   I N S T A L L I N G   P R O G R A M S

Your startup disk (that is, the disk that you boot from, usually your hard disk) must have only one System folder. If you have more than one, your Mac will have trouble deciding which to use; this will almost certainly lead to errors and possibly even data loss. Since the most likely way for you to get extra System folders is by installing old software, whenever you install programs, particularly old programs, you should check to see whether you have copied an extra System folder to your hard disk. If so, drag that folder to the Trash and then choose Empty Trash from the Special menu. (Don't worry. You can't throw out the wrong one at this point because the Mac won't allow you to discard the copy of the System that you are currently running.)

Making a duplicate copy of a floppy disk is easy if you have two floppy-disk drives: Just put the original disk in one drive and the disk you want to use as your duplicate in the other. (Make sure that the duplicate disk is either empty or contains data that you don't mind overwriting.) Then move the icon for the first disk (the original) on top of the icon for the second disk (the duplicate). When the Finder asks if you want to replace one disk's contents with those of the other, choose OK.

If your Mac only has one drive, duplicating a floppy is a bit more complicated. First, insert the disk you plan to use as a backup into the drive. Then choose Eject Disk from the Special menu. The disk will be ejected but its icon will remain on the desktop (even though it's now dimmed). Next write-protect the original disk (the one you want to duplicate) by closing the write-protect notch in its corner. (See Chapter 3 for details.) This will prevent you from accidentally overwriting the original disk rather than the backup. Then insert that disk into the drive and drag its icon to the dimmed icon for the backup disk. When you're asked whether you want to replace the backup disk's contents, select OK to begin the copy operation. You will probably be prompted to switch disks a few times during the process.

WORKING WITH FLOPPY DISKS

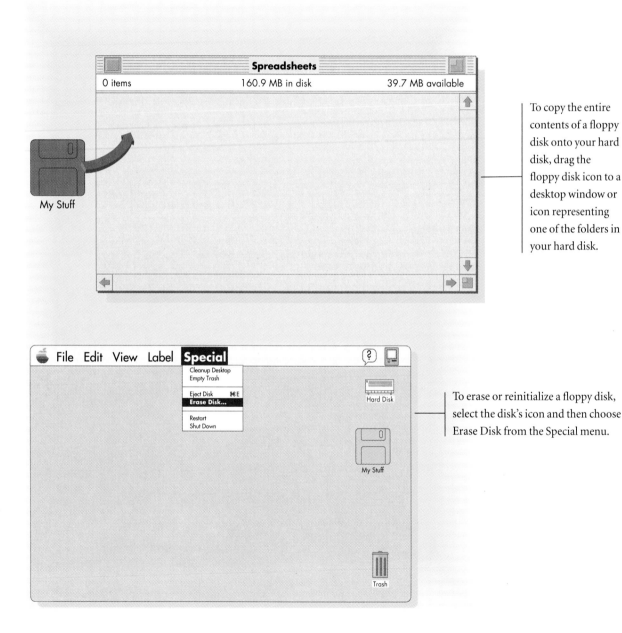

To copy the entire contents of a floppy disk onto your hard disk, drag the floppy disk icon to a desktop window or icon representing one of the folders in your hard disk.

To erase or reinitialize a floppy disk, select the disk's icon and then choose Erase Disk from the Special menu.

As you learned in Chapter 3, new floppy disks must be formatted or, as they say in Mac-speak, *initialized* before you can use them. Whenever you insert an unformatted disk, the Mac assumes you want to initialize it. If you've inserted a double-density rather than high-density disk, you'll be given a choice of one-sided or two-sided formatting. In most cases, you will choose two-sided formatting. The Mac will then warn you that all information already on the disk will be erased. Since the disk is presumably blank anyway, it doesn't matter.

To erase the entire contents of a floppy disk, first select the icon for that disk and then select the Erase Disk option from the Special menu. Since erasing a disk actually initializes it, you will be asked to confirm the operation. If you are erasing a high-density disk, select Initialize to proceed. Otherwise, choose Two-Sided.

LAUNCHING AND SWITCHING PROGRAMS

Starting, or, in Macintosh lingo, *launching*, a program is a simple matter of double-clicking the icon for that program or for any document created within that program. If you double-click a document icon, the Macintosh starts the program and then immediately opens the specified document. You can also open an application by dragging a document icon on top of it, which is particularly useful in those rare cases when you want to open a document that was created in another application. (This will only work if the data is stored in a format, such as text-only, that is acceptable to the application.)

NOTE *You can also launch programs by selecting a program or document icon and selecting Open from the File menu, but double-clicking is usually easier.*

LAUNCHING AN APPLICATION

Launching a program on the Macintosh is a simple matter of double-clicking the icon for the program itself or for any document created within that program.

When you launch some applications, the program assumes that you intend to create a brand new document and therefore presents you with an empty document window. In other programs, you will simply see the menu bar change and you'll need to select New from the File menu if you want to create a new document. In contrast, when you launch an application by either double-clicking a document icon or placing the document icon on top of the program icon, you get a document window containing the specified document.

If you want to be able to launch a program or access a document from more than one folder, you can create what's known as an alias. An *alias* is a means of representing a program or document in multiple folders without actually making a copy of the file. You can think of it as a kind of pseudo-icon or duplicate icon that contains information on where the file itself is stored. (You can, for example, make it possible to open a particular letter from any one of three folders by placing the document's icon in one folder and place aliases for that document in the other two.) See your *Macintosh User's Guide* for details on creating and using aliases.

Once you start launching programs, it can get a little difficult to tell which program is active at any given moment. Regardless of which program is currently active, the last item on the menu bar is the application menu icon. This icon indicates which program is currently active. If it resembles a computer, the Finder is active. If an application program is active, you'll see a logo for that program.

There are three ways to switch from one open application to the next:

▶ *You can click in the window for the application that you want to activate.*

▶ *You can open the application menu (by pointing to its icon and pressing the mouse button) and then select the desired program from the list of programs at the bottom of the menu.*

▶ *You can click the grayed icon for the application itself.*

Clicking the close box in a document window or selecting Close from its File menu does not actually close the application. It merely closes the document window and any document that is currently displayed inside of it. (If you haven't saved all your changes to the document, the Mac will ask if you want to save them before unloading the document from memory.)

The program remains open and active until you activate either another window or the desktop. This can be confusing because in most cases, the screen will be largely empty (as it was before you started the program). The only ways you can tell that the program is still active is that the Application menu icon in the upper-right corner of the screen shows the icon for that program, and the menu bar still shows the choices for that particular program rather than the Finder menu. (Remember that if you see the word "Special" in the menu bar, you know that the Finder is active.) You can tell that an application is running, even it's not currently active, because its program icon will be completely gray and its name will appear in the bottom section of the Application menu. You can activate the program by double-clicking its grayed icon, selecting it from the document window, or clicking inside its document window (if one is open). Even if you activate another window or the desktop, the application remains running and in memory. To switch back to that application, simply select it from the Application menu.

If you actually want to close a program—that is, remove it from memory—select Quit from the File menu. (In most programs, you can also use the keyboard shortcut ⌘Q.) You should close programs when you are done working with them so that they don't take up room in memory and slow down the performance of any other programs you are running.

NOTE *It's quite easy to accidentally click on the desktop while you're working in an application. If you do so, you will inadvertently activate the Finder and the contents of the menu bar will change accordingly. You'll then need to reactivate your application (usually by simply clicking within the document window) before you can use any of its menus.*

VIRTUAL MEMORY

If your computer has limited random access memory or you like to open lots of programs at once, you may need to make use of a feature known as virtual memory. *Virtual memory* allows your system software to treat a hard disk as an extension of RAM, copying programs from memory to your hard disk whenever you run out of room in RAM, and copying them back to memory as needed. See your *Macintosh User's Guide* for details.

THE CLIPBOARD

The Macintosh operating system has a feature, called the Clipboard, that allows you to copy or move data from one place to another. Think of the Clipboard as a tool that you use to transport data. (I sometimes picture it as a tote bag for carrying data from place to place.)

Moving or copying data via the Clipboard involves four steps.

▶ *Select the data that you want to move or copy. In most cases, the easiest way to select data is to simply drag across it with your mouse. (When data is selected, it appears in a different color.) You can also often select a set of data by moving the cursor or insertion point to one end of the data and then holding Shift while you move to the other end. (You can position and move the cursor/insertion point by either clicking with your mouse or using the arrow keys.)*

▶ *Either copy or "cut" (move) that data to the Clipboard, using either the Copy or Cut option on the Edit menu. (You can also use the shortcut ⌘C to copy data or ⌘X to cut it.)*

▶ *Move to the desired location—be it in the same file, a different file, or a file in another application.*

▶ *Paste the data from the Clipboard using the Paste command on the Edit menu (or the ⌘V shortcut).*

Bear in mind that data remains in the Clipboard until you either shut down the system or replace it with something else (by issuing another cut or paste command). This means that you can easily paste the same set of data into several different spots.

If you want to save the contents of the Clipboard so that you can reuse it in future work sessions, you can paste from the Clipboard to the Scrapbook. The Scrapbook is actually a file that consists of multiple "pages" of data which you can easily copy to the Clipboard and then paste wherever you like, select the Scrapbook option from the Apple menu (the first icon on the menu bar). Then choose Paste from the Edit menu or press ⌘V to paste the contents of the Clipboard into the Scrapbook. It will be added to the Scrapbook as the last "page." Then, anytime you want to paste that data somewhere else, move to that page, and select Copy from the Edit menu (or press ⌘C) to paste it into the Clipboard. (You can move from one page to the next using the scroll bar at the bottom of the Scrapbook window.) Then you can paste from the Clipboard as usual. To remove a page from the Scrapbook, move to that page and then select the Clear option from the Edit menu. To copy a page to the Clipboard while removing it from the Scrapbook, move to that page and select Cut from the Edit menu.

BALLOON HELP

One of the easiest ways to learn your way around the desktop is by using a feature known as *Balloon Help*. When this feature is on, every time you point to a particular element on the screen—like a menu option, an option in a dialog box, a window, or part of a window such as the title bar or zoom box—a description of that element is displayed. The description always appears inside a little balloon, like the ones used to display dialog in comic books. Hence the name Balloon Help.

To turn on Balloon Help, open the Help menu (represented by a question mark near the right edge of the menu bar) and select Show Balloons. To turn it off again, open the Help menu and choose Hide Balloons.

BALLOON HELP

When Balloon Help is turned on, every time you point to a particular item on the screen, a description of the item appears in a little balloon. (To turn on Balloon Help, select Show Balloons from the Help menu.)

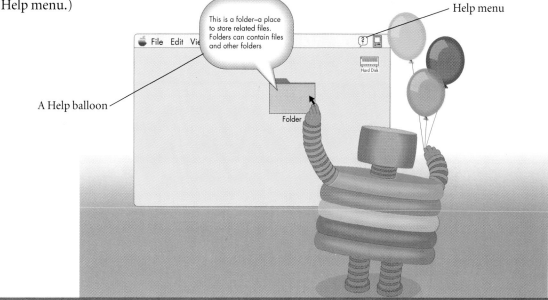

NOTE *The Help menu also contains an option named Finder Shortcuts that displays a window full of tips on manipulating icons and windows. Use the buttons in the lower-right corner of the window to move to the next or previous "page" of information.*

INPUT

OUTPUT

CHAPTER 8

APPLICATIONS SOFTWARE

Word Processing

Spreadsheet Programs

Database Management Programs

Some General Advice on Choosing Software

Installing Programs

Learning an Application Program

8

In a sense, application programs are the most important part of your computer system. They're what enables your computer to actually do something useful, like create documents, perform calculations, or even play games. Unless you decide to become a dedicated programmer, they're also responsible for what appears on your screen 90 percent of the time.

There are dozens of types of application programs available. In this chapter, I'll delve into only three of the most commonly used types: word processing programs, spreadsheet programs, and database management programs. In each case, I'll tell you what such programs do, what they look like and how you use them. I'll also provide some pointers on how to choose one of the dozens on the market.

What I won't tell you is the exact series of steps needed to accomplish particular results in particular programs. (You won't learn how to underline a word in the WordPerfect word processing program, or how to copy a set of data in the Lotus 1-2-3 spreadsheet, for example.) Instead, I'll focus on the basic concepts and metaphors used in all word processing, database, and spreadsheet programs, and the range of feats each of those programs can perform. I'll give you the foundation you need before you get to the "which keys to press" or "which items to click on" stage—a foundation that's often overlooked in the manuals.

WORD PROCESSING

At its simplest, word processing on a computer is just electronic typing. Instead of pressing keys on a typewriter, you press keys on a computer keyboard that looks much like a typewriter. But there is one essential difference. In word processing, the process of composing a document is separate from the process of printing.

WORD PROCESSING IS LIKE ELECTRONIC TYPING

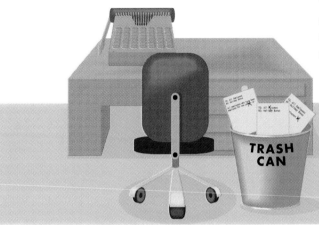

When you type something on a typewriter, the characters are immediately recorded on paper. If you change your mind or notice mistakes, you need to erase characters or retype a page or more of text.

When you type something using a word processing program, the characters you type are simply stored in your computer's memory. You can make any changes you like and print whenever (and as often as) you want.

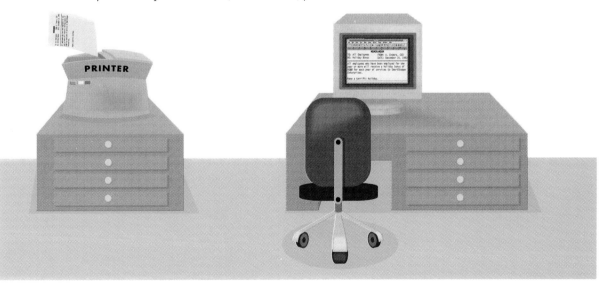

This separation of typing from printing, of electronic document from printed copy, makes all the difference in the world. It lets you erase, amend, and rearrange your document without retyping any of the existing text. If you erase characters, the program automatically closes up any gaps left behind. If you insert characters, it pushes existing characters to the right or downward to make room for the new text. If you decide that a particular sentence or paragraph really belongs somewhere else in your document, you simply move it to the desired spot and let your program rearrange the rest of the document (including your page breaks) to accommodate the change. Most word processing programs even let you change your mind about such editorial changes, providing you with an undo and/or an undelete command that reverses the effects of the last deletion or move.

Whenever you are ready to print your document, you simply issue a print command. (This procedure varies from one program to the next, but it's usually quite simple.) If you are less than thrilled with the resulting printout, just return to your electronic document, make additional changes, and print it again.

For many people, the separation between composing a document and printing it takes some of the anxiety out of the writing process itself. Since you can start typing without committing yourself to paper, the move from thinking about writing to actually starting may feel less momentous or intimidating. Knowing that your work is so easy to fix can make it easier to start.

The ability to insert, delete, and rearrange text without retyping is word processing's main selling point, and this alone is worth the price of admission. But word processing programs offer other features that typists never dreamed of. For starters, most word processing programs can perform the following basic tasks:

▶ *Display and print characters in a variety of typefaces and sizes, and with different attributes such as boldfacing, underlining, and italics.*

▶ *Search for and replace a specified set of characters. This feature can prove particularly useful if you find that you've misspelled someone's name throughout a document. You can also use it to save yourself typing. You can, for example, type some obscure character like the ~ every time you want to display your company's name and then later replace every occurrence of ~ with the name itself.*

▶ *Automatically center text or align it with the right margin*

▶ *Right-justify text, so that characters line up at the left as well as the right margin (as they do in books)*

▶ *Automatically print page numbers either at the top or bottom of each page. This saves you the trouble of entering page numbers within the text and then moving them around when your editing causes the page breaks to move slightly.*

▶ *Print headers and footers—that is, specified sets of text at the top or bottom of each page. These headers and footers can include the current page number if you like. Some programs let you specify different headers or footers on facing pages.*

▶ *Format and manage footnotes and endnotes. Most word processing programs let you attach footnotes or endnotes to particular spots in your document. If you add additional footnotes or rearrange text, the program automatically moves and renumbers the notes as necessary. If you use footnotes (rather than endnotes), the program automatically figures out how much room is required for notes at the bottom of each page, and correctly prints the footnotes exactly where they belong.*

▶ *Automatically hyphenate words at the end of a line. Most programs use their built-in dictionaries to break words in between syllables and ask you to specify a location for the hyphen in words not found in that dictionary.*

▶ *Arrange text in two or more columns (as it appears in many leaflets and most periodicals).*

▶ *Check your document for misspelled words, a process known as spell-checking.*

▶ *Locate synonyms for a selected word. This thesaurus feature can prove invaluable when you find yourself using the same word over and over, or when you can't quite pinpoint the word you want.*

▶ *Enter special characters that you can't generate on most typewriters, including foreign language characters, bullets, and mathematical symbols*

▶ *Create "personalized" form letters and labels. This feature, commonly known as mail merge, lets you "merge" a set of names and addresses with a letter or other document. The result is a set of letters (or whatever) that includes an individual's name, address, and any other personal information you specify.*

▶ *Incorporate lines, boxes, and even pictures within a document. This capability is particularly useful for producing newsletters or fancy reports.*

▶ *Print envelopes and mailing labels. Some high-end word processing programs can even print envelopes by automatically pulling the name and address from the top of your letter, so that you don't have to retype it.*

Few people actually learn or use all of these features. Within the vast collection of bells and whistles offered by the majority of word processing programs, most people identify a few features that they can't live without and ignore the rest. (I, personally, am hooked on the thesaurus. For you, however, the best thing about word processing may be the spell checker, or the ability to mix and match fonts.)

N O T E   Font *means a specific combination of typeface and point size (although a few people use the term to mean typeface, regardless of size). Arial 12-point font means the Arial typeface and a size of 12 points. Helvetica 10-point font means the Helvetica typeface and a size of 10 points. (A point is* $\frac{1}{72}$ *of an inch. The more points, the larger the character.) You'll learn more about fonts in Chapter 9. People frequently use fonts with a larger point size for titles or headings within a document, and sometimes use different typefaces for different elements within the document. In this book, for example, the typeface used in headers at the top of each page is different from that used in the text itself.*

SPELL CHECKERS

Spell checkers can prove invaluable, especially to those who always finished last in spelling bees. (Never send out a resume without using one.) They are, however, no substitute for human proofreading. For one thing, spell checkers only check whether a particular word exists; they don't tell you if it's the right word for a particular context. If you type "here" when you mean "hear," for example, or "major" instead of "mayor," the spell checker will not blink.

WORD PROCESSING FEATURES

Most word processing programs can automatically check your document for misspelled words and suggest alternatives.

All word processing programs include a search and replace feature that lets you replace each occurrence of one set of characters with another set of characters.

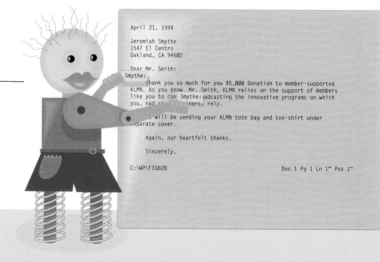

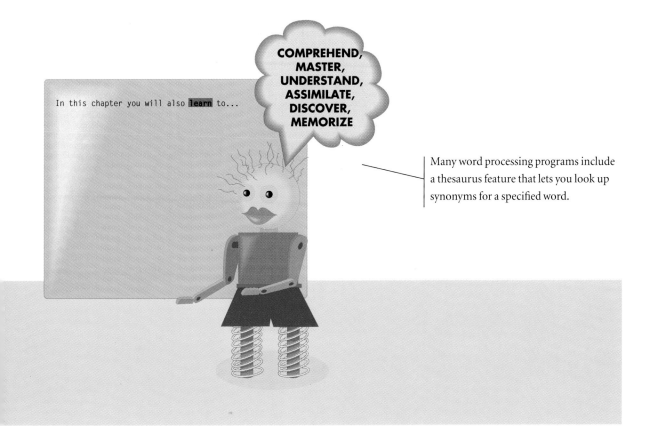

In this chapter you will also **learn** to...

COMPREHEND,
MASTER,
UNDERSTAND,
ASSIMILATE,
DISCOVER,
MEMORIZE

Many word processing programs include a thesaurus feature that lets you look up synonyms for a specified word.

Almost all word processing programs let you generate "personalized" form letters (a feature known as *mail merge*).

April 17, 1994

Dear Mr. Edgewater:

You are one of the lucky few who will have the opportunity to test drive EcoMow's state of the art compost-powered lawn mower.

Doc 1 Pg 1 Ln 1" Pos 1"

PRINTER

Some word processing programs offer even more esoteric features, including

▶ *Special editing tools. Several high-end word processing programs provide a variety of tools that facilitate editing, or writing by committee. These tools allow you to insert or delete text provisionally, subject to the author's approval, or to insert comments into the text, which are visible on screen but skipped over when you print.*

▶ *Tables. Many word processing programs have tools for creating and managing tables of information (that is, text entered in a grid of rows and columns). Most programs allow you to adjust the width of columns after you enter your text, and some let you apply special formatting— such as shading every other row.*

▶ *Create and use styles. Styles are stored collections of typographic, margin, and line spacing formats. Many high-end word processing programs allow you to create styles for various types of documents. Some include various preset styles—for bibliographies or legal pleadings, for example.*

▶ *Outlining features. Some programs include outliners that help you sketch and then refine the overall structure of a document. Such features let you create a preliminary outline with headings and one or more levels of subheadings, and then rearrange these headings, often simply by dragging with your mouse. Some outliners also let you expand part or all of your outline—to display subheadings and/or descriptions—and collapse them so that you see only the headings themselves.*

▶ *Math capabilities. Some word processing programs have built-in basic math features, allowing you to total or subtotal columns of numbers, for example, or to calculate the difference between an amount charged and amount paid on an invoice.*

▶ *Indexes. Some programs permit you to mark words or phrases that you want included in an index and then create an index of all those words, with their page numbers, on your command.*

▶ *Table of contents. In some programs you can mark section headers in the document and then automatically generate a table of contents, with section names and the page on which they appear.*

▶ *Line numbering. Some programs can automatically number the lines in a document, a feature that can prove particularly useful in producing legal documents.*

▶ *Grammar and style checkers. Some programs let you scan your document for grammatical problems such as incorrect punctuation, double negatives, and split infinitives, and/or for stylistic problems, such as overuse of the passive voice or use of redundant expressions.*

▶ *Macros. Some word processing programs allow you to "record" a set of keystrokes and then play them back whenever you like. The process is analogous to speed dialing a telephone: When you press one or two keys, the machine responds as if you had pressed a whole sequence of keys. You can use macros to automate any set of steps that you repeat frequently. You might create a macro to enter the closing for business letters. Then every time you pressed the key(s) to play back that macro, the program would automatically type the word "Sincerely" followed by a comma, press Enter/Return three times, and type your name. Some word-processing programs also let you create more sophisticated macros using a macro programming language.*

▶ *Equation editing capabilities. Some programs let you create, edit, and print complex mathematical equations. Be forewarned that the process is often pretty complicated. You should also be aware that equation editing features help you display and print equations, not solve them.*

Choosing a Word Processing Program

There are three different approaches you can take to selecting a word processing program:

▶ *Talk to friends and colleagues who word process and find out what they like and don't like about the programs they're using. Try to concentrate on people who are producing the type of documents that you plan to create.*

▶ *Make a list of any special requirements you have. Figure out what, exactly, you need the program to do. (You may decide that you don't need any fancy features at all, and prefer to focus on finding a program that's simple, streamlined, and easy to learn.*

▶ *If at all possible, take the top contenders for a test drive. Either visit the home or office of an advocate of each program, or spend an hour or two at your local computer store.*

For many people, the real advantage offered by word processing is the luxury of changing your mind—of editing, rearranging, and reformatting the document until it's just about perfect. The ease with which you can accomplish the day-to-day operations therefore outweighs the assortment of fancy features. If you can, make sure that the program makes it easy to accomplish the types of things you'll want to do all the time, like moving a paragraph, deleting and un-deleting a block of text, and printing. If you use a lot of bulleted lists or outlines, find out how easy (or hard) it is to create them. If you need to print envelopes, make sure that the program you choose makes it as painless as possible.

WINDOWS VERSUS DOS

If you have a PC, the first question to consider is whether you want to use a Windows-based or a DOS-based word processing program. Because they are graphics-based, Windows word processing programs prove particularly useful if you use a lot of fonts and design elements such as lines, boxes, or pictures because you get to see exactly (or close to exactly) what the document will look like when printed. In addition, using a Windows word processing program makes it easier to exchange data with other Windows programs. You can, for example, easily pull in data from a spreadsheet or database program to augment a report, or copy a picture or logo from a graphics program into a newsletter. On the other hand, many people don't need these advantages and not everyone likes the way that text looks in graphics mode. (I personally find it much easier to read, write, and edit text in a text-based word processor and only prefer graphics-based programs when I'm using a lot of fonts.)

USING A WORD PROCESSING PROGRAM

Explaining how to use every word processing program, or even the major few, is beyond the scope of this book. But I can tell you something of what your word processing program will look like. I can also describe the central metaphors and concepts involved in word processing—topics that are often skipped over in manuals and books on the subject. Knowing a bit about the lay of the land will also help if you decide to try out a few word processing pro-grams at your local computer store before you buy.

When you first start up a word processing program, your screen is largely blank. You are, in a sense, confronted with the electronic equivalent of a blank sheet of typing paper. As soon as you start typing, this page becomes filled with the characters that you have pressed on your keyboard.

Most word processing screens also contain a menu (set of options) at the top of the screen and in some cases a set of icons (pictures) representing additional choices. (You'll need to refer to your software manual for information on what each of the menu options and icons do.)

Every word processing screen also contains a symbol that serves as a "you are here" marker. (When you first start the program, this symbol appears in the upper-left corner of the typing area.) If you are entering text, this symbol indicates where the next character will appear. If you are deleting text, it tells you which character you are about to erase. If you are using a DOS-based word processing program, you will probably see a cursor (a little blinking line or rectangle). If you are using either a Windows-based or a Macintosh word processing program, you will see a vertical line known as the insertion point.

The insertion point is not the same as the mouse pointer. Most of the time when you're working in a Mac or Windows word processing program, the mouse pointer looks like a vertical line with a wishbone at the top and the bottom. (This symbol is often called a t-bar.) You use the mouse pointer to select options from menus, to select blocks of text that you want to move, copy, or delete, and to reposition the insertion point. (To move the insertion point, just move the mouse to the desired spot and then click.) If you have trouble distinguishing the pointer from the insertion point, just remember that the insertion point blinks and the pointer has wishbones. The pointer also moves when you move the mouse itself.

You can move the cursor or insertion point around using cursor-movement keys and, in many cases, the mouse. The cursor/insertion point also moves as you add or erase characters.

One of first things to understand about word processing programs is that they scroll text. Most documents are too long to display on screen at once. As soon as you fill up the screen with characters, the program starts scrolling lines off the top to make room for additional text.

The best way to get used to this is to start thinking of the work area on your screen (the part below the menu and/or icons) as a window in which you edit and view documents. Since most documents are too long to fit in the window at once, you need to move the window up and down to view different parts of the text. In other words, even though part of your document may disappear from the screen, it's not erased from memory. You can always scroll upward or downward to bring it back into view.

A central feature of all word processing a feature known as word-wrap. *Word-wrap* means that as you type, the program automatically "wraps" the text to the next line when you reach the right margin. There's no need to press Enter or Return (the electronic equivalent of a carriage return). In a sense, the computer handles your entire document as one long ribbon of characters that wraps from one line to the next. If you erase some characters (removing a section of the ribbon), the program pulls the rest of the ribbon leftward or, if necessary, pulls it up a line to close the gap. If you add characters in the middle (inserting a new section of ribbon), the rest of the ribbon is pushed forward and/or down.

If you learned to type on a typewriter, you may find your old habits hard to break. In particular, you'll have to train yourself not to press the Enter or Return key when you get near the right margin (that is, the right side of the screen). Not only is pressing Enter/Return unnecessary, it can actually create problems.

YOUR SCREEN AS A WINDOW

All word processing programs scroll text. As soon as you fill up the
screen with text, lines start disappearing off the top to make room
for new lines at the bottom.

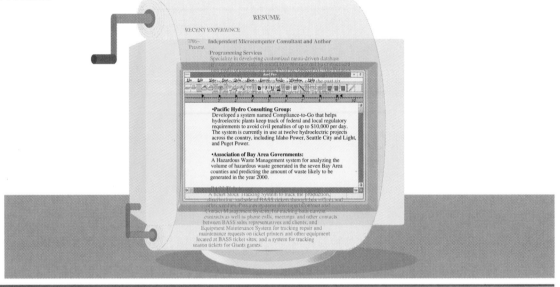

When you press Enter/Return, the program inserts what is known as a
hard return—a code that tells the program "go the next line here, no matter
where you are in relation to the margins." Whenever the program encounters a
hard return, it breaks the line at that spot, even if there are only two words on
the line. If you inadvertently press Enter/Return at the end of a line and later
delete characters from that line, the line break will not change accordingly.

The moral of the story is that you should only press Enter/Return at the
end of a paragraph, at the end of a line that you want to be abnormally short
(like an address line), or when you want to insert a blank line between paragraphs. The rest of the time, just keep typing and let the program handle the
line breaks for you.

WORD-WRAP

Word processing programs treat documents as a continuous ribbon of text. Whenever you reach the right margin, the program automatically wraps this ribbon around to the next line.

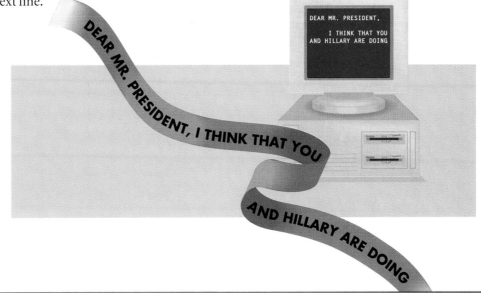

N O T E   *In most word processing programs, you can't move the cursor/insertion point past the last character in the document. If you want to start typing three lines down from the top of a blank screen, for example, you can't just move the cursor/insertion point down three lines. You need to either press Enter/Return a few times instead, inserting hard returns and thereby pushing the cursor/insertion point downward.*

Although they are usually invisible, hard returns are characters, just like letters or numbers. Each one occupies a mailbox (byte) in memory. And it can be deleted or moved just like other characters. To get rid of a hard return, place your cursor or insertion point on or to the left of the first character on the subsequent line, and then erase the character right before that spot by pressing the delete key if you're using a Mac or the Backspace key on a PC.

HARD RETURNS

Whenever you press Enter/Return in a word processing program, you are inserting a special code called a *hard return* that directs the program to move to the next line.

```
                                    September 27 [NEXT LINE]
[NEXT LINE]
Dear Myrtle, [NEXT LINE]
[NEXT LINE]
     It was so nice to see you, Mortimer, and your three
lovely childeren. (Matt really does look EXACTLY like
Mortimer.) [NEXT LINE]
[NEXT LINE]
     Those games of golf were a joy, and Mort drives a golf
cart like a caddy! I especially enjoyed our afternoon at the
Miracla Mall. What a sale! [NEXT LINE]
[NEXT LINE]
     Hope you can visit us in Fresno again next year. [NEXT LINE]
[NEXT LINE]
                              Your friend, [NEXT LINE]
[NEXT LINE]
                              Mable Maplethorpe [NEXT LINE]

                              Doc 1 Pg 1 Ln 1" Pos 1"
```

SPREADSHEET PROGRAMS

In a nutshell, a *spreadsheet* is a grid of rows and columns in which you enter numbers and text. Spreadsheets were actually invented centuries ago as a means of performing and recording calculations. For their first two or three hundred years, spreadsheets' format—a book of pages divided into rows and columns—remained essentially unchanged. Then in the late 1970s, someone got the brilliant idea of automating the spreadsheet—that is, of displaying the same grid of rows and columns on a computer screen and having the computer do the work of performing the calculations. The result was an extremely successful program known as VisiCalc. Since then, spreadsheet programs such as Lotus 1-2-3, Quattro Pro, and Excel have become some of the most widely used types of computer software (second only to word processing programs).

Spreadsheet programs are the number crunchers of the computer world, although they can be used to manipulate text as well. Think of them as powerful, multi-purpose calculators, capable of everything from adding two plus two to calculating a loan amortization schedule to projecting the likely impact of an increase of an energy tax on your cost of goods sold. Spreadsheets excel at performing both calculations on given numbers (what's the total of these 439 expense items?) and at what-if computations (how much will my monthly mortgage payment increase if I change the term from 30 years to 15 years?).

Although the appearance of spreadsheet programs varies a bit from one program to the next, they all have features in common. In almost all cases, the screen is largely occupied by a grid of rows and columns, frequently known as the *work area* or worksheet area. The columns are identified by letters shown at the top of the work area. The rows are identified by numbers (shown at the left side of the work area). The boxes formed by the intersection of individual rows and columns are known as *cells*. Cells are identified by the combination of their column letter and row number. The fifth cell in the second column is known as cell B5, for example. (The letter always comes first.) This is known as the cell's address or cell coordinates.

At any given moment, you are positioned in a single cell, generally known as the *current cell*. You can always tell which cell you are in at the moment by looking at the position of the cell pointer—a highlight that you can move from one cell to the next. (You can move the cell pointer from one cell to another using the cursor movement keys or your mouse.) The address of the current cell is usually displayed on a line just above the work area, in an area usually known as the cell address indicator.

When you create a new spreadsheet, the grid of rows and columns is empty. You start with the equivalent of a blank sheet of ledger paper—a tabula rasa waiting for your data.

ANATOMY OF A SPREADSHEET SCREEN

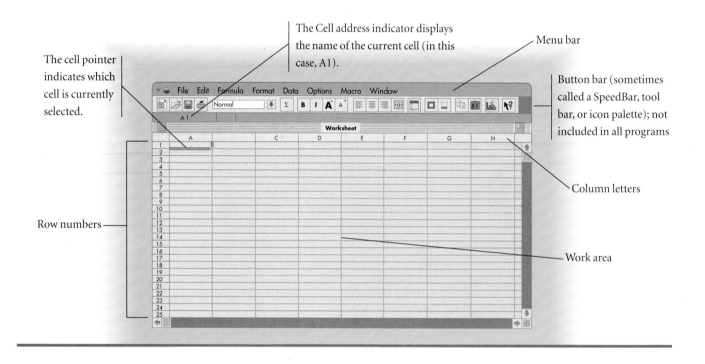

The Cell address indicator displays the name of the current cell (in this case, A1).

Menu bar

The cell pointer indicates which cell is currently selected.

Button bar (sometimes called a SpeedBar, tool bar, or icon palette); not included in all programs

Column letters

Row numbers

Work area

The size of this "piece of paper" is actually quite huge. Most spreadsheets contain at least 256 columns and 8192 rows (about 2 million cells). What appears on the screen, however, is a small portion of that "page," usually about 8 columns and 20 rows. In order to find your way around the spreadsheet, you need to imagine the work area as a movable window, just as you do in a word processing program. But in this case, you can move the window sideways (to view additional columns) as well as up and down (to view additional rows).

In addition to the work area, most spreadsheets contain a menu bar at the top of the screen. This menu bar is either visible all the time or is invoked by pressing a key (usually the slash key) when you want to use it. We're not going to cover the use of the menu system, since the menus vary from program to program. But in general, you use menu commands to do things like moving, copying, and erasing blocks of data, inserting or deleting columns and rows, printing, saving, and changing the appearance of the data in various ways.

YOUR SCREEN IS A WINDOW ONTO THE SPREADSHEET PAGE

Think of the work area section as a movable window through which you can view different sections of a spreadsheet.

Quattro Pro for Windows

Edit   Block   Data   Tools   Graph   Property   Window   Help

BOBS.WQ1

	D	E	F	G	H	I	J	
	FTE	CLASS	Annual Cost	Year 1 Staffing	Year 1 Cost	Year 2 Cost	Year 3 Cost	Cost
	3.00	Psych Social Worker	46,160	0%	0	138,480	141,250	
	3.00	Psych Socela Worker	46,160	0%	0	138,480	141,250	
	1.00	MH Associate	36,480	0%	0	36,480	37,210	
	2.00	Probation Officer	40,400	0%	0	80,800	82,416	
		Fiscal Tech 1	33,120	0%	0	33,120	33,782	
					0	427,360	435,907	
					0	106,840	108,977	
					0	534,200	544,884	
					20,000	20,000	20,000	
					48,360	48,360	48,360	
					55,000	55,000	55,000	
					55,000	55,000	55,000	
					20,000	20,000	20,000	
					10,200	10,404	10,612	
					208,560	208,764	208,972	

NOTE *In some spreadsheet programs, individual files are referred to as worksheets or spreadsheet notebooks rather than spreadsheets.*

HOW SPREADSHEETS WORK

Although spreadsheets are capable of calculating almost anything you can imagine, they're not set up in advance to perform any particular calculations. It's your job to fill in the grid by entering text, numbers, and instructions (formulas) that direct the computer to perform particular calculations.

Let's take a simple example. Suppose that you wanted to calculate the net income for a company. You might start by entering the numbers for total revenue in one cell and for total expenses in another. (You might also enter text identifying these numbers in two adjacent cells.) Then you would need to enter a formula telling the program to subtract the expenses from the revenue and display the result. You do this by moving to a blank cell and typing in an instruction describing the desired calculation in terms of cells. If cell B3 contains the figure for revenue and cell B4 contains your expenses, for example, you would enter a formula such as +B3-B4 or (B3-B4) or =B3-B4. (The exact syntax for formulas varies from one spreadsheet program to the next.) You can think of this formula as "take whatever value currently appears in cell B3, subtract the value that currently appears in cell B4 and then display the result in this cell." Then, whenever you change the value in cell B3 or B4, the result of the formula will be automatically—and, in most cases, instantly—updated.

This feature is known as automatic recalculation, and it is one of the main advantages that spreadsheets offer over calculators. Once you tell the spreadsheet what you want it to do, you are free to change the raw data as much and as often as you like, and the program does the work of recalculating the results.

Automatic recalculation actually offers two benefits. First, it lets you change a few of your numbers and have the program recalculate the results. You don't have to reiterate your instructions or reenter any data that didn't change.

The advantages grow even more obvious when you have more formulas, and when some of those formulas "piggy back" on top of others. The "Stuffed Animal Sales Spreadsheet" figure illustrates this concept. If you changed the dollar amount of dinosaurs sold in January, the total for January at the bottom of that column would automatically be recalculated, as would the total dinosaur sales at the right edge of the row. (Both of those totals are based on formulas that add up all the other values in that row or column.) Then because the total dinosaur sales figure changed, the grand total in the lower-right corner would be recalculated as well, because that number is the result of a formula that adds up all the other values in the column (that is, the total for each type of stuffed animal). If there happened to be another formula based on the grand total, that formula would be recalculated as well.

To put this in more general terms: Every time you change the value in a cell, any formulas that refer to that cell are updated. As those formulas are updated, any formulas that refer to their results are updated as well. In this way, a single change in value may set off a chain reaction, instigating changes in several cells throughout the spreadsheet.

The other advantage of automatic recalculation is that it lets you "play" with numbers. If the Stuffed Animal Sales spreadsheet represented budgeted rather than actual sales amounts, and you wanted to get your total sales up to 20,000, you could try adjusting various numbers to see exactly what it would take to get the desired total.

STUFFED ANIMAL SALES SPREADSHEET

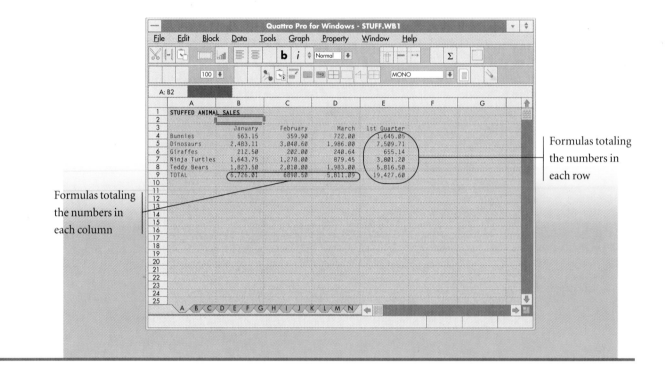

Formulas totaling the numbers in each row

Formulas totaling the numbers in each column

As mentioned, automatic recalculation is only one of the main advantages that spreadsheets offer over calculators. The others include:

▶ *Functions. All spreadsheet programs feature something known as func-tions—built-in tools for performing calculations other than simple arithmetic (addition, subtraction, multiplication, or division). Most major spreadsheet programs offer around 100 different functions, which allow you to calculate averages, square roots, depreciation, payments or earnings on annuities, and standard deviation (to name just a few).*

▶ *Database management capabilities. Most spreadsheet programs offer at least a few tools for managing lists. At a minimum, they allow you to sort a set of rows alphabetically or numerically, and to select items that match specified selection criteria. Bear in mind that if your list exceeds a hundred items or if you need to produce formatted reports or mailing labels, you are better off calling in an expert—namely, a database management program—rather than testing the limits of your spreadsheet program.*

▶ *Formatting tools. Many spreadsheet programs offer desktop publishing tools, enabling you to mix and match fonts within a single spreadsheet, to print spreadsheets sideways, and dress up your spreadsheets with lines, boxes, shading, and graphic elements like pictures and logos.*

▶ *Macros. As described earlier in this chapter, macros are a means of automating an entire series of steps and then "playing them back" with one or two keystrokes. Some spreadsheet programs allow you to record macros—that is, to "memorize" a series of actions as you perform them and then repeat them on demand. Others require you to construct macros by typing commands into cells of the spreadsheet, much as a programmer would type in the lines of a computer program. (In fact, many spreadsheet macro languages are really programming languages in themselves—with all the implied power and potential difficulty.)*

▶ *Three-dimensionality and linking. Many spreadsheet programs offer tools for linking multiple spreadsheet files, so that a formula in one file can refer to cells in other file. Others let you store multiple sets of information—almost like individual spreadsheets—within a single file. (This is called a* three-dimensional spreadsheet.*) Such features can prove extremely useful if you need to consolidate information from several departments or time periods, or want a way to organize several distinct but related sets of information.*

▶ *Graphing tools. Most spreadsheet programs offer some means of representing the numbers within your spreadsheets in graphical form as a bar chart, line chart, or pie chart (among others). Some offer sophisticated graphing features that let you create dozens of different types of graphs, and also allow you to dress up your graphs with lines, boxes, ellipses, text, and other design elements.*

CHOOSING A SPREADSHEET PROGRAM

When comparing two or more spreadsheet programs, start with the basics. See how you like the menu structure. (You may find some more intuitive than others.) Find out the procedure for doing simple things, like entering dates, or copying an entry from one cell to another, or inserting a row. For many people, the ease with which you can accomplish mundane tasks—like entering and formatting data—is at least as important as the high-powered extras.

The first step in choosing a spreadsheet program is determining which special features you need, if any. For example, if you plan to use your spreadsheet to perform crosstabs (that is, to summarize data by two sets of variables, like age and ethnicity, or color and size), make sure that the program supports that type of calculation. (Not all do.) If graphs are critical to your work, check out the graphing talents of various programs: what types of graphs can they generate, what tools do they offer for customizing or annotating graphs, how easy it is to print graphs, can you produce graph slide shows?

Another area to explore is how easily you can exchange data with other programs. Can you easily move data from a spreadsheet into a word processing document? If you also plan on using a database program, how well can the spreadsheet program "talk to" various database programs? As always, data exchange tends to be less of a problem with Mac and Windows programs because they can usually exchange data via the Clipboard feature.

A SPREADSHEET WITH A GRAPH

Some spreadsheet programs let you display graphs as part of your spreadsheet. Others can only display graphs on a screen by themselves.

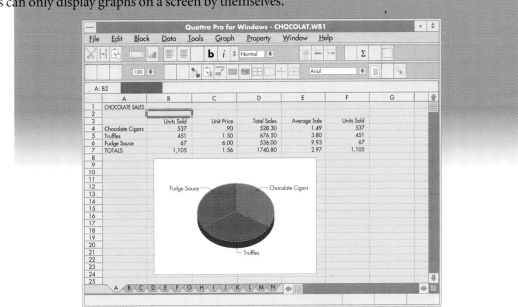

If you want your spreadsheets to look desktop published—with various fonts and accoutrements such as lines and boxes—see how such features are implemented in the program. In some spreadsheet programs, for example, the desktop publishing features are treated almost like a separate program within the program—you need to switch to a different screen, with a different set of menus, to use them. You may or may not like this separation of features.

DATABASE MANAGEMENT PROGRAMS

Most offices are teeming with files and filing systems, not to mention stacks of paper waiting to be filed. Database management programs are designed to help you manage such masses of data. Their purpose is to turn the names, notes, facts, and figures involved in running a business, a non-profit organization, or a research project into manageable and, hopefully, useful information. You can think of database programs as a cross between filing clerk and research assistant: They help you both store and retrieve information, and make some sense of it all.

To put it more mundanely, database management programs help you manage and use databases. A *database* is simply a structured collection of information about people (like customers, vendors, members, or employees), things (such as products on hand or documents on file), or events (orders received, services provided, or sales calls made).

You've probably dealt with many databases already, even if you've never touched a computer. Library card catalogs, inventory systems, rolodex files, and collections of customer ledger cards are all databases. Managing such databases involves the same basic processes, regardless of whether you perform them with the aid of a computer. Those operations include

▶ *Entering new data*

▶ *Locating previously entered data*

▶ *Changing and deleting existing data*

▶ *Selecting portions of your data, such as all the customers in San Francisco or all the orders that are past due*

▶ *Arranging the data into different sequences, such as in alphabetical order by last name, or by zip code, or by state and within state by city.*

▶ *Producing reports and other printed output, including form letters and mailing labels*

▶ *Generating statistics—for example, counting the number of orders for a particular item, or determining the average dollar amount of all orders placed in the last year*

EXAMPLES OF DATABASES

The types of information you might store in a database include inventory lists, a list of rental properties, and a set of student registration data. You might also create databases to track data on company employees, orders received from customers, tickets sold for a performance, current sales contracts, or video rentals, for example.

ALFREE'S ANIMAL SUPPLY

Item No.	Description	Cost	Selling Price
X20-0084	Pack, petite dog bones	$ 1.02	$ 2.20
X20-0085	Pack, regular dog bones	$ 1.54	$ 3.00
X20-0096	Pack, giant dog bones	$ 1.90	$ 4.00
Y04-1233	4 1/2" frisbee	$ 2.20	$ 4.00
Y04-1596	9" frisbee	$ 6.00	$11.00

RENTAL PROPERTIES

Address: 104 Park Forest
City: Flint
No. of Bedrooms: 2.5
No. of Baths: 1
Rent: $650.00
Available as of: 3/1/94

STUDENT REGISTRATION FORM

Student I.D. no.: 555-113442
Name: Jennifer Wriggins
Address: 645 West Lake Drive
City: Cambridge State: MA Zip: 03345
Telephone: (617)555-1134
Enrollment Date: Fall '93
Anticipated Date of Graduation: Sp. '97
Concentration: Philosophy of Law

Notice that all of these operations can be accomplished without a computer. In this sense, maintaining a shoe box full of index cards can be called database management. The main advantages of computerizing are

▶ *Speed. In general, putting a database on computer won't save you much time on the input side of things. (It takes about the same amount of time to type a customer's name and address on the keyboard as it does to scribble it on a rolodex card, maybe even a bit more.) Where the time savings occur is on the output side of the equation—once you've got the information in there, you can "massage" the data in any way you like with relatively little time or effort: sorting it into 12 different orders, printing it in a variety of formats, selecting all the customers that live in Cincinnati and like to order red plaid hiking shorts.*

INPUT AND OUTPUT

When you use a database management program, you can input (enter) data once and then output it in a variety of forms—generating lists, labels, form letters, and statistical reports.

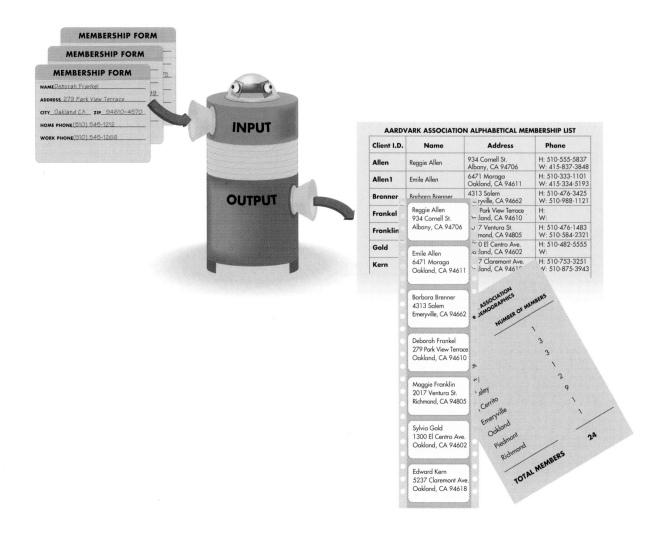

▶ *Increased accuracy in calculations. Assuming they receive the right instructions, computers are generally more reliable at performing calculations than people are.*

▶ *Fewer errors and greater consistency in the data. If you have a lot of data, you want some way to ensure its accuracy. Many database programs let you prevent simple data entry errors by defining rules for what data is acceptable in a field by specifying an allowable numeric range for a field, or a list of valid entries. Some programs also let you define particular items as mandatory, or fill in default values whenever an item is left blank. And some let you set up automatic formatting rules, so that all letters entered in an entry are automatically capitalized, for example.*

Before you get too enthusiastic about how a database management program is going to change your life, there's one limitation you should know about. Database management programs do not turn you into an organized person (or your office into an organized office). If you can't keep your desk in order, you're not likely to fare much better with a database program. On the other hand, if you're serious about the process of setting up a database, the transition to computers can force you to standardize the way you structure and manage information. Since most database programs require you to define in advance exactly which items of information you are going to enter, you'll need to think through exactly what you want to know. Similarly, since computers can't make value judgments, you need to define clear-cut rules about issues like when old customers should be deleted from your mailing list, whether you want to allow the entry of overpayments, or what codes you will use for departments in your personnel list. (If you don't standardize, it will be difficult to find everyone in a department later.) In other words, computerizing a database can force you to be more thoughtful and systematic than you'd otherwise be, at least during the design phase.

Most database programs are not free-form. They don't allow you to just jot down whatever information you want on each customer or inventory item. Instead, they make you decide, in advance, exactly which items of information you're going to collect. (You can change your mind about this structure, but it takes a little time and effort.) Note: There are exceptions to this rule. Some database programs—known as *free-form database programs*—are more open-ended, allowing you to enter data in whatever format you like.

To take a simple example, suppose that you have decided to use a database program to manage a personnel database. The first step is to set up a structure for your data, specifying what categories of information you intend to include for each employee.(You can think of this as making a mold into which you plan to pour your data.) Only after you have defined this structure can you start entering data.

In database terminology, these individual categories of information are known as *fields* and the entire set of information related to each person, thing, or event is known as a *record*. When the data is laid out in a tabular or spreadsheet-like form, as it is in the figure "Database Terminology," fields occupy columns and records occupy rows.

In the case of the personnel database, the fields might include first name, last name, address, phone extension, home phone number, department, supervisor, date hired, social security number, department, position, and salary. The entire collection of data for each employee—that is, the full set of fields— is one record. You may leave one or more of these fields empty in some records, but every record has the same set of fields. You also cannot have one or two records with extra fields that don't exist in the other records.

DATABASE TERMINOLOGY

A table is a collection of records that share the same structure—that is, include the same set of fields. This is a table of data on animals in a wildlife refuge.

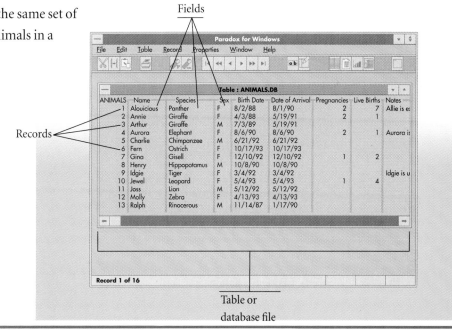

Fields

Records

Table or database file

NOTE *In many database programs, besides specifying the number of fields and their names, you need to specify the type of data you will enter (numbers, text, dates, or pictures) and, in some cases, the amount of space you want to reserve for each field.*

Some people refer to a collection of records with the same structure as a *database file,* and others call it a *table.* I'll use the latter term. Many databases consist of a single table; others consist of two tables or more.

Unlike word processing and spreadsheet programs, database programs do not share a common metaphor or a similar look. All they have in common is a comparable set of standard features. Specifically, most database programs have tools for:

▶ *Designing new tables. All database programs have a feature for creating and structuring new tables. Usually, when you issue the command for*

A CUSTOM DATA ENTRY FORM FOR ENTERING EMPLOYEE DATA

Most database programs let you design customized data entry forms.

creating a table, you see a screen with columns for field name, type of data, and in some cases the field size.

▶ *Viewing and updating data. Most database programs offer one or two standard forms for entering data—often a tabular form and a one-record-at-a-time form. Most also include commands for searching for, changing, and deleting individual records.*

▶ *Creating customer data entry forms. If your database is fairly small and includes relatively few fields, you may find the standard data entry forms sufficient. If you're going to be entering a lot of data, you may prefer to design a customized form. Most high-end programs let you design your own forms—placing fields wherever you like, including descriptive text or instructions, and adding window dressing like lines or boxes to make the data easier to read.*

▶ *Designing reports. All database programs have tools for producing reports. Most have features known as report designers that allow you to select and arrange the fields that you want to include, to perform calculations like totals or averages, and, in most cases, to group records into some meaningful order. You might, for example, print a list in which employees are grouped by department, including a count of the number of employees in each department and the average salary at the end of each departmental group.*

▶ *Selecting data. Most database programs provide some tools to help you select subsets of your data. Probably the most common selection tool is something called* query-by-example *(QBE). (As the name implies, you use query-by-example to pose questions about your database—questions like what are the name of all the customers with a past due balance, or how many clients are there in each city.) The figure "A Query for Selecting Employees in the Art Department" shows a typical query-by-example feature at work.*

▶ *Macro features or programming languages. Some database programs include macro features or even full-fledged programming languages that allow you (or a professional programmer) to automate repetitive tasks.*

CHOOSING A DATABASE PROGRAM

One of the first questions you need to answer when choosing a database program is whether your database is likely to include one table or many. Sometimes all the information related to a particular business problem is stored in a

Query-by-example is a feature that lets you select records from a table by checking off fields and entering selection criteria in a query form. (This is a query for selecting the Name, Sex, and Birth Date from records in which the Species is Giraffe.)

single table. If your database is a list of customers, for example, and you just need to maintain their names and addresses so that you can periodically send out product or sales announcements, a single customer table is all you need. However, many business applications are not this simple. If you are running a mail order business, for example, and many of your customers place multiple orders, you might have one table for customers and a second one for the individual orders they place. The customer table would include name, address, phone numbers, and other information that is the same for each order. The order table would include the date of the order, the amount, the quantity, product code, price, and so on—the items that vary from one order to the next.

MULTIPLE-TABLE DATABASES

Most orders databases contain at least two tables: one for customers and another for orders. For each Customer record, there may be one or more Order records.

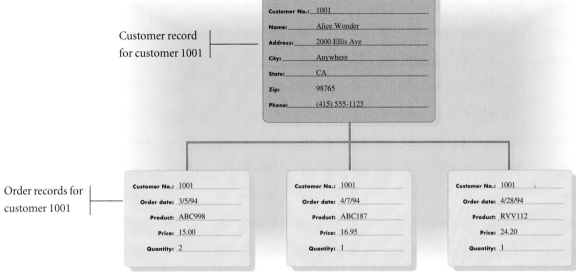

Customer record for customer 1001

Order records for customer 1001

In most cases, if you are dealing with any kinds of events or transactions, your database should include at least two tables: one for the people or things involved in the transaction/event, and a second for the transactions/events themselves. Typical examples of such two-table databases include Patients and Visits, Donors and Donations, Clients and Services Provided.

Not all database management programs are designed to manage multiple-table databases. Those programs that let you work with two or more tables at once—and to find and display matches between tables—are known as *relational database management programs*. Relational database programs let you:

▶ *Match up data in two or more tables*

▶ *Transfer data between tables (posting data from an orders table to a balance due field in a customer record, for example)*

▶ *Ask questions related to multiple tables (such as what is the name and address of each customer who placed an order for x)*

▶ *Display related data from two or more tables in reports and data entry forms*

The better relational database programs also help you maintain consistency between tables, preventing deletion of a customer who has orders on file, for example, or making sure that if you change a customer's I.D. number, the I.D. number in all related orders records is changed as well.

Database programs that only let you work with one table at a time are known as *flat file managers*. In general, flat file managers tend to be a little easier to learn and use and a bit less expensive.

Once you have decided whether you need a relational database program, there are several other factors to consider.

▶ *If you have very specific reporting needs—like reports that include lots of text that you need to word wrap in a column, or reports that must include graphics such as a company logo—make sure the program can handle them.*

▶ *Make sure that the program supports the type of data you have. Almost all database programs let you enter text, numbers, and dates. Some but not all databases can handle graphics (pictures), free-form text fields (fields capable of accommodating any amount of text), and other types of data as well.*

▶ *If you have a relatively small database—say, 2,000 records or less—speed is not likely to be much of a problem. Any database program should be sufficient. But if you have a database of 20,000 or 60,000 or 200,000 records, it will be. You may want to see results of performance tests (often called* benchmarks) *or have someone demonstrate the program on a large database. Also, many programs have a limit on the number of records you can enter, or on the size of each record. Make sure these limits are high enough for your needs.*

▶ *Decide whether you need to move data back and forth between your database program and another program—like your spreadsheet or word processing program. If so, make sure that either your database program can export data in a form the other program can read, or that your other program can read data in your database program's own file format. In most cases, you can move data from one Windows program to another via the Clipboard.*

▶ *Check whether it has a query-by-example (QBE) feature or something comparable that makes it fairly easy to select subsets of your data and generate statistics.*

▶ *Determine how easy it is to design data entry forms, reports, and labels.*

▶ *Find out if it includes tools for automating operations, such as macros/scripts, application generators, or a programming language.*

Learning to use a database management program is usually more demanding than learning a word processing or even a spreadsheet program—unless someone has already set it up for you and tailored it to your needs. If you're starting from scratch, expect to spend at least a few days getting started, much more if your needs or your program are particularly complex. If you find the process to be more work and more of a challenge than you're ready for. In this case, you have two choices.

▶ *Find a customized database package. If it's likely that many other people are trying to do exactly the same thing as you, you can try looking for a customized database package—that is, a program designed to do exactly what you need. There are, for example, customized database programs designed to manage medical offices, track and solicit donations to various types of nonprofits, and help schools keep track of teacher and student schedules. Finding such programs is not always easy. If there is a magazine or journal devoted to your particular line of business, you may want to scan its ads. Even better, if you can manage it, talk to people who are already using such packages to find out what they like and dislike about them. (If you belong to a professional organization, try asking around at a meeting.)*

If you are going to buy a customized package, make sure that the company that distributes it has been around for a while and is likely to last a while longer. If you have any doubts about the company's longevity, make sure that the program is written in a widely-used language and that you have the source code (the original form in which the program was written—a form that other programmers can read and modify). Otherwise, if the company folds next week and you discover a very troublesome bug the week after, you're out of luck.

▶ *Hire a programmer/consultant. There are lots of people who design small databases for a living. Some can help you find a custom package or simply guide you through the creation of a particularly sticky report. You can also hire consultants to develop a completely customized "turn key" system—that is, a system that is built to your specifications and requires no special knowledge of computers or your database program to use. Again, be sure to get the source code.*

There are two potential advantages to buying a customized package rather than having someone write one from scratch. It will usually (although not always) cost less, and it will hopefully have been tested by previous users and therefore have fewer bugs. The disadvantage is that you may have more trouble getting support should problems arise, and the system may never fit your needs exactly. Unless you are lucky enough to find a package that does exactly what you need, you'll have to decide how much you're willing to change the way you do things to fit the system.

If you think you may need expert help, don't buy an obscure package. You'll have a lot more trouble finding someone to help you out with Joe Blow's Database Manager than with a major database program. (The major ones include Paradox, Access, FoxPro, dBASE, Q&A, Approach FileMaker Pro, 4th Dimension, FoxBase Mac.)

SOME GENERAL ADVICE ON CHOOSING SOFTWARE

Throughout this chapter, I've offered advice on what to look for and what questions to ask when you're selecting various types of software. Following are some more general considerations that apply for buying programs of any type.

DO YOU KNOW SOMEONE WHO'S BOTH HAPPILY USING A PARTICULAR PROGRAM AND IS WILLING TO HELP YOU OUT IF YOU GET STUCK? Finding a friend or colleague willing to bail you out for free (or for a few minor bribes) can be a godsend. Although some people prefer figuring out everything on their own, most of us sleep easier knowing there's someone to call in emergencies.

HOW IS THE COMPANY'S TECHNICAL SUPPORT DEPARTMENT? Most software companies offer some degree of technical support to their customers, meaning that you get to call them up and ask questions. In some cases, this support is free. Sometimes it's free for a limited period only. Sometimes it's free but involves a long-distance call and a good chance that you'll be on hold for 20 minutes. But while cost is crucial, it's only half of the issue here. The other half is what the support is actually worth. Technical support personnel can range from helpful, knowledgeable, and patient to rude, incompetent, and/or impossible to understand.

WHAT KIND OF BUILT-IN HELP DOES THE PROGRAM OFFER? Many programs have some kind of built-in help feature, which furnishes information about the program and its various features. In some cases, the help feature may be cursory or nonexistent. In others, the entire program manual is available "online," making it possible to use the help feature to actually learn the program, rather than just to refresh your memory periodically. Some software packages also offer tutorials (a set of detailed lessons) that step you through the basics of using the program.

HOW'S THE DOCUMENTATION? All commercially available programs are sold with one or more manuals. Some are clear and easy to use; others are incomprehensible. If at all possible, try to flip through the manuals before you buy the program. In particular, check out the index. Since you're likely to use the manual primarily as a reference, the index may be its most important feature.

ARE THERE ANY BOOKS AVAILABLE ON THE PROGRAM? Even when a program's documentation is relatively clear and comprehensive, you may still want to buy a book on the subject. Program manuals are designed as reference books. Many beginners need tutorials instead—books that take you through the process of creating a document, spreadsheet, or database step by step. There's another reason to see if there are any books on the subject: If there aren't, it may mean that the program's too small-time to merit a book. This should raise some questions about whether it's likely to be supported next year, to produce upgrades, and so on.

WILL THE PROGRAM WORK WITH YOUR HARDWARE? And if not, what will it cost to replace or upgrade your equipment? Before you go shopping for software, make sure that you know the answers to all of the following questions:

▶ *Which operating system are you running and which version?*

▶ *In the case of DOS machines, what kind of CPU chip does your computer contain. If you're using a Mac, which model do you have?*

▶ *How much memory does your computer contain?*

▶ *What type of monitor do you have, with what type of graphics display, if any? (You'll learn about various types of graphics display modes, like EGA, VGA, and Super VGA, in Chapter 9.)*

▶ *What size and density of floppy disks can your computer use?*

▶ *What's the capacity of your computer's hard disk, in megabytes, and how much of that space is currently available?*

▶ *What type of printer do you have?*

If there is any chance that you'll forget the answer to any of these questions, write down all the answers and bring them with you (or have them handy when you pick up the phone). Then, before you buy, make the salesperson swear that the program will work with your hardware and that you can return the program for a full refund if it doesn't.

INSTALLING PROGRAMS

The process of installing a program can take anywhere from a few minutes to half an hour, depending on the size of the program and the speed of your computer. Most programs come with their own installation program— that is, a program designed solely to copy the main program onto your hard disk and, in most cases, acquire some information about your hardware. With luck, your manual will explain, in fairly coherent terms, how to use the installation program. Look for an installation section in the manual or, in some cases, a separate manual labeled something like Installation or Getting Started. Occasionally, the program's installation instructions will be printed on the box the program is sold in or the envelope containing the disks, or even on the disks themselves.

The first step in installing a program is locating the installation disk. Look for a disk labeled Install or Installation Disk or something similar. If no such disk exists, try looking for one labeled Disk 1. Insert that disk into your floppy-disk drive. The next step varies from one operating system to the next.

▶ *In DOS, you must get to the DOS prompt if you're not already there. Next either log onto drive A, by typing A: and pressing Enter, and then enter either INSTALL or SETUP (check your manual); or enter A:INSTALL. You usually don't get to choose between these two alternatives: You need to read your manual to find out which procedure to use.*

▶ *In Windows, you must get to the Program Manager, open the File menu, and select Run. Then type A:INSTALL in the box labeled Command Line and press Enter or click OK.*

▶ *On a Macintosh, look for an icon labeled Installer in the floppy disk's window and double-click it.*

Once you have started the installation program, that program takes over, asking questions as necessary and periodically prompting you to insert additional disks. With luck, the questions will be at least somewhat comprehensible. In general, you should just accept the program's suggestions on where to place the program files or what to call things. If you are offered a choice between a standard or quick installation and a custom installation, pick the standard/quick one. Sometimes installation programs make you use a key other than the Enter key—like F2 or Tab—to move from one question to the next. If you press Enter and nothing happens, scan the screen for information on which keys do what.

M O D I F Y I N G   C O N F I G U R A T I O N   F I L E S

The installation programs for many PC programs like to modify various configuration files on your hard disk. Polite programs will ask whether this is OK with you before proceeding. (Others will make the changes without your permission.) If you do see a message asking if it's OK to modify AUTOEXEC.BAT, CONFIG.SYS, or WIN.INI, select Yes.

Most programs are shipped with a file named README or README-.DOC which contains late-breaking news about the program. Sometimes it contains information on anomalies in the program. (In most cases, "anomaly" is a code word for bug, used because no manufacturer wants to admit that their program isn't perfect.) Sometimes it contains minor corrections to the manual. If you are using a Mac, you can read the README file by double-clicking the ReadMe icon. If you are using DOS, enter TYPE README > MORE at the DOS prompt to display the file one screenful at a time. If you are using Windows, you can launch the Windows Notepad and then use the File Open command to read the file.

LEARNING AN APPLICATION PROGRAM

Once you've chosen and installed a new program, you still need to go about learning it. There are several approaches that you can take toward this process:

▶ *Use the tools that come with the software—namely the manuals, the on-line tutorial (if there is one), and the built-in help system (if any).*

▶ *Buy a book on the subject at your local bookstore or computer store. Many bookstores carry several different books on the major software packages. My strategy for finding the right one is simple. Start by look-ing in the index for any operation that you know you'll need to perform. If you can't find your topic in the index, choose another book. (Since much of the time you'll be using the book as a reference, the index may be its most critical feature.) Assuming you can find your topic, go ahead and read what the book says about it. If the explanation seems clear and complete, place the book in your stack of "books under consideration" and try out a few others. When you're done, buy the book with the ex-planation you liked best.*

▶ *Take a class at a computer school or a community college. (Check local computer magazines, computer stores, and your local yellow pages for computer school locations.)*

▶ *Find a friend who is willing to help you get started. (Since most pro-grams take more than an hour or two to master, don't expect your friend to hold your hand the whole route.)*

Which of these approaches will work depends on your own learning style—some people learn best on their own; others need the enforced discipline or camaraderie of a class. Once you've read through this book, you should know enough buzzwords and have enough understanding of computers to manage either a book or a basic class. (If you have trouble with either, you can probably assume there's something amiss with the author or teacher.)

The one general piece of advice I would offer on learning a new program is to take some time to get your bearings. As you've seen throughout this chapter, most programs work with some kind of metaphor—that is, they treat your screen "as if" it were something more familiar, like a piece of typing paper or an accountant's ledger. One way or another, they present you with a little world. Your first step should therefore involve discovering what kinds of objects populate that world, how you move around in it, and what tools—like menus or sets of icons or function keys—you can use to make your mark. In other words, when you first approach a new program, don't get immediately caught up in accomplishing a specific task. Instead, picture yourself as Alice stepping through the looking glass. Your first task should be exploring the new world. (You can worry about how to get to the next square later.)

COMPUTER USERS GROUPS

If you're at all partial to clubs or other social gatherings, and you live in a metropolitan area, you may also want to hunt for a local computer user's group. User's groups are membership organizations of people who use or are learning to use computers. Most user's groups have members that range from absolute beginners to professional programmers and computer consultants, although some groups lean more toward one end than the other. Such groups can be a tremendous source of free advice and technical support. The larger user's groups usually have several special interest groups (commonly known as SIGs) on various types of software or computer-related topics. The larger computer groups—like the Boston Computer Society and the Bay Area Macintosh User's Group (BMUG)—have dozens of SIGs on almost anything you can imagine doing with a computer. Many computer user's groups also feature a question and answer period where confused or frustrated members can pose questions to the membership at large. With any luck, someone in the audience will know exactly where the problem lies and how to solve it. If you are in the market for a new computer, user's groups are also an excellent source for tips and warnings about local vendors. Finally, many user's groups receive discounts on both hardware and software.

9

MORE ABOUT HARDWARE

Monitors

Printers

Storage Devices

Networks

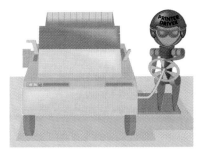

9

Back in Chapter 2, you were introduced to the basics of computer hardware. In this chapter, you'll go a little further, learning some of the finer points about peripherals (namely monitors, printers, and storage devices) that I didn't want to overwhelm you with earlier in the book. You'll also learn a bit about networks: what they are, what they're for, and how you use them.

MONITORS

The monitor is your computer's primary output device—its tool for displaying information, soliciting information, and responding to your requests. It's also likely to be the center of your attention most of the time you are using the computer. As a result, it's hard to underestimate the importance of a good monitor, meaning one that's clear, easy to read, and free of glare and flicker. A good monitor can make staring at the screen for eight hours bearable. A bad one can cause headaches, fatigue, and eye strain (not to mention grumpiness).

Computer monitors come in three main types: monochrome, gray scale, and color. Monochrome monitors display images in a single color against a contrasting background. The combinations you'll encounter most often are green, amber, or white characters against a black background. Gray scale monitors are monitors capable of displaying various shades of gray as well as black and white. In general, gray scale and color monitors are more expensive than monochrome ones. They are also more likely to be capable of displaying graphics. (You'll learn more about displaying graphics in the next section.)

Just because gray scale and color monitors are generally more expensive than monochrome ones doesn't mean that they're better. If all you

VARIETIES OF MONITORS

Monitors come in a variety of shapes and sizes.

want to do with your computer is write the great American novel using a DOS-based word processing program, a monochrome monitor is probably the best tool for the job. Not only will it cost a lot less, it will also be easier on your eyes.

All three types of monitors come in a wide range of sizes. (Monitor size is almost always measured diagonally across the screen.) At the small end are the 9-inch screens on Mac Classics, which are actually not separate monitors at all, but are built into the system unit. At the large end are full-page and two-page screens designed for desktop publishing. These let you display either one or two full pages of text at once, rather than the half-page of text typical of other monitors. The majority of monitors range from 14 inches to 20 inches in size.

NOTE *Never buy a monitor until you see it running the applications software that you plan to use. Some monitors are great at displaying color photographs and horrible at displaying text, and vice versa. Make sure that your monitor is well-suited to the particular task you have in mind.*

The monitor itself is only one of the pieces of equipment involved in displaying images on your screen. The other is something known as a *video adapter*, a set of circuitry that translates instructions from your computer into a form your monitor can use.

In most personal computers, the video adapter is an expansion board that fits into a slot on your computer's motherboard. On some Macs, however, video circuitry is built into the motherboard itself and you only need a separate video card for special monitors or for increased speed. You may hear video adapters called things like display adapter card, video card, or video hardware. You might also hear the acronyms for various types of video cards, like EGA and VGA. (You'll learn about those shortly.)

TEXT MODE VERSUS GRAPHICS MODE

Text display modes use your computer's built-in character set.

Graphics modes construct every element on the screen, including each character, out of dozens or even hundreds of individual dots.

TEXT MODES VERSUS GRAPHICS MODE

There are basically two methods of displaying characters and other objects on a computer screen: text mode and graphics mode.

▶ *Text mode uses the computer's built-in character set and a preset grid of rows and columns. Most text modes use a grid of 25 rows and 80 columns to display data, but some use 40 or 50 rows and as many as 132 columns.*

▶ *In graphics mode, each element on the screen—be it a character, a picture, or a box—is composed of dozens or even hundreds of individual dots. Although drawing images dot-by-dot is time-consuming, graphics mode offers tremendous flexibility because the results are not limited to a predefined set of characters or a fixed set of locations on the screen. You can draw just about anything, anywhere you like.*

The difference between text mode and graphics mode is like the difference between typesetting and calligraphy: The first is more efficient, while the second leaves more room for creativity.

Most DOS-based programs display images in text mode, although some give you a choice. Both Windows and Mac programs use graphics modes, which is why their screens tend to be more picture-oriented and visually interesting. (Since displaying images in graphics mode takes more time, this is also why Windows programs tend to be slower than their DOS counterparts, at least when it comes to displaying or redrawing things on the screen.)

The video adapter you are using determines whether you can display graphics. If you have what's known as a *graphics adapter,* you'll be able to display images in one or more graphics modes.

N O T E   *If you want to be able to display graphics on a PC, you're probably going to want a color or gray scale monitor. Although there are some graphics adapters that let you display graphics on monochrome monitor (the most well-known one is the Hercules graphics card), the effects are usually not as clear or as attractive as those you'll get with gray scale or, better yet, with color.*

But the type of images you see on your screen is not determined by hardware alone. Ultimately, the display mode your monitor uses is an issue of software. On PCs, some programs use text mode and others use graphics mode. If your program uses a text mode, characters will be displayed using the monitor's built-in character set regardless of your adapter's graphics capabilities. In other words, your hardware's graphics capabilities only matter if the software itself uses a graphics mode.

GETTING A PICTURE ON THE SCREEN

The process of getting an image onto your screen involves several players. You type a character, draw a shape, or issue a command to a program. The program sends instructions to a video driver that translates them into a form that your monitor can understand.

You draw a square in the Paintbrush program.

Paintbrush tells the video driver to draw a square.

The video driver provides the monitor with explicit instructions on how and where to construct the image.

VIDEO STANDARDS AND SCREEN RESOLUTIONS

Some monitors and video adapters are capable of displaying images at various resolutions by using different numbers of dots per inch. When you use a lower resolution, the image expands: you see less on the screen but everything you do see is larger, as if you were looking through a magnifying glass. When you use a higher resolution, everything on the screen shrinks, allowing you to see more information at once. Using a higher resolution may therefore make it possible for you to compose your annual report in one window while viewing a spreadsheet with this year's income statement in another window, for example, or to view a dozen more columns and/or rows of spreadsheet data at one time. The only reason to switch to a lower than normal resolution is if you have trouble seeing and want to display larger characters or images on the screen.

Screen resolution depends on three things: your monitor, your video adapter, and your software. As you already know, the monitor determines whether you can display images in color. It also sets the upper limit of the screen resolution—that is, how many dots per inch you can display on screen. Some monitors are designed to display images at only one resolution. Others, known as *multisync monitors,* can display images at various resolutions.

Resolution is described in terms of number of pixels. A *pixel,* which is short for *picture element,* means a dot used to construct screen images. In the Mac world, resolution is usually described in terms of number of dots (pixels) per inch (dpi), with 72 dpi as the norm. (This means 72 dots horizontally and 72 dots vertically.) In the PC world, resolution is usually described in terms of the number of pixels displayed horizontally by the number of pixels displayed vertically across the entire screen (rather than within an inch). The most common resolution in graphics mode is 640x480 (640 pixels horizontally and 480 vertically).

AN IMAGE AT DIFFERENT RESOLUTIONS

A spreadsheet in
640x480 resolution

The same spreadsheet
in 800x600 resolution

NOTE *There is one fundamental difference in the way that Macs and PCs handle screen resolution. On Macs, images are normally displayed at 72 dots per inch (dpi), regardless of the size of the monitor. This means that, by default, you will see more information on a larger screen than on a smaller one. On PCs, the default resolution is usually 640x480 pixels, regardless of the size of the monitor. This means that you will normally see the same amount of information on a 20-inch monitor as you do on a 14-inch monitor, but on the 20-inch monitor, the image will be larger. (Every menu, picture, or character on the screen will be almost one-and-one-half times as big.) If you want to take advantage of the larger monitor to display more information, you need to change to a different resolution, as you'll learn to do shortly.*

As mentioned, the video adapter you are using determines whether you can display graphics and, if so, which of several video standards and resolutions you can use. Among PC graphics adapters, there are several standards for video cards. Currently, the most widely used standard is something called VGA, which stands for Video Graphics Array. A regular VGA adapter displays images at 640x480 resolution (meaning 640 dots horizontally by 480 vertically) and either 16 colors, or, if you have a special video driver, 256 colors. (You'll learn about video drivers shortly.) Super VGA is an enhancement of the VGA standard. It allows for higher resolutions (800x600, 1024x768, and in some cases 1280x1024) and for more colors. If you are buying a monitor tomorrow, be sure to get a Super VGA adapter and a monitor capable of taking advantage of it.

NOTE *You don't need to have a color monitor in order to use VGA. Most gray scale monitors are designed to display images in what's known as gray scale VGA, using various shades of gray rather than different colors to display graphic images.*

Many laptop and notebook computers feature gray scale VGA displays since they're both less expensive and less demanding on batteries than color displays.

Some of the older video standards are CGA (for Color/Graphics Adapter) and EGA (Enhanced Graphics Adapter), both of which are now all but obsolete. A few others you may encounter are MCGA (MultiColor Graphics Array), which is a subset of the VGA standard that is used on some low-end IBM PS/2 computers; and PGA and XGA, which are used primarily in high-end drafting and design applications.

Finally, there's the question of software. There are actually two types of software involved in displaying images on your screen. First, there's your operating system and/or applications software and the types of display modes it's capable of using. The other type of software that affects your screen display are *video drivers*—programs that allow your operating system or application programs to converse with your video board. In many cases, you select a video driver when you install a program, by answering questions about the type of monitor you are using. After that, you'll only need to think about video drivers if you want to change to a different screen resolution.

PC In Windows, you can select a different video driver by choosing Setup (usually located in the Main program group) and then using the Options menu option to change the Display system setting. (See your Windows manual for details.) Windows comes with several generic drivers for some standard screen resolutions. If they don't work with your graphics adapter, you need to get Windows drivers from the adapter's manufacturer. Once you have selected a driver that works with Windows, that driver will determine how data is displayed in all your application programs. In DOS, on the other hand, the display mode is determined by the application program. In some cases, you can issue a command to switch from one display mode to another (in effect, selecting a different video driver). In other cases, the display mode changes automatically when you issue certain commands. Most DOS-based spreadsheet programs, for example, switch from text mode to graphics mode automatically whenever you issue the command for displaying a graph. Some DOS-based word processing programs switch to graphics mode when you request a "print preview"—that is, an on-screen approximation of what a full page will look like when printed.

MAC Macs always display images in graphics mode. You can change to a nonstandard resolution if you have a multisynch monitor and a relatively fancy video card. See your video card manual for the details.

HOW MONITORS WORK

The monitors for most desktop computers work just like television sets: They use something called a *cathode ray tube* (CRT) to project images onto a screen. A CRT is essentially a vacuum tube with an electron gun at one end and a flat screen at the other. The electron gun "shoots" a single stream of electrons at the screen. The inside of the screen is coated with special particles, known as *phosphors*, that glow when struck by the electrons.

In monochrome monitors, there is one electron gun and each phosphor dot results in one dot on the screen. In color monitors, there are three phosphor guns and each screen dot consists of three phosphor dots: one red, one green, and one blue. The color of the dot on screen depends on the intensities of the various electron streams. If a particularly high-intensity beam is directed at the red phosphor dot, for example, the screen dot is very reddish. If the green dot is hit with a high-intensity beam, you get a very greenish dot on the screen.

In both types of monitors, each of the electron beams is directed at one spot at a time, but the beams themselves move, scanning horizontally across a single line of the screen, then dropping down a line and scanning across that one, dropping down another line, and so on. Think of these beams as moving search lights that continually and repeatedly pan across the screen. As various phosphors are struck by the electron beam(s), they glow for a fraction of a second and then fade again. To keep the image from fading or flickering, the monitor must hit the same phosphors with electrons dozens of times in one second. The term *refresh rate* means the amount of time it takes the monitor to scan across and down the entire screen, "re-zapping" all the phosphors.

HOW CRTS WORK

Inside a CRT, one or more electron guns at the back of the monitor shoots electrons toward the screen. When the electrons hit phosphors on the inside of the screen, the phosphors glow, creating patterns of dots on your screen.

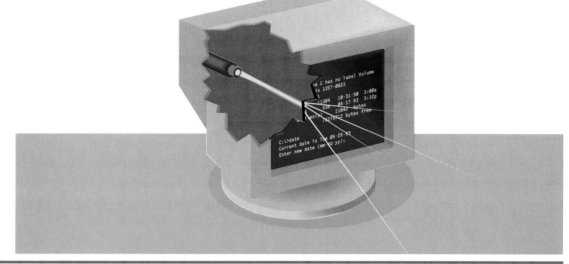

If you leave your monitor on for a long period of time with the same image displayed on the screen, the phosphors responsible for displaying the image can become worn out. Once this happens, you'll see a shadow of that image superimposed on anything else you display on the screen, kind of like a permanent ghost image. This problem, often called *phosphor burn-in,* is particularly common on monochrome monitors. There are two ways to prevent phosphor burn-in. You can turn your monitor off whenever you're planning to leave your computer unattended for a while, or you can use a special program, known as a screen saver, that either blanks out the screen or displays a moving image (like changing geometric shapes or fish swimming in an aquarium or a set of flying toasters) whenever you haven't touched the keyboard or mouse for a certain amount of time. As soon as you press any key or move your mouse, the previous screen image is restored. (Windows comes with its own screen saver programs. You can also buy screen savers from just about any store or mail order company that sells software.)

Another way to pamper your monitor (and your own eyes) is to clean the screen periodically. Most monitors pick up an inordinate amount of dust, not to mention fingerprints. You can often get rid of both by wiping the screen with a soft, dry cloth. You can also safely clean most monitors with a glass cleaner such as Windex, provided that you spray the cleaner on a cleaning cloth rather than directly on the screen. (If you spray it on the screen itself, you run the risk of soaking some of your monitor's circuitry.) A few monitors have special coatings designed to cut down on glare, which may not take kindly to cleaners. If you have an expensive monitor, be sure to check the monitor manual for warnings and advice before you apply anything but a dry cloth to the screen.

Then there's the issue of taking care of yourself while you use a monitor. Most monitors have contrast and brightness controls, usually on the front of the monitor but sometimes on the side or back. Use these to adjust the image so that it's clearest and easiest on your eyes. And remember that a badly positioned monitor can be, literally, a pain in the neck. As mentioned in Chapter 4, you can minimize neck strain by positioning the monitor so that its upper edge is at or just below eye level. Most monitors also have swivel stands that you can use to adjust the angle of the screen to eliminate glare and/or neck strain.

COMPUTER MONITORS MAY (OR MAY NOT) BE HAZARDOUS TO YOUR HEALTH

Virtually all desktop computer monitors emit some amount of electromagnetic radiation (EMR). So do many household appliances, including microwaves, electric blankets, radios, and TVs. Now before you panic, bear in mind that the type of radiation that all these devices emit is something called nonionizing radiation, which is quite different from the ionizing radiation emitted by nuclear reactors and weapons.

There is substantial evidence that, at high levels, electromagnetic radiation is harmful to health. Studies have found an increased incidence of certain types of cancer among children living right next to power plants, which emit very large amounts of EMR. But as yet there is no definitive answer on whether the amount of EMR emitted by computer monitors is dangerous. Although a few studies have shown a link between extensive computer use and increased rates of miscarriage, others have found no link at all.

If you use a computer only occasionally, the issue is probably not worth worrying about at all. However, if you plan to spend most of your workday in front of a CRT and you like to err on the side of safety, here are a few precautions you can take to minimize your risk.

▶ *Turn off your monitor when you are not using it. (Don't just dim the screen or use a screen saver program, as this has no effect on EMR emissions.)*

▶ *Sit at least 24 inches away from the monitor, or more if possible. (The amount of radiation is inversely proportional to the square root of your distance from the screen. In other words, if you're twice as far from the monitor, you receive one quarter the radiation. If you're three times as far, you receive one ninth the dose.)*

▶ *Avoid sitting near the sides or back of CRT monitors, since they emit more EMR than the front.*

▶ *Buy a monitor shield designed to block EMR.*

▶ *Buy a low-emission monitor. The Swedish government has developed a standard, called MPR II, defining acceptable levels of EMR. You can now buy many monitors in the U.S. that meet these standards, although it's easier to find monochrome monitors that meet the test than color ones. In general, smaller monitors have lower emissions than larger ones, and monochrome monitors have lower emissions than color ones.*

Whatever the risks of extensive monitor use turn out to be (if any), they're likely to be greatest for fetuses, particularly in the first trimester. Until more research is done, you may therefore want to be especially careful if you are pregnant.

NOTE   *The screens on laptop and notebook computers use a completely different type of technology than that used in desktop computer monitors, and do not emit EMR.*

LAPTOP AND NOTEBOOK DISPLAYS

The screens on most laptop and notebook computers use a technology known as liquid crystal display (LCD). Briefly, LCD screens work as follows: Liquid crystals (a fluid that reflects light) are sandwiched between two polarized pieces of glass or plastic. These polarized sheets shut out all light waves except for those that are parallel to their particular plane. Inside the display, tiny electrodes pass current through the crystals, causing them to form spirals that bend the light to a greater or lesser degree. The amount of current determines the amount of spiraling, which in turn determines how much of the light actually makes it through the front of the screen. (In areas where the light is not bent at all, the beam is completely blocked and the screen remains dark.) In the case of color LCD screens, the light passes through various color filters.

LCD screens are often characterized as either passive or active matrix displays. In passive matrix displays, groups of pixels (screen dots) share the same electrodes. In active matrix displays, which are considerably more expensive, each pixel gets a transistor of its own. The resulting images are much clearer and easier to read. Active matrix displays also drain batteries much faster than passive matrix displays, making them less appropriate for long airplane flights and other work sessions conducted without the benefit of an electrical outlet.

NOTE *Some laptop computer screens use a completely different technology known as* gas plasma. *Gas plasma screens consists of tiny neon-like bulbs which glow orange (a color that many people find unattractive). On the positive side, gas plasma displays have a much faster refresh rate than LCD screens, which leads to less blurring. (On LCDs, the slow refresh rate causes the mouse pointer to disappear temporarily when moved because the screen can't keep up with the movements.) On the negative side, there's the color and the fact that they're quite a bit heavier than LCD displays.*

PRINTERS

For years people have predicted that computers would make paper obsolete. While this may be true in the long run, in the short run they seem to be having the opposite effect. By giving people the power to endlessly manipulate and analyze their data, computers have facilitated the production of mountains of reports and memos that we had somehow previously managed to live without.

For most of us, printing is still the final step in any project we undertake on the computer. When you finish the letter, you print and send it. When you get done calculating how much money you could make if only you did x, you print out the spreadsheet and show it to your spouse, boss, or coworkers. Sooner or later, you'll want a hard copy, if for no other reason than that it's easy to carry around and show to others.

There are several different types of printers used with personal computers; by far the most common types are dot-matrix, laser, and ink jet printers.

DOT-MATRIX PRINTERS

Dot-matrix printers work by striking a cloth, nylon, or mylar ribbon with a set of small wires. The resulting characters are composed of a pattern of dots, just like characters displayed on a monitor. There are two types of dot-matrix printers, characterized by the number of wires (or pins) they use. 9-pin printers are less expensive (costing as little as $150) but produce poorer quality output. 24-pin printers cost a bit more but are capable of generating "near letter-quality" print, meaning print that looks almost typewriter quality.

SETUP STRINGS

Most printers have their own codes for doing things like switching from normal-sized print to compressed print, or from normal page orientation to landscape (sideways) orientation. These codes are known as control codes or escape sequences because they usually start with either the ASCII code for a control character (a character produced by holding Ctrl while you press another character) or with the ASCII code for the Escape key. If your application program has a special setting or command for one of these special print effects, you're in luck; assuming that you have the right printer driver selected, the program should take care of sending the necessary code to your printer. If not, you may need to send the code to your printer yourself. This is commonly known as sending a "setup string"—that is, a string of characters designed to set up your printer for a particular type of printing. The first step in sending a setup string is finding the appropriate code. You do this by looking in your printer manual, under printer commands, setup strings, or programming your printer. The exact steps for sending this code to your printer vary from one program to the next. In some programs, you issue a setup string command and then type in the code. In others, including many spreadsheet programs, you precede the setup string with a special character like the vertical bar (|) character. To undo the effect of a setup string, you either send another setup string to your printer, press the printer's Reset button if it has one, or turn the printer off and then on again.

THE MAIN TYPES OF PRINTERS

The three types of printers most commonly used with personal computers are laser, ink jet, and dot-matrix printers.

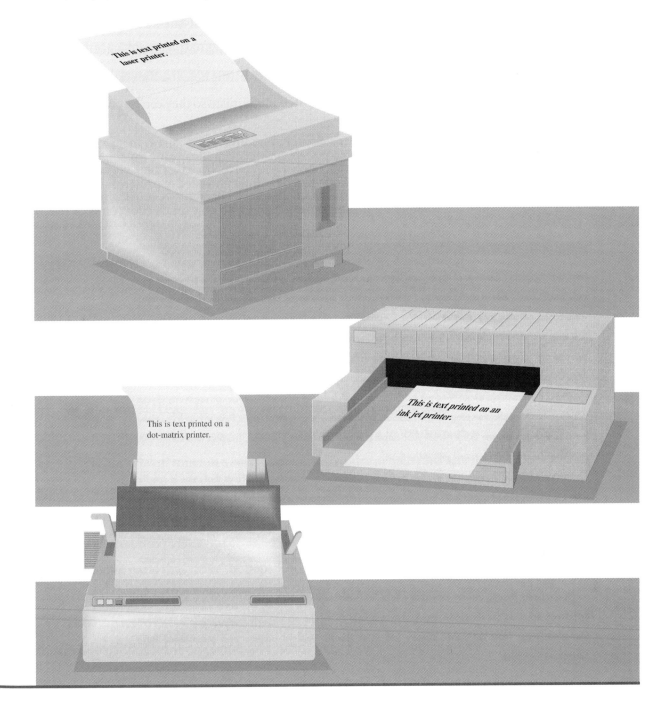

This is text printed on a laser printer.

This is text printed on an ink jet printer.

This is text printed on a dot-matrix printer.

PRINTER BUFFERS AND SPOOLERS

In general, printers are far slower than computers. Your computer can send data to a printer much faster than the printer can print it. Most printers have some built-in memory that serves as a *printer buffer*—that is, a kind of holding pen for data that is waiting to be printed. This is why if you interrupt printing, your printer keeps going for a while. In this case, you can often stop the printer more quickly by turning it off and then on again. This effectively erases the printer's memory.

In most cases, the printer buffer will be quite small—enough to hold a few lines of data in the case of dot-matrix printers, a few pages on laser printers. As soon as the printer buffer fills, the computer needs to stop and wait before sending the next chunk of data. If you are printing a very long report, this could effectively tie up your computer for several minutes or even hours.

There are special programs, known as *print spoolers*, that solve this problem by sidetracking data en route from your computer to your printer and storing it either in RAM or on disk. Then, when your printer is ready for more data, the print spooler sends it. In the meantime, you're free to get back to work in your application program.

STORAGE DEVICES

In Chapter 3, you learned about various types of disks. Following is a brief account of some of the other technologies available for long-term storage.

▶ *Tape drives are designed primarily as a means of backing up the contents of hard-disk drives. Many tape drives can record up to 120 megabytes or more on a single cassette tape. Just like more conventional tape recorders, however, they access data sequentially, and are therefore suited for backup rather than regular data storage.*

HOW PRINTER BUFFERS AND SPOOLERS WORK

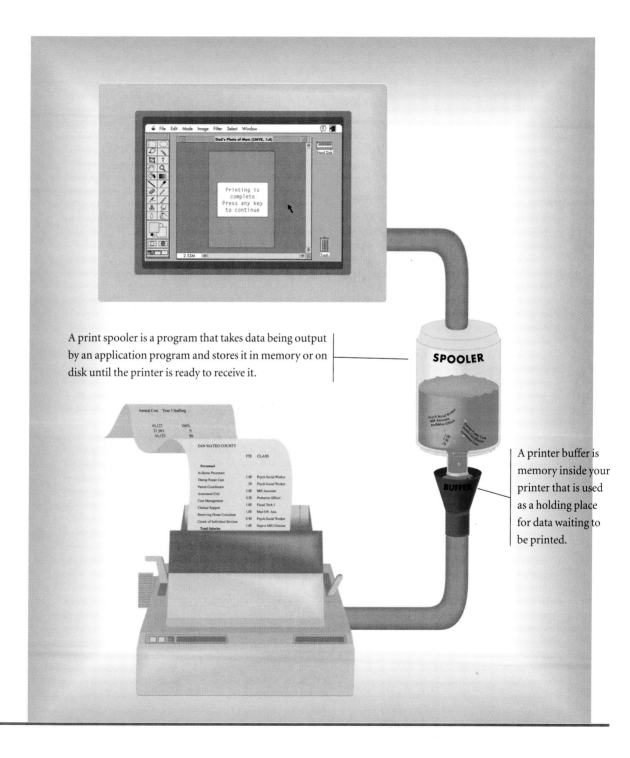

A print spooler is a program that takes data being output by an application program and stores it in memory or on disk until the printer is ready to receive it.

A printer buffer is memory inside your printer that is used as a holding place for data waiting to be printed.

▶ *Removable-media drives* combine the best features of floppy and hard drives. Like floppy drives, they use disks that are removable. Like hard drives, they store dozens of megabytes (usually somewhere between 20 and 150 megabytes) on a single disk. This makes them perfect for backing up data and transferring large amounts of data from one computer to another. In addition, removable-media drives allow you to keep expanding your computer's storage capacity indefinitely at a relatively low cost. Every time you run out of space, you just buy another cartridge. There are two basic types of removable-media drives: Bernoulli (pronounced Ber-new-lee) drives, which use cartridges containing a flexible, floppy-like disk; and Syquest drives, which use rigid disks more like the platters used in hard drives.

▶ *CD-ROM drives* allow your computer to read information recorded on compact discs, or CDs, much like the ones you buy at the music store. The ROM in CD-ROM stands for read-only memory, meaning that you can use CD-ROM drives to read information on CDs but not to record any information. Some CD-ROM drives fit inside your system unit, much like most floppy-disk drives. Others are external units that plug into your system unit. Although CDs are about the same size as many floppy disks, they hold between 550 and 640 megabytes of data (which is more than most hard disks). They are frequently used for storing reference works, like encyclopedias, dictionaries, legal precedents, catalogs, and census information—things that you want to look up or display but not change. CDs also play an important role in the multimedia world, where their ability to store digitized audio (sound in computer-readable format) as well as data makes them ideal for interactive educational software and full-motion video.

▶ *WORM (Write Once/Read Many)* **drives** *contain disks that you can record on only once. Whatever you record on the disk remains there permanently, as if written in indelible ink, that you can neither erase nor overwrite. For this reason, WORM drives are perfect for archiving large amounts of data, and are frequently used by banks and accounting firms as a means of maintaining a permanent, unalterable audit trail.*

▶ *Magneto-optical (MO)* **drives** *may be the wave of the future. These drives, which are also known as erasable optical (EO) drives, use both a laser and an electromagnet to record information on a cartridge, the surface of which contains tiny embedded magnets. These cartridges can be written to, erased, and then written to again. Magneto-optical drives are, at this point, both considerably slower and more expensive than hard drives, but both of these characteristics are changing fast.*

NETWORKS

Networks are groups of computers that are linked together. There are three reasons to network computers:

▶ *To enable multiple computers to share peripherals, such as expensive printers, scanners, and fax equipment.*

▶ *To allow people to exchange messages via computer (a process known as* electronic mail*) and to easily transfer files from one computer to another.*

▶ *To allow computers to share data and/or programs—so that, for example, three people in a department can write a report together, or work with the same spreadsheets. This capability is particularly useful in the case of databases, which may need to be accessed and changed by many different people in an organization.*

The term *Local Area Network* (LAN for short) means a network in which the computers are all connected with wire cables. (This generally means that they're in the same part of a single building.) LANS are contrasted with Wide Area Networks, aka WANs, in which some of the links in the chain are connected by modems and phone wires or satellites.

The details of setting up a network are best left to experts. But to make a long story fairly short, there are three essential steps in the process:

▶ *Special expansion boards, generally known as* network cards, *must be installed in each of the computers.*

▶ *The computers must be physically connected in some way, usually via wire cables.*

▶ *Network software designed to control the flow of information across the network must be installed on each of the computers.*

The business of running a network can also be fairly complicated. For this reason, most networks of any size are assigned a full- or at least part-time network administrator. (If your report won't print or your computer starts displaying error messages, the network administrator is the person to see.) Nonetheless, there are a few pieces of information that everyone on the network should know, if for no other reason than to help you communicate with the network administrator.

Most networks include one or more computers that are designated as file servers. A *file server* is a computer whose hard disk is accessible to other computers on the network. Its job is to "serve" data and program files to these other

A NETWORK CONFIGURATION

Networks are groups of computers that are linked together in order to share data, programs, or peripherals, and/or to facilitate communication and file exchange within an organization.

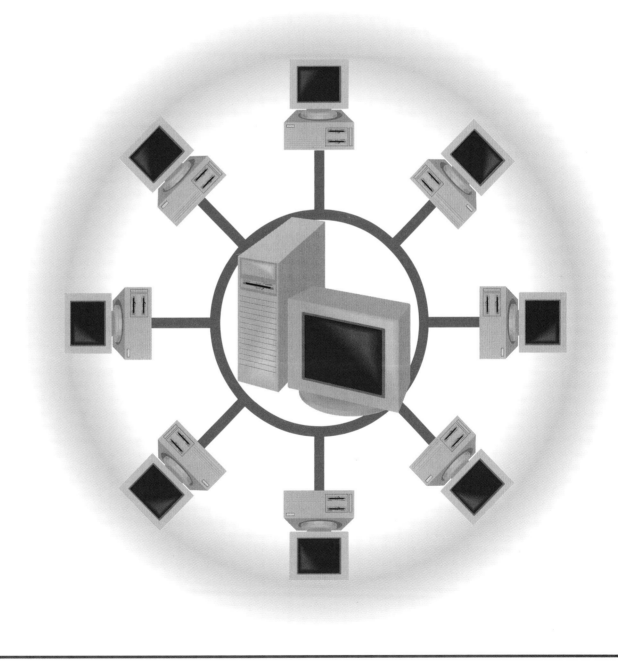

machines via cables or other network connections. On some smaller networks, each computer can access the hard disk of any of the other computers, and there is no one computer (or more) dedicated to the task of delivering goods to the others. Such networks are known as *peer-to-peer networks*, because all the computers in the chain are on roughly equal footing.

When there is a dedicated file server—that is, a computer that's used for nothing other than serving the other computers on the network—the other computers are usually called either *nodes* or *workstations*.

Even if your computer is part of a network, you need to explicitly "log on to" the network in order to use it. The procedure for logging on varies from one type of network to another. In most cases, you'll either start by typing LOGIN (pronounced log in) or your computer will be set up to type it for you. Next, you'll be asked for your user name (that is, the name you're known by on the network) and then a password. Assuming that the network recognizes both your name and password, it goes ahead and gives you access to other computers and resources on the network.

In most cases, you will be able to access the file server's hard disk just as you would any other disk. On a PC, the server's hard disk is usually assigned one or more drive letters (just as your own hard disk is usually labeled C). On a Mac, network drives are represented by icons at the right side of the desktop, just like other drives.

NOTE *Most networks have built-in security features that allow the network administrator to limit access to sensitive data (such as personnel or financial data). In such cases, your user name determines which data files and programs you can use.*

When you're done using the network, you should "log out," meaning disconnect from the network.

A FILE SERVER SERVING FILES

A file server is a computer that "serves" data and program files to
other computers on a network.

ELECTRONIC MAIL

Most networks have electronic mail (e-mail) programs that enable people on
the network to send messages to other people on the network via computer.
Once you get used to it, you may well find this mode of communicating supe-
rior to both answering machines/voice mail and interoffice memos. It can
eliminate the need for "phone tag" and make it easy to convey information
that's too involved to leave on voice mail. (E-mail also has the advantage of
being easier to store and review later.) In addition, e-mail is easier and faster
than printing and then delivering memos. In some organizations, it's the preferred vehicle for sharing ideas, making announcements, scheduling meetings,
and so on.

When you want to send a message to someone using electronic mail, you type in the message and then request that it be sent to a particular person's electronic "mailbox." (Many e-mail programs let you send the same message to several mailboxes at once.) In most cases, this means that the message is stored, as a small file, in a subdirectory of the file server's hard disk that has been reserved for a particular person's "mail." In some e-mail programs, as soon as your message has been sent, a window appears on the recipient's screen indicating that a message is waiting. He or she can then read and/or print the message whenever it's convenient. In other programs, the recipient only finds out about your communiqué when explicitly asking for messages.

MULTIUSER SOFTWARE

By allowing multiple users to access files on the same disk, networks open a potential Pandora's box. What happens when more than one person tries to change the same spreadsheet or decides to edit the same report?

Suppose, for example, that a company's customer list resides in a database file on the network's file server. This makes it possible for more than one person to access and update the same list. Whenever someone looks up a particular customer, a copy of the data for that customer is copied into memory on that person's computer and displayed on his or her screen. Now suppose that two people look up the same customer, and then both decide to edit the data. (Say one person wants to update the customer's address and the other wants to revise the credit limit.) If the database program allowed both people to change the record simultaneously, one person's changes would cancel out the other one's. If the person making the address change saved the record first (by moving to another record or leaving the database), the revised copy of the customer record that exists in their computer's RAM would be copied back to the file

SHARING DATA

Multiuser application programs prevent two (or more) users
from updating the same file or, in the case of databases, the
same record simultaneously. Otherwise, whoever saves the
data last will overwrite changes just made by another user.

server. Then, as soon as the person changing the credit limit saved his or her version of the record, their version of the data—which includes the old address—would replace the version on the file server.

Most major application programs come in multiuser as well as single-user versions and the multiuser versions are designed to prevent exactly this type of mishap. Different application programs handle the problem of simultaneous editing in different ways.

▶ *Some won't allow anyone to use a file that is in use by someone else.*

▶ *Some let other users view a file that is being used by someone else, but not change it.*

▶ *Still others let multiple people view the same data, but only allow one person at a time to change it. In the case of word processing, spreadsheet, or graphics programs, this generally means only one person at a time can change a file. In the case of database programs, it usually means that only one person at a time can change a particular record within a file.*

NETWORK ETIQUETTE

Following are some guidelines on how to use a network without aggravating your coworkers.

▶ *Don't run programs from the server if you don't have to. Whenever you run a program that resides on the file server's disk, you are tying up some of the server's brain power. In certain cases, this is unavoidable, but if you simply want to create a spreadsheet for your own use and you have a copy of the spreadsheet software on your own hard disk, there's no need to tie up the server.*

▶ *Don't run single-user software from the server. If someone else tries to use it at the same time, you're likely to bring down the entire network (and possibly ruin a dozen people's day).*

▶ *Don't hog the printer. If you are sharing a printer with several other people on a network, try to avoid printing huge reports in the middle of the work day. Since the printer will handle various people's print jobs one at a time, you will prevent everyone else from printing until your report is completed.*

▶ *Don't delete files that you don't recognize. If you get an irrepressible urge to clear space on the file server, make sure you don't delete anyone else's files, at least not until you've determined how important they are.*

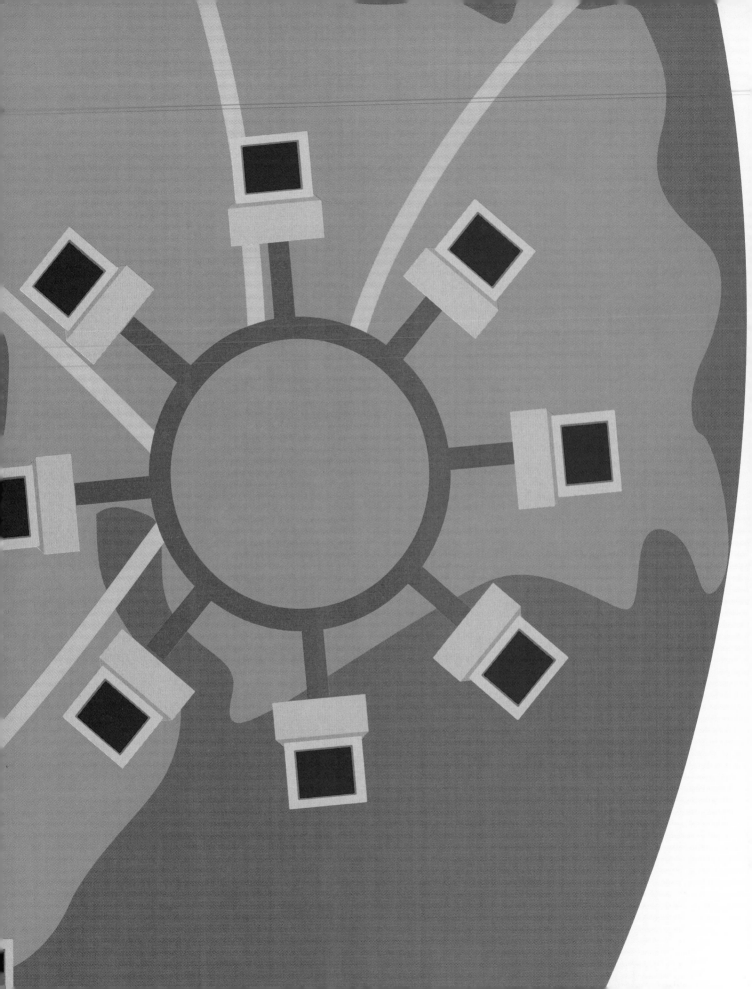

CHAPTER

10

TELECOMMUNICATIONS

How Computers Communicate

Communications Software

Using a General Communications Program

Information Services

Bulletin Board Systems

Modems are your computer's link to the outside world. It's been estimated that over ten million computers in the U.S. alone are equipped with modems. The number worldwide is probably two or three times that. Once you install or attach a modem, the people behind all those computers become potential teachers, clients, collaborators, or even friends.

The list of things you can do with a modem includes

▶ *Exchanging data with colleagues and friends. You could use a modem to obtain a report or spreadsheet from an associate in another city, for example, or to send a coworker a file of orders received while you're on the road.*

▶ *Accessing your office computer from a computer at home or a laptop in a hotel room, making use of the same programs and data that you would have if you were actually sitting in your office.*

▶ *Using on-line information services, such as CompuServe, Prodigy, and America Online to obtain technical support on computer programs, look up stock prices, make plane reservations, read the latest news from the wire services, go shopping, pay your bills, participate in a college seminar, solicit advice on when and how to prune your roses, or send electronic mail to clients, coworkers, or friends.*

▶ *Using bulletin board systems to carry on electronic conversations on everything from politics to gardening to science fiction.*

N O T E   *We'll get more into the specifics later, but for now, just know that the main difference between information services and bulletin board services is* *that information services cost money and provide a wealth of services, like up-to-the-minute news and weather, stock quotes, and access to reference literature. Bulletin board services are generally free (although you will pay for the phone call, which can get expensive if the service is across the country). They also tend to offer fewer services and often focus on specific topics. There are bulletin boards specifically geared towards mathematicians, real estate agents, and people interested in 12-step recovery programs, to name just a few.*

This chapter covers all the basics of telecommunications—that is, of transmitting information between two computers via modems and phone lines. It starts with an overview of the hardware and software involved, and a description of what the process is like. Then you learn about different types of modems and communications programs: the programs that provide the interface between you and your modem, and that guide the transmission of data from one system to the other. Next, you delve into some of the complexities involved in getting computers to "talk" and exchange files. The chapter will end with a brief description of electronic information services, bulletin boards, and the Internet (a kind of global computer network for distributing information).

HOW COMPUTERS COMMUNICATE

There are two prerequisites to telecommunication. On the hardware side, you need a modem. On the software side, you need a communications program that can tell the modem what to do and handle the technical details of transmitting and receiving data.

NOTE *Once your modem has successfully established a connection to another modem, you are said to be "on line." When no such connection exists, you are "off line."*

COMPUTERS ON LINE

In order for two computers to communicate, they must both have modems and be running communications programs.

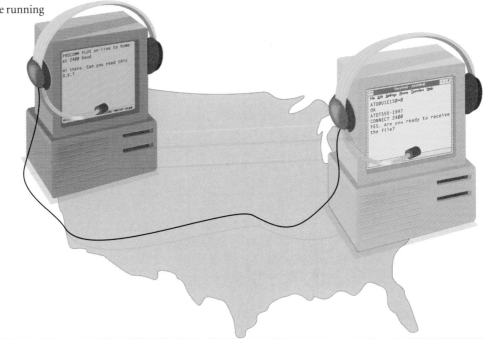

The main purpose of the modem is to translate data from a form palatable to a computer into a form palatable to a telephone and vice versa. Most computers are digital devices. They store and manipulate information by turning on and off sets of tiny electronic switches. At any given moment, a switch is in one of two possible states, on or off; there are no gradations. (When turned on, a switch represents the number one; when off, it represents the number zero.) Transmitting digital data is a bit like sending morse code: At any given instant, the signal must represent either a dot or a dash. Telephones, in contrast, transmit data as an analog signal (sound wave) that varies in frequency and strength, rather like the line drawn by an electrocardiograph machine.

ON BITS AND BYTES

As mentioned in Chapter 1, computers store and manipulate information as numbers, regardless of whether the information in question consists of numbers, letters, pictures, or any other type of data. Internally, computers represent all numbers using base 2, a numbering system that employs only two digits—0 and 1. (Humans, in

DIGITAL AND ANALOG SIGNALS

The purpose of modems is to transform digital information generated by a computer into an analog form that can be transmitted over phone lines (a process called *modulation*) and to transform analog signals received over the phone line into digital codes that your computer knows how to use (*demodulation*).

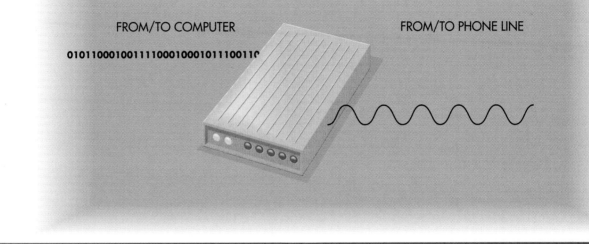

FROM/TO COMPUTER   FROM/TO PHONE LINE

0101100010011110001000101110011

contrast, like to think in base 10, which involves ten digits: 0 through 9.) Base 2 is often referred to as binary notation or a binary numbering system. The reason computers "think" in base 2 is that they represent information in terms of the presence or absence of an electrical or magnetic charge. The number 1 is used as the numeric equivalent of on, or charged. Zero is used to mean off, or uncharged.

In computer terminology, the electronic representation of a 0 or a 1 is known as a *bit* (short for binary digit) and there are eight bits to each byte of information. (That is, it takes eight 0s and/or 1s to represent a single character.) For example, the pattern used to represent a lowercase "a" on a personal computer is 01100001. As mentioned, when bits are stored inside a computer, they are stored as electrical or magnetic charges. When information is transmitted from one part of the computer to another or from a computer to a modem, bits are represented by small bursts of electricity—where a single burst represents an on bit (a number 1) and a pause between bursts represents an off bit (a number 0). A lowercase "a," for example, is represented by a pause, two bursts of electricity, four pauses, and another burst of electricity.

You won't actually have to think about bits very much. People always describe the capacity of a disk or the size of a program in terms of numbers of bytes rather than bits, for instance. As you will see later in this chapter, however, you will encounter the term in discussions of modem speed, since modems transmit data one bit at a time.

The primary function of a modem is to translate digital signals into analog ones and vice versa. When you send data, the modem converts the digital information from the computer into analog signal that can be transmitted over phone wires: a process known as *modulation*. When you receive data, the modem converts the analog signals received from the phone into digital codes that your computer can manage (a process known as *demodulation*). The term modem is a hybrid of the terms modulate and demodulate.

There are basically two types of modems:

▶ *Internal modems, which are expansion boards that are installed inside your system unit.*

▶ *External modems, which look like flat plastic or metal boxes (about the size of a rather thin hardback book) that usually plug into the back of your computer.*

Internal modems are often cheaper and consume none of your precious desk space. External modems offer the advantage of visible status lights—little lights on the front end of the device that can help you (or the expert you get on the phone) figure out where the problem lies if you have trouble establishing a connection with another computer. External modems are also easily transferred from one computer to another. This can save you the expense of buying two modems if you have both a desktop computer and a laptop, for example.

FAX MODEMS

You can also purchase a device that serves as both a modem and a fax machine. Like regular modems, these fax modems come in both internal and external varieties. They are particularly useful for sending documents and graphics created on your computer because they eliminate the need to print the data first. On the down side, if you want to use a fax modem to transmit data that you have only in "hard copy" (that is, on paper), you need to first scan it into your computer using a scanner. In terms of receiving, fax modems have both advantages and

INTERNAL AND EXTERNAL MODEMS

Internal modems are circuit boards that fit into expansion slots inside your computer.

External modems are little boxes with lights on the front that you connect to your computer with a cable.

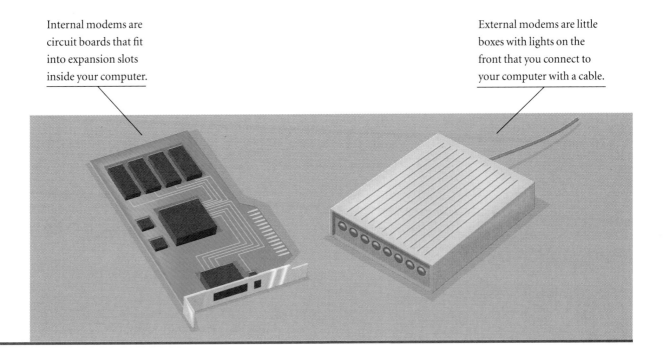

disadvantages relative to regular fax machines. On the plus side, you can read faxes on your computer before deciding whether they're worth printing. And if you do decide to print, you can print on regular paper rather than fax paper. On the other hand, it usually takes a little longer to print a fax on a printer than on a fax machine. If you have a page printer (laser or ink jet as opposed to dot-matrix), you'll also need a fair amount of memory. In addition, you can only receive faxes when your computer is turned on, which means that you either have to tell your associates only to send faxes during your regular hours or leave your computer on during off hours. Learning to use a fax modem also takes much more time and effort than learning to use a fax machine. Even if you talk someone else into setting it up for you, you need to learn the fax software.

Bear in mind that even if a fax consists entirely of text, your fax modem will receive it as a graphic image. This means that you won't be able to edit it afterwards. If you want to be able to change the document, have it sent as a file via modem. (You'll learn about transmitting files later in this chapter.)

Aside from living quarters, what distinguishes one modem from the next is the speed at which it can transmit data. The speed at which modems send and receive data is typically measured in bits per second (bps), with 1200 being the low end these days and 19200 being the rarely used high end. Most modems now in use transmit data at a maximum of either 2400 bps or 9600 bps.

You may also hear the term baud rate used to describe modem speeds. These days, baud rate is actually an outdated term. In slower modems, baud rate (which measures the number of times the frequency of the analog signal changes per second) was equivalent to the number of bits transmitted per second. In faster modems, however, two or three bits may be transmitted for every frequency change—making bps a different and more useful measurement. Nonetheless, if someone says they have a 9600 baud modem, they probably mean a modem that can transmit data at 9600 bps.

Modem speed doesn't matter that much if you are using your modem strictly to send short messages via electronic mail or carry on on-line conversations with friends or colleagues. Speed does matter, however, when you are sending or receiving files. It takes four times as long to transmit a file at 2400 bps as it does at 9600 bps, and eight times as long at 1200 bps. Try transmitting a file that's 50K or more and the difference will be very noticeable.

MAKING SENSE OF BPS

As a rule of thumb, you can divide the bps rate by 10 to determine the number of characters (bytes) transferred per second. A 60K (60,000-character) file will take approximately 62.5 seconds to transmit at 9600 bps (60,000 divided by 960) and approximately 250 seconds at 2400 bps (60,000 divided by 240). This rule of thumb is only approximate because the actual transmission rate varies slightly depending on the amount of interference on the phone line (if any) and the protocols you use to transmit the data. (You will learn about communications and file transfer protocols under "Using a General Communications Program" later in this chapter.)

Another factor to consider when purchasing a modem is compatibility. One of the earliest and most popular modem manufacturers is a company named Hayes. Hayes modems use a set of commands—a simple language really—that has become a standard for modems in general. The phrase "Hayes-compatible modem" means a modem that understands the Hayes commands for dialing, checking to see whether a modem has answered the phone, hanging up the line, and the like. Most modems currently manufactured are Hayes compatible. Make sure yours is one of them.

PLUGGING IN YOUR MODEM

External modems come with an intimidating number of connectors. There are at least three connections to be made:

▶ *From your modem to a power source*

▶ *From your modem to your computer*

▶ *From your modem to the telephone line*

If you are using a single phone line for both the modem and voice communications (that is, if you plan to talk on the same line that you use to telecommunicate), you may want to connect your modem into your telephone as well.

To connect your modem to a power source, you simply plug its power cord into a wall outlet or power strip. (The power cord features a little transformer box and a standard electrical plug.)

To connect an external modem to your computer, you plug a cable running from the modem into a serial port at the back of your system unit. As explained in Chapters 2 and 9, ports are data channels designed to carry data and instructions between your computer's memory and an I/O (input/output) device. Most computers feature two types of ports: serial ports, which are generally used for modems and mice and occasionally printers, and parallel ports, which are always used for printers. At the back of the system unit, you will usually find one or two serial ports that serve as gateways into the computer's internal communication channels.

PC On PCs, serial ports are always "male" (that is, have pins sticking out) and have either 9 or 25 pins. Most PCs have either one or two serial ports, but it's possible to have neither. (If you don't have a serial port, you either need to use buy a circuit board that includes a serial port or use an internal modem.)

9 TO 25 PIN ADAPTERS

If the connector on the end of your modem cable has the wrong number of holes for your particular serial port (say your modem cable has 25 holes and your serial port has only 9 pins), you'll need to get a special 9 to 25 pin adapter from your computer store. This is rather like buying an adapter that lets you plug a three-prong plug into two-prong electrical outlet.

MAC Most Macs come with two serial ports: one identified by a telephone symbol and another by a printer symbol. Although you can actually plug your modem into either one, it's best to use the telephone port since this is the one that communications programs will assume you are using.

PC The internal communications channels inside PCs are known as *COM ports*. (Although many people use the term serial port and COM port interchangeably, technically a COM port is an internal data channel and a serial port is the connector at the back of your computer that lets you connect an external device, like a modem, into that data channel.) All COM ports start with the letters COM. If you have only one serial port, it's connected to the COM port named COM1. If you have two serial ports, they're connected to COM1 and COM2.

PLUGGING IN YOUR MODEM

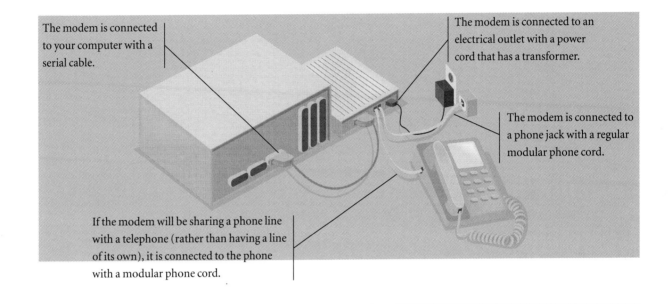

The modem is connected to your computer with a serial cable.

The modem is connected to an electrical outlet with a power cord that has a transformer.

The modem is connected to a phone jack with a regular modular phone cord.

If the modem will be sharing a phone line with a telephone (rather than having a line of its own), it is connected to the phone with a modular phone cord.

If you have an internal modem, it's still configured for a particular COM port (usually COM1 or COM2), but the connection into that communication channel is made entirely inside your computer. When you set up your communications software, you need to tell it the name of the COM port your modem is connected to. If you don't know, try telling your software that you're using COM2 if you have a mouse and COM1 if you don't. If this doesn't work, try the other setting. The actual command for telling your software which port you're using will, of course, vary from one program to the next. Look for commands named setup, settings, or configuration, or, better yet, read your manual.

Some communications programs will ask which port your modem is connected to during the installation process, but all of them let you change the port setting later if necessary. A few communications programs let you select an "autodetect" option during the installation process, directing the program to test the various serial ports to determine which has a modem attached.

MAC The serial ports on Macs are called simply the modem port and the printer port.

Finally, all modems—both external and internal—need to be connected to phone lines. If you have a separate phone line for your modem, you will generally run a modular phone cord from a phone jack on your wall to the back of your external modem, or to the piece of your internal modem card that protrudes from the back of your computer. If you don't have a phone line just for this purpose, you run one cord from the modem into the phone and another from the modem into the phone jack. This way, you and your modem can share the same line. (In most cases, there are specific parts for connecting to the phone line and to the telephone itself. Check your modem documentation to determine which is which.)

N O T E *Try not to attach a modem to a phone line that has call interrupt. Otherwise, an incoming call may either break the connection between modems or introduce a signal that your modem will not know how to interpret. (If you happen to be in the middle of transmitting a file, such errant signals can ruin the file transfer or make it necessary for you to retransmit the file from scratch.)*

COMMUNICATIONS SOFTWARE

Hardware (namely a modem) is only half of the telecommunications equation. The other is software or, more specifically, a communications program that serves as the intermediary between you and your modem, and that handles all the technical details of telecommunication. Communications programs provide tools that let you tell your modem what and when to dial or when to answer the phone, that let you send messages to the computer on the other end of the phone line, and that allow you to send and receive files.

There are three basic types of communications programs:

▶ *General communications programs allow you to connect to information services, bulletin board systems, electronic mail services, and regular modem-equipped PCs. Some of the more popular commercial general communications programs are Procomm Plus, Crosstalk, Smartcom, Versaterm, White Knight, and Blast. There are also shareware programs like Procomm, Qmodem, and Telix that you can often get from user's groups or bulletin board systems. (Shareware programs are distributed for free but if you like the program, you are supposed to send a small fee to its creator.) Windows comes with its own general communications program called Terminal. Occasionally you will find general communications programs bundled with modems.*

▶ *Front-end programs are programs designed to help you access and navigate through informational and electronic mail services. Some services—like Prodigy—can only be accessed through a front-end program. Others, like CompuServe or America Online, can be accessed through either general communications programs or front-end programs, but the latter can make it easier to find information or explore particular topics (saving you money as well as time). Bear in mind that front-end programs are tailored to a particular service: You can't use Prodigy's software to access CompuServe, or the CompuServe Information Manager program to access America Online.*

▶ *Remote-control programs let you operate one computer from another computer. You can use such programs to access your office computer from home or, if you're a computer wiz, to troubleshoot a client's system without leaving your office. Once you have connected to a computer using a remote-control program, you see on your screen exactly what appears on the other computer's screen, and you can operate the other computer as if you were sitting in front of it—running that computer's programs, creating and saving files, and even printing. In most cases, if there's a person at the remote computer, he or she can use the computer as well, perhaps demonstrating a problem he or she is having so that you can fix it. Some of the more popular remote-control programs are PCAnywhere, Carbon Copy, Blast, and Remote2.*

The difference between using a front-end program and a general communications program is a little like the difference between riding a bus and driving a car. In one case, you don't need to do much work, but you can only go to specified places (namely one information service). In the other case (general communications programs), you can go anywhere you want, but the driving's up to you. Front-end programs already know everything they need to know about CompuServe or America Online or whatever service you're using to properly configure your modem. You don't have to do much of anything until the connection is already made. With general communications programs, you need to understand and deal more with the technical details of connecting to another computer and transferring files. (You'll learn about these details in the next section.) The down side of front-end programs, of course, is that you can't use them for anything else but accessing one particular service.

The amount of work involved in using a remote-control program depends on which end you're on. If you're the "remote"—that is, the side that's dialing in—you'll need about the same amount of knowhow that you need to run a general communications program. If you're the "host"—that is, the side that's being dialed into—you don't need to do much of anything. In fact, much of the point of remote-control software is that little or nothing needs to happen on the host end of things, allowing someone to call a computer that's completely unattended or attended by someone who knows little or nothing about modems (or computers for that matter).

The type of program that's right for you depends on what you plan to do with your modem.

▶ *If you'll just be calling a particular information service, get a front-end program designed for that service.*

▶ *If you plan on calling bulletin boards or exchanging files directly with other PCs, and perhaps occasionally use an on-line service, get a general communications program.*

▶ *If you need to call into your office computer and access files while you're not there, or exchange data with someone who's not very computer literate, get a remote-control program.*

If you want to be able to do some combination of these things, you'll probably want more than one program.

USING A GENERAL COMMUNICATIONS PROGRAM

Many computer users who are perfectly comfortable building spreadsheets or commandeering databases freeze at the prospect of using a general communications program. In large part this is because both the manuals and the user interfaces of these programs often resemble those of ten years ago—that is, they look like they were designed by and for computer nerds. Not only do the manuals assume that you already know about things like data bits and parity checking, the programs themselves often disdain such user-friendly doodads as on-screen prompts and menus, let alone context-sensitive help.

Once you understand some of the basics, however, general communications programs are actually easy to manage. Before delving into the details, let's start by examining the steps involved in using a general communications program to establish a connection between your computer and the computer of a friend or colleague (as opposed to an information service or bulletin board). The process works like this:

▶ *You and the person on the other end decide who will call whom and which communication protocols you will use. (You'll learn all about communications protocols in the next section.)*

▶ *You both turn on your computers and, if you have external modems, your modems as well. (You don't need to turn on internal modems.)*

▶ *You both start up your communications programs.*

▶ *One of you issues a command directing your modem to dial the other modem's phone number and the other person issues a command directing his or her modem to answer the phone when it rings.*

▶ *If you're the person who initiates the call and your modem is equipped with a speaker (most are), you'll actually hear a dial tone and then the sound of your modem dialing the phone. Then you'll hear a high-pitched tone—your modem's equivalent of "Hi there. Are you a modem?" (Think of it as a modem mating call.) Meanwhile, the modem on the other end answers the phone and returns a slightly higher-pitched tone to indicate "Yes I am a modem." The two modems then exchange information about how they intend to exchange data, a process known as a* handshake. *If you're on the receiving end of the call, you'll probably hear the sound emitted by the remote modem and then the answering tone of your own. In most cases, you'll then see a message such as "Connect 2400" or "Connect 9600," indicating that a connection has been established at the specified transmission rate.*

▶ *At this point, you can test the connection by typing a short message. If there's a problem with the connection—maybe the systems are using incompatible communications settings—the person on the other line will either see nonsense characters or nothing at all. If all goes well, however, you'll be able to type a message on your keyboard and have it show up on your friend's screen and vice versa. At this point you're ready to exchange files.*

The procedure is similar when you call up an on-line service or BBS, except that the modem on the other end is already set up to answer the phone when you call. In addition, as soon as a connection is established you'll usually be asked to "log in," meaning identify yourself and, in most cases, enter a password.

What happens once you are on line depends on who you're calling and what you're trying to accomplish. If you are calling or receiving a call from a person at another personal computer, the next step will probably be exchanging files. (You'll learn about file transfers a little later.) If you're calling an information service, you'll probably see a menu of choices and will begin navigating through the system, seeking out information to read, choosing files that you want to copy to your computer, leaving messages for other people, or joining in an electronic conversation with others currently logged into the system.

THE MODEM HANDSHAKE

As soon as one modem answers a call from another, the modems trade information about how they intend to exchange data. This process is known as a *handshake*.

In any case, when you're done "telecommunicating," you either log out of the information service or bulletin board system or type good-bye to your friend or colleague, and then direct your modem to hang up the phone, severing your electronic connection. Then you exit from your communications program.

A similar set of steps occurs when you use a front-end or remote-control program, but many of the technical details are either managed by the program itself or are handled ahead of time when you define settings during the program installation process.

COMMUNICATIONS PROTOCOLS

Modems can only connect over phone lines if both systems send and receive data in similar ways. Both need to transmit data using the same transmission speed, number of data bits, type of parity (if any), and number of stop bits. (You'll learn the meaning of the last three of these shortly.)

In most cases, you don't need to worry about any of these things if you are using a front-end program, since the program already knows everything it needs to know about the information service's settings and directs your modem to communicate accordingly. If you are using a general communications program or if you're setting up a remote-control program, however, you need to direct your modem to transmit data in a manner acceptable to the modem on the other end of the line.

Speed is the first thing your modems need to agree upon. In order for modems to communicate, they must both be sending and receiving data at the same rate. This means that if your modem can send and receive data at 9600 bps but the computer on the other end of the line can only send and receive at 2400 bps, the connection must be made at 2400 bps. In some cases, a high-speed modem will sense the slower speed of the remote modem and decelerate accordingly. In others, you'll need to explicitly tell your modem to use the slower speed using your communications software before your modem dials or answers the incoming call.

The meaning of the other settings, commonly known as communications protocols, is a bit more obscure. If you want to know all the details, refer to the sidebar called "Parity, Data Points, Stop Bits, and Duplex". If you'd prefer being spared the details, all you need to know is that you'll almost always use one of two combinations of settings:

▶ *8 data bits, no parity, and 1 stop bit (referred to as 8N1)*

▶ *7 data bits, even parity, 1 stop bit (referred to as 7E1)*

The most commonly used combination is 8N1, although some on-line services require 7E1. (If you have trouble establishing a connection to an information service using one combination, try the other.)

DEFINING COMMUNICATIONS PROTOCOLS

In some communications programs, you define your communications protocols once and then only change them as necessary. This is the dialog box used for defining communications protocols in Terminal, the communications program built into Windows.

PARITY, DATA BITS, STOP BITS, AND DUPLEX

The number of data bits refers to the number of bits used to represent each character. When you connect to another PC, you usually set this to 8. When you connect to on-line services, you frequently need to change it to 7.

The parity setting determines whether the modems will employ a type of error correction known as parity checking. When you connect directly to another PC, you will usually leave Parity set to None. When you connect to an on-line information service, you may need to set Parity to Even. (The information service itself will tell you which settings you need to use.)

A stop bit is a signal used to mark the end of a character. In PC communications, you always use a single stop bit.

Some communications programs also ask you to define a duplex setting. The *duplex* setting indicates whether your modems can send and receive data at the same time. When duplex is set to half, both modems can send and receive data, but only one of them can transmit data at any one time. When duplex is set to full, your modem can send and receive data simultaneously. These days, nearly all systems are capable of full-duplex communications.

Most communications programs allow you to define default settings for your transmission speed and communications protocols through some kind of setup command or setup menu option. Some also have a dialing directory feature that lets you store both the phone numbers of systems that you call regularly and the settings that you want to use when calling those numbers. If your friend Joe has a 2400 baud modem, for example, you can store that speed along with his phone number. Knowing that CompuServe likes the settings 7E1, you can store those settings along with the CompuServe number. Then, whenever you issue the command for dialing a number in your directory, the program automatically uses the appropriate protocols.

TERMINAL EMULATION MODES

When you connect to another computer via modem, your computer is temporarily transformed from a computer in its own right into a "dumb terminal"—a passive input and output device. The other computer, often known as the host computer, calls all the shots. As you enter characters they appear on the other computer's screen (and sometimes are "echoed" to your screen). If you are using an information service or remote control program, as you enter commands, the host computer carries them out and then sends back output to be displayed on your screen.

Sometimes the host computer expects a particular type of terminal at your end of the line. You can tell your computer to act like a particular type of terminal by changing its terminal emulation setting. In most cases, you don't even need to think about this setting: You can just leave it as is. If you are having trouble establishing a connection to a BBS, an information service, or the company mainframe, however, changing the terminal emulation setting is a good place to start. If you are accessing a bulletin board, try setting the terminal emulation mode to ANSI. Otherwise, set it to VT-100. If neither of these works, try TTY.

Some communications programs feature dialing directories that let you store the name, phone number, and communications protocols for people, bulleting boards, or information services you call regularly. This is a dialing directory in the ProComm Plus program.

Data bits

Parity

Speed

Stop bits

Duplex

```
DIALING DIRECTORY: PCPLUS

        NAME                      NUMBER     BAUD P D S D  SCRIPT
  1 CompuServe              1-415-482-0190   2400 E-7-1 F
  2 Miriam Liskin                 555-1234   2400 N-8-1 F
  3 E. Bay dBASE BBS              652-1763   2400 N-8-1 F
  4 Quanto BBS              1-415-255-2981   2400 N-8-1 F




  PgUp Scroll Up   ↑/↓ Select Entry    R Revise Entry   C Clear Marked
  PgDn Scroll Dn   Space Mark Entry    E Erase Entry(s) L Print Directory
  Home First Page  Enter Dial Selected F Find Entry     P Dialing Codes
  End Last Page    D Dial Entry(s)     A Find Again     X Exchange Dir
  Esc Exit         M Manual Dial       G Goto Entry     T Toggle Display
  Choice:
  PORT: COM2  SETTINGS:  9600 N-8-1   DUPLEX: HALF   DIALING CODES:
```

FILE-TRANSFER PROTOCOLS

One of the main reasons for using a modem is to be able to send and receive files (reports, academic papers, spreadsheets, programs, whatever) across phone lines.

When you send a file from your computer to the remote computer, it's called *uploading*. When you receive a file from the remote computer, it's called *downloading*. The easiest way to remember the terms is to imagine the remote computer as hovering above you somewhere, so that sending a file entails moving it up to the "computer in the sky" and receiving a file means bringing it down.

In most cases, when you transfer files via modem, you don't simply send them character by character; you use what's known as a *file-transfer protocol* to control the flow of data and check for errors. Think of a file-transfer protocol as a carefully choreographed strategy that two communications programs use to

UPLOADING AND DOWNLOADING FILES

Uploading means sending a file to a remote computer and *downloading* means receiving a file. The easiest way to remember the terms is to think of the remote computer as hovering somewhere above you.

ensure that the data sent on one end matches the data received on the other. The program sending the data performs a calculation on each block of data it transmits and sends the results along with the data. The program receiving the data performs the same calculation and checks its result against the result transmitted by the other program. If an error is detected in a particular block, that block retransmitted. (If you see a message on your screen about errors in the transmission, it doesn't mean that the data you got is bad; it just means that it took the modems a few tries to get it right.) In order for this strategy to work, the communications programs on both ends need to be using the same file-transfer protocol.

In some programs, you define your file-transfer protocol ahead of time. (Look for a settings or setup command, and then an option for file transfers or something similar). In other programs, you choose a protocol when you issue the command to send or receive.

ZMODEM is considered by many to be the best file-transfer protocol, but not all communications programs support it. If ZMODEM isn't available on both ends, try either XMODEM or YMODEM. (YMODEM offers the advantage of letting you transmit a group of files at once.)

If you are using an on-line service or bulletin board, you will often be asked to specify a file transfer type as well as a file transfer protocol. Your choices will include text files (sometimes called ASCII files) and binary files. (They may include other more specialized file types as well.) The only files that can safely be transmitted as text files are files that only contain characters with ASCII codes under 128. This includes letters, numbers, and most punctuation. Be sure to transmit all other files, including most word processing files, as well as programs, spreadsheets, databases, and graphic images, as binary files.

FILE COMPRESSION

File compression means translation of a file into a coded format that occupies less space than the original file. The amount of space you'll save by compressing a file depends on the file type, but it's not unusual for compressed files to take up half the space of the originals or less. (Graphic files and database files tend to compress the most.) There are two reasons to compress files:

(1) To save room on disk. If you have files that you use infrequently but still want to keep on your hard disk, for example, you might compress them to free up disk space. You might also compress large files in order to fit them on floppy disks.

(2) To save time when sending data from one computer to another and thereby minimize bills from both the phone company and information services. (The smaller the file, the less time it takes to transmit.)

Bear in mind that you cannot actually use files in their compressed form. Rather, you need to decompress (expand) them to their original size.

If you plan to send files via modem, you may want to investigate compression programs to minimize your phone bills. If you download programs from computer bulletin board, you may have to learn about compression programs because the files you receive will probably be compressed and will need to be decompressed before you can use them.

The most widely used file compression program is a shareware program named PKZIP. Files that have been compressed with PKZIP have an extension of .ZIP and are often referred to as zipped files. (Anytime you download or are handed a file that has a .ZIP extension, you can assume that it has been zipped and that you need to unzip it before you can use it.) In order to unzip such files, you need to use a program named PKUNZIP.

The easiest way to get a copy of PKZIP and PKUNZIP is to download them from a BBS. Usually, you'll get a file named PKZ*xxxx*.EXE (with *xxxx* being the version number), which is what's known as *self-extracting* EXE file—that is, a compressed file that contains the information it needs to extract (decompress) itself. To decompress the file, just enter its name. If the file is named PKZ204G.EXE, for example, enter PKZ204G at the DOS prompt. (You can create self-extracting EXE files yourself, using a program named ZIP2EXE, which is usually distributed along with PKZIP and PKUNZIP.)

Assuming you have a copy of PKUNZIP, you unzip a file using the format PKUNZIP *filename*, where *filename* is the name of the compressed file. For further instructions on using PKUNZIP, enter PKUNZIP /H. (The /H switch stands for Help.) For basic instructions on how to use PKZIP, enter PKZIP /H.

If you can't find a copy of PKZIP and PKUNZIP, you can purchase them, along with a printed copy of the user's manual, from

PKWARE, Inc.
9025 N. Deerwood Dr.
Brown Deer, WI 53223-2427
(414) 354-8697 (Voice)
(414) 354-8559 (Fax)
(414) 354-8670 (BBS)

PKARC is another file compression utility that is often used on information services and bulletin boards. Files that have been compressed with PKARC have an extension of ARC. To decompress such files, you must use a program named PKXARC.

There are Mac utility programs for decompressing files created with PKZIP. The compression program usually used on Macs is called StuffIt.

INFORMATION SERVICES

One of the main reasons to buy and use a modem is to gain access to on-line information services. There are already over a dozen national information services and more are introduced nearly every month. Some, like the Dow Jones News/Retrieval Information Service (which focuses on financial information and services), are quite specialized. Others, like CompuServe,

Prodigy, GEnie, America Online, and Delphi are broader in scope and try to offer at least a little for everyone.

The services that you'll typically find on the general-purpose information services include

▶ *Electronic mail services—that is, the ability to send and receive messages and files via "electronic mailboxes" (a folder of files on the information service's hard disk). Whenever you call into the service, you are automatically informed if you have mail waiting and can either read it on-line or download it to your own computer to read or print later.*

▶ *News, weather, and sports information, including Associated Press clippings and, on some services, more extensive press clips from UPI, Washington Post, and Reuters World and Financial Reports.*

▶ *Travel information and services that let you find out about airline flights, hotels, motels, and car rentals and then make reservations on line.*

▶ *Financial information and services, including current stock market price quotes, access to on-line brokerage firms, and access to home banking services*

▶ *On-line databases including access to encyclopedias, Consumer Reports, dictionaries, and health-related databases that provide up-to-date information on disabilities, and diseases such as AIDS and cancer.*

▶ *Forums (aka special interest groups), which are essentially ongoing electronic conversations on a particular topic. Depending on the topic and the people involved, they resemble an electronic version of a clubhouse, lodge, study group, professional network, café, or singles bar. There are forums on cooking and wine-tasting, religion, national politics, working from home, raising various species of pets, and hobbies like photography, gardening, coin and stamp collection, sailing, and genealogy. Compu-Serve features a White House forum on which you can debate politics with fellow citizens or download copies of press releases or transcripts of presidential press conferences. Many information services offer professional forums that allow various types of professionals (including doctors and nurses, entrepreneurs, journalists, musicians, lawyers, and computer programmers and consultants) to exchange information and advice, generate ideas, and collaborate on projects. Finally, most information services offer dozens of forums on computer hardware and software.*

▶ *Games, both single player and multiple player. In single-player games, you play against yourself or the computer. In multiple-player games, you play against one or more people currently on line.*

▶ *Shopping services for everything from clothes to cameras to computer hardware and software. You can even have gourmet food or flowers delivered anywhere in the country.*

Some information services have monthly fees. Others charge only for time spent on line. Most have additional charges for special services and a few offer discount rates for calls before or after prime time (which starts somewhere between 6 and 8 a.m. and ends between 6 and 7 p.m., depending on the service).

NOTE *Most information services can be accessed through local telephone numbers, so that you don't need to pay for long distance charges.*

THE COMPUSERVE MENU

This is the first screen you encounter on CompuServe, currently the largest information service. (The items listed change from week to week.)

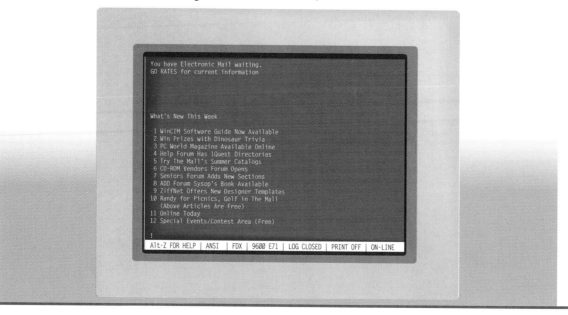

GETTING TECH SUPPORT ON LINE

As mentioned, most general-purpose information services offer forums on various types of hardware and software. Some of these forums are exclusively devoted to technical support and are monitored by the technical support staff of the manufacturer. Others also feature information-sharing, conversation, and exchanging of sample files and utilities. If you post a question in such a forum, you may either get an answer from the manufacturer's tech support staff or from an experienced user who happened to get there first. One advantage of using forums for tech support is that you don't have to limit yourself to regular business hours. If you have a Monday deadline and a problem crops up on Friday, you can post a message and, with luck, some knowledgeable user will dial in over the weekend and offer a solution. Some hardware and software manufacturers also have their own bulletin board systems, on which you can post questions, read product announcements, and download technical information or even program updates. (Bulletin board services are discussed in the next section.)

Although there is plenty of overlap among information services, they each have their own "personalities" and strengths. CompuServe probably has the most extensive research tools and databases, and the widest range of forums on computer hardware and software. America Online offers an exceptionally smooth, easy-to-use interface. Delphi is known for its friendliness and sense of community, and offers full access to the Internet. (You'll learn about the Internet at the end of this chapter.) Prodigy is strong on news stories, and on services for children.

Depending on your needs and interests, you may pick a service because of the particular services or forum topics it offers. Or it may be a question of ambiance. If your main reason for using an information service is to send e-mail to a particular set of people, your choice may also depend on which services your intended recipients are using.

If you're interested in sampling a service, keep your eyes out for free introductory offers. Many software packages come with a free introductory subscription to CompuServe, for example, in part because the software company wants to encourage you to use CompuServe rather than your telephone to solicit technical support.

As mentioned, if you plan to use an information service regularly, you'll probably want to get a front-end program that makes it easier to navigate through the system and find the information you want. If you use the CompuServe Information Manager program, for example, you can specify services and forums that you're interested in or files that you want to upload or download before you go on line. Once you are on line, the program takes care of as much work as it can automatically—logging you into the forum, sending or retrieving your mail and so on. It also provides you with menus that you can use to browse through services, forums, and files, sparing you the need to memorize cryptic commands. If you regularly participate in one or more forums, you can automate the process even further with programs like Tapcis or Ozcis, which will dial up CompuServe, download the descriptions of any new messages or files posted to the forum since your last call, and then immediately disconnect. You can then look through the list of messages and files, check off the ones you are interested in, and let the program dial in again to retrieve them for you. One good way to find out about front-end programs is to request opinions on line from other users of the service.

N O T E   *Always leave an information service by issuing the proper command for doing so. (In many cases, you can type **bye** or **off**, or select Exit from a File menu.) If you simply disconnect or turn off your modem without explicitly signing off the service first, it may take a while for the service to notice that you're no longer on line. In this case, you will be charged for any time that elapsed between the moment when you actually disconnected and the moment that the service recognized your absence.*

H O W   T O   S I G N   U P

Here are contact phone numbers for some of the major on-line services:

America Online	(800) 227-6364
CompuServe	(800) 848-8199
Delphi	(800) 695-4005
	(617) 491-3393
GEnie	(800) 638-9636
Prodigy	(800) 776-3449

ELECTRONIC MAIL SERVICES

There are some services—like MCI Mail and AT&T Mail—that specialize in e-mail. These services generally charge by the number and length of the messages sent rather than by time spent on line. Although they don't offer information services per se, they do offer e-mail services beyond those available on the more general-purpose information services.

Even if the person you want to reach doesn't have a modem or a subscription to your e-mail service, you can save some money on courier or express mail services by sending a letter to MCI mail and having someone print it out locally and deliver it from there.

There are front-end programs for MCI Mail available for both PCs and Macs. PC users can use Lotus Express. Mac users can use Desktop Express.

NOTE *MCI Mail has a special connection (known as a gateway) to CompuServe, enabling MCI Mail subscribers to send mail to users of CompuServe and vice versa.*

BULLETIN BOARD SYSTEMS

A bulletin board system (BBS) is a computer with a modem and a reasonably large hard disk that acts as repository for files and messages. In order to serve as a BBS, a computer must also be equipped with a special type of communications software, known as bulletin board software, that logs in users as they call and maintains a database of files and messages. Most BBSs run 24 hours a day so you can call whenever the fancy strikes you and unlike information services most are free to use. The person who administers the bulletin board (and usually owns the computer) is called the *sysop* (sysop is short for system operator and is pronounced sis-op).

In most cases, you use a bulletin board service to leave mail for other users of the board, to send and receive files, and to participate in ongoing "conferences" (discussions consisting of a series of messages sent in by callers, usually relating to a particular topic). If friendly discussion is what you had in mind, your choice of BBS will be based on what types of conferences it offers.

A BULLETIN BOARD MAIN MENU

Some BBSs are open to the general public. Others are available only to people in a particular field, or who belong to a particular organization (like a user's group), or who are friends of the person who set up the bulletin board. Some BBSs are private—run by computer consultants or companies to facilitate the transmission of data to and from clients and/or employees.

You can often find bulletin board listings in computer magazines, especially local ones. Many bulletin boards also have lists of BBSs in their file libraries. Look for a file that starts with the characters USABBS##.ZIP (where ## are digits representing the month).

If you hear about a BBS that seems potentially interesting, try calling up to see what it offers. (Your best bet is to set your communications settings to 8N1 and your terminal emulation to ANSI.) Once you're connected, press Enter once or twice. You will then be asked to "log in," meaning identify yourself. Once you enter your name, the BBS will see if you're already a registered user. If so, you'll be asked to enter your password. If not, you'll probably be asked a series of questions and then asked to define a password. After you log in, you'll generally see a menu of choices. If you need help, there's usually a help key or help command available. (Scan the screen for details.)

NOTE *Bulletin boards have traditionally been one of the major sources of computer viruses. See Chapter 3 for information on how to protect your computer from infection.*

THE INTERNET

To its devoted participants, the Internet represents the true promise of telecommunicating. The Internet is a federation of networks—many centered in universities—that have agreed to share information and resources across extremely fast information channels. Started as a tool to let scientists and researchers access expensive computer resources, the Internet links computer networks located at colleges and universities, governmental agencies, and, more recently, private businesses in one huge international information web. Once you connect to the Internet, you can access information stored on tens of thousands of computers throughout the world. The current number of users of the Internet has been estimated to be approaching one million.

Until recently, the only way to gain access to the Internet was through one of the participating networks. (You can't just join the Internet the way you can an information service.) The Internet was therefore primarily the province of professors, students, and government employees (mostly at the Department of Defense). Now there are companies that provide public access for a fee. (See the sidebar "Accessing the Internet.")

THE INTERNET

The Internet is a global matrix of computer networks
that allows users to access information stored on tens
of thousands of computers throughout the world.

ACCESSING THE INTERNET

Following are some of the companies that provide public access to the Internet for a fee.

HoloNet
Voice: (510) 704-0160
Free demo via modem: (510) 704-1058
To find out local access numbers, via modem: (800) NET-HOLO

DIAL N 'CERF
Voice: (800) 876-2373
(619) 455-3900

Delphi (the information service)
Voice (800) 695-4005
(617) 491-3393

Through the Internet, you can get to some of the same services you get
through an information service—like UPI news feeds and weather reports—as
well as some similar forums (on the Internet, they're called lists or newsgroups).

But you also gain entry to the library catalogs of thousands of universities, access to millions of articles and academic papers, and the ability to converse with a "global community" of users. Since almost all academics are part of the Internet, you're also more likely to find conversation and files on technical topics. If you're looking for information on computer education in the third world or are trying to find someone to collaborate with on a research project, the Internet is the place to look.

NOTE *Most of the major information services allow you to exchange mail with the Internet's users, but not to access the Internet's database and research services. As of this writing, the only national on-line service that provides full access to the Internet is Delphi.*

INDEX

text mode, 311–312

text-only files, 77

386 computer, 34

title bar, in Macintosh operating system, 234

tower case, 34

trackball, 36, 125

transistors, 33

Trash, in Macintosh operating system, 246–247

TREE command, 175–177

tree panes, File Manager, 212–213

trees. *See* directory trees

TSRs (terminate-and-stay-resident programs), 95–96

turning off your computer, 127–129

turning on your computer, 100–105

typewriter keys on a keyboard, 106–110

U

UNDELETE command, 162–164

undeleting files

    in DOS, 162–164

    in Windows, 216

uploading files, 370

user interface, 13

users groups, 305

V

VDT (video display terminal), 37. *See also* monitors

VER (version) command, 141–143

VGA (Video Graphics Array), 316

video adapter, 310, 313

video drivers, 313, 317–318

virtual memory, 254

viruses, 93–97

Visicalc, 276

W

WAN (Wide Area Network), 340

wide directory listings, 151–153

wildcard characters in DOS commands, 148–149, 150

windows

    changing your view of, on a Mac, 239–241

    in Macintosh operating system, 233–239

    manipulating on a Mac, 238

Windows, 26, 188–221

    Clipboard feature, 207–210

    File Manager, 193, 211–217

    Help system, 217–220

    Program Manager, 193, 194–197

    application windows, 193–194

    changing the size of, 201, 202

    closing windows in, 201

    control menu, 197–201

    copying files in, 214–216

    deleting files in, 216

    dialog boxes, 189, 190

    document windows, 193–194

    formatting disks in, 217

    getting help in, 217–220

    icons, 189, 190

    keyboard shortcuts, 210–211

    leaving, 221

    loading application programs in, 204–205

    manipulating, 197–201

    maximizing windows in, 197–199

    menus, 201–204

    minimizing windows in, 199

    moving windows in, 199, 202

    program groups, 195–196

    renaming files in, 217

    resizing, 201, 202

    restoring, 198–199

    running DOS programs in, 205, 221

Arrrgh!

Don't you just hate it when software doesn't work the way you expect? When simple problems block your progress for hours? When your resident techie isn't around, the technical support hotline is constantly busy, on-line help is no help at all, the manual is hopeless, and the book you have tells you everything except what you really need to know?

Don't you just hate it?

ISBN: 099-8
Price: $29.95

We do too. That's why we developed *HELP!*, a groundbreaking series of books from Ziff-Davis Press.

HELP! books mean fast access to straight answers. If you're a beginner, you'll appreciate the practical examples and skill-building exercises that will help you work confidently in no time. If you're already an experienced user, you'll love the comprehensive coverage, highly detailed indexes, and margin notes and sidebars that highlight especially helpful information.

ISBN: 014-9
Price: $27.95

We're launching the *HELP!* series with these all-new books:

ISBN: 039-4
Price: $27.95

ISBN: 151-X
Price: $29.95

HELP! WordPerfect 6.0—WordPerfect insider Stephen G. Dyson has created the most complete single source of techniques, examples, and advice that will help you clear the hurdles of WordPerfect 6.0 quickly and easily.

HELP! Microsoft Access—Best-selling author Miriam Liskin gives you fast access to the complete feature set of Microsoft's leading-edge Windows database program. Sample databases included on disk!

HELP! Paradox for Windows—Popular database and spreadsheet authority Lisa Biow provides one-stop solutions to the challenges of Borland's high-powered new database manager.

HELP! Windows NT 3.1—Windows authority Ben Ezzell has the answers to your NT questions in this highly effective quick-access format.

HELP! Lotus Notes 3.0—Learn how to harness the power of Lotus Notes with this easy-access reference guide from the ultimate Notes guru, John Helliwell.

ISBN: 160-9
Price: $29.95
Avail.: November

So if you hate struggling with software as much as we do, visit your favorite bookstore and just say *HELP!*

Available at all fine bookstores or by calling 1-800-688-0448, ext. 101.

ZIFF-DAVIS
ZD
PRESS

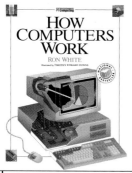
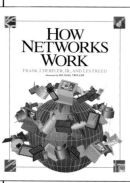

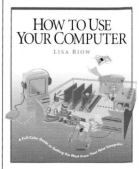
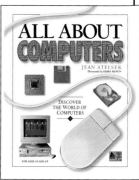